DATE DUE			

The Journal and Order Book

of

Captain Robert Kirkwood

KENNIKAT AMERICAN BICENTENNIAL SERIES
Under the General Editorial Supervision of
Dr. Ralph Adams Brown
Professor of History, State University of New York

The Journal and Order Book

of

Captain Robert Kirkwood

of the

Delaware Regiment of the Continental Line

PART I

"A Journal of the Southern Campaign"
1780-1782

PART II

"An Order Book of the Campaign in New Jersey, 1777"

———

"The brave, meritorious, unrewarded Kirkwood"

———

EDITED BY

REV. JOSEPH BROWN TURNER

KENNIKAT PRESS
Port Washington, N. Y./London

973.345
K63j
77615
Feb. 1972

THE JOURNAL AND ORDER BOOK OF CAPTAIN ROBERT KIRKWOOD

First published in 1910
Reissued in 1970 by Kennikat Press
Library of Congress Catalog Card No: 78-120882
ISBN 0-8046-1275-7

Manufactured by Taylor Publishing Company   Dallas, Texas

KENNIKAT AMERICAN BICENTENNIAL SERIES

FOREWORD

"Render, therefore, to all their dues;
Honour to whom honour is due."

So far as Robert Kirkwood is concerned neither the State of
Delaware nor the Historical Society of Delaware has obeyed
this injunction. One of the most intrepid and fearless men
Delaware has produced has received little notice and scanty
praise. The MSS. volumes containing his "Journal" and his
"Order Book" have been allowed to accumulate dust on a shelf
of the library of the Historical Society for thirty-four years.
In justice to a brave son of the State they are now published,
with the following letter containing his ancestry:

Bloomington, Indiana, July 14, 1876.

Dr. Lewis P. Bush:

Dear Sir—

When I saw you in Newark a few weeks since you requested me to furnish you a statement of any facts in my possession in regard to the ancestry and early history of Captain
Robert Kirkwood. With this request I cheerfully comply,
although at this distance of time perhaps little new can be given
on the subject.

The family from which Captain Kirkwood was descended
removed from Scotland to the vicinity of Derry in the north of

Ireland in the latter part of the seventeenth century.   In 1731 the captain's father, Robert Kirkwood, then a youth of perhaps 18 or 20 years of age, emigrated to this country in company with the widow and two infant children of an elder brother, William, then recently deceased.   Robert Kirkwood, some years after his arrival in Delaware, married a Miss Sarah McDowell, a native of England and a member of the religious society of Friends.   They lived on a farm about two miles north of Newark—a farm recently owned by Andrew Gray, Esq., and adjacent to the lot on which the White Clay Creek Presbyterian church now stands.   They had nine children, eight of whom were daughters.   Robert, the only son, was born in 1756.   Of his childhood nothing is now known but the fact of his early manifesting a fondness for reading and study—a fact which decided his father to educate him for the ministry.   He was accordingly placed in the Newark Academy where he pursued his classical studies with great diligence and success.   On the commencement of the revolutionary war, however, the young student at once abandoned his literary pursuits and promptly espoused the cause of his country.

You informed me in conversation that the manuscripts of Captain Kirkwood had been deposited in the library of the Delaware Historical Society by his grandson, Gen. R. K. Whitely.   It is therefore unnecessary that I should attempt any account of his public services.   You are probably aware also that an interesting biographical sketch of Captain K., by P. Benson Delany, M.D., may be found in Graham's Magazine for March, 1846.

Of the family that came over from Ireland with Robert Kirkwood the descendants are now very numerous.   The widow, Mrs. Sarah Kirkwood, some time after their arrival in Delaware, married a Mr. Gallagher, then a member, I think, of

White Clay Creek church. Her son, Robert Kirkwood, who died in Harford county, Maryland, in 1810, was my grand-father.

With pleasant recollections of my former residence in Delaware, I remain, dear sir,

Yours very truly,

DANIEL KIRKWOOD.

To the above it may be added that Capt. Kirkwood married Sarah, a daughter of Joseph England, Jr., of White Clay Creek hundred, who was, as his mother had been, a member of the Society of Friends. His father was for many years a Ruling Elder in the White Clay Creek Presbyterian Church. At the very beginning of the Revolution Robert Kirkwood, Jr., was commissioned, January 17, 1776, First Lieutenant of Capt. Darby's Company, Colonel Hazlet's Regiment. He received his commission as Captain, December 1, 1776, and was transferred to Colonel Hall's regiment as second Ranking Captain, and served to the end of the war as Senior Captain in command of the Delaware Battalion. He was brevetted Major, Sept. 30, 1783. The State of Virginia alone recognized and rewarded his services. In 1787 he received from Virginia a grant of 2000 acres of land in the North West Territory, in what is now Southeastern Ohio. His land was probably in Belmont Co., whither he removed soon after the grant was made. He was a Justice of the Peace in "the North West Territory" in 1790, and a carefully written copy of the laws promulgated by Gen. Arthur St. Clair is found in the back of his journal, together with some interesting items from his docket. On the 4th of March, 1791, Kirkwood was commissioned Captain in the Second Regiment U S. Infantry, and marched under General St. Clair in his unfortunate expedition against the Indians. In the battle near Fort Recovery,—his thirty-third engagement,—he refused to retreat with the defeated army, and died with his face to the foe on the 4th of November, 1791, at the age of forty-five.

Captain Kirkwood left two children:

1. A son, Joseph Kirkwood, who removed with his father to the Ohio Territory. His children as late as 1875 were still in possession of the lands granted to their grandfather in 1787.

2. A daughter, Mary, who married Arthur Whitely, of Dorchester Co., Md., and was the mother of General R. H. K. Whitely, by whom the Historical Society was made custodian of these valuable MSS.

JOSEPH BROWN TURNER.

Dover, Delaware,
    December 6, 1910.

Part I

JOURNAL

of the

Marches of the Delaware Regiment

of the

Continental Line

in the

Southern Campaign
1780-1782

Kept by

Captain Robert Kirkwood

JOURNAL OF MARCHES FROM MORRISTOWN, EAST JERSEY, SOUTHERLY

When	Year 1780	Miles
April		
13th.	I left Morristown four days before the Maryland and Delaware Line, and arrived at Newark, in the Delaware State....................................	120
	From thence went to Lewes town, and returned back to Newark...................................	260
May		
8th.	Set sail from the Head of Elk, in Compy with 50 sail of vessels, being the Second brigade in the Maryland Line, Destin'd for Petersburgh, Virginia, at which Port the vessel I was in arrived the 23 Inst......	350
30th.	Decamped from Petersburgh, and marched to Rockaway Court House.................................	15
31st.	Marched to Jones's Bridge, and Encamped..........	17
June		
1st.	Marched to Commissarys Lambs, Brunswick County...	15
2nd.	Marched to Short's Ordinary.....................	16
3rd.	Marched to Stony Creek.........................	18
4th.	Marched to Roanoke which we crossed at Taylor's Ferry and lay upon its Bank, (this river is about 350 miles long)...................................	8
6th.	Marched into Granvill County, North Carolina......	18
7th.	Marched this day to Genl. Parsons...............	10
		847

When	Year 1780	Miles
June		847
21st.	Marched from Genl. Parsons, and encamped on the South Side of Flat River......................	20
22nd.	Marched this Day to Hilsborough..................	15
30th.	Marched and crossed Haw River...................	15
July		
1st.	Marched and lay in the woods....................	6
2nd.	This day marched to Chatham Courthouse..........	18
5th.	Marched this day to Deep River which we crossed....	14
18th.	Marched to Wilcoxes Iron Works.................	12
19th.	Marched to Hollinsworth's Farm on Deep River.....	18
25th.	This Day the Honble. Majr. Genl. Gates arrived and took Command of all the Southern Troops.	
27.	Marched this day to Spinks Farm Randolph County, No. Carolina.................................	18
28.	Marched this day to Cottons Farm................	18
29.	Marched to Smiths Mill, on little River...........	18
Augst.		
1st.	Marched to the River Pee Dee and crossed at Masseys Ferry, incamped on Ingram Farm, Hanson County..	10
2nd.	Marched this Day to Mays Mill...................	18
3rd.	Marched to Thompsons Creek. The line at this place divides North & South Carolina..................	18
4th.	Marched this day near Hendersons Cross roads.......	17
6th.	Marched and encamped in the pines, received Information that the Enemy was advancing..............	5
8th.	Marched to Big Linches Creek....................	16
10th.	Marched and encamped in the Pines...............	7
11th.	Marched to Little Linches Creek to gain the Enemys right	16
		1114

When	Year 1780	Miles
Augst.		1114
12th.	Marched this Day and lay on our arms all Night....	6
13.	Marched to Ridgleys Mill......................	16
15.	Marched this Night at 10 OClock................	6
16.	About one in the morning met with the British Army at Black Swamp and Drove in their Advance Guards we then Halted and formed the line of battle the 2nd Brigd. on the Right the first in the Center, and the Militia on the left, and Lay on our arms untill Break of Day when the British advanced and attacked our Left Flank where the Militia Lay, who gave way which gave the enemy's horse an opportunity to gain our Rear, their Infantry at the same time gaining our Flank, and their Line advancing in our front which Caused the Action to become very Desparate; which continued for the space of half an hour. In this Action Lt. Col. Vaughan, Major Patten, six officers and Seventy Rank and file of our Regt. were taken Prisoners, with all the Cannon and Baggage of the Army—I can give no account of our Marches on the Retreat untill we came to Sallisbury which we arrived at on the 21st...............................	123
24th.	Marched and crossed the Yadkin River............	7
	From thence we marched to Guilford Courthouse.....	50
	And from thence to Hilsborough..................	45
Octb.		
7.	This Day three Companies of Light Infantry were Chosen, one under the Command of Capt. Bruen from Virginia, Second by Capt. Kirkwood, & the third by Capt. Brooks the Whole Under the Command of Col. Morgan.	
		1367

When	Year 1780	Miles
Octbr		1367
8.	Began our march from Hilsborough under Command of Col. Morgan, and arrived at Salsbury the 15th Inst.	95
18th.	Marched this Day to Col. Locks Farm............	5
19th.	Marched to Fifers Mills........................	15
21st.	Marched about two below Esq., Alexander's........	23
22nd.	Marched to Six mile run there joined the No. Carolina Militia under Command of Genl. Davidson.......	16
25th.	Moved our Encampment in Front of the Militia this Neighbourhood is Called New Providence and within 14 Miles of Charlotte. While we Lay at this place Col Morgan Received his Commission of Brigadier Genl. From Congress.	
Nov.		
4.	This Day Genl Morgan's Infantry with Col. Washingtons Horse, marched Down to Ridgely's Mill, within 13 miles of Cambden; reconoitre the Enemy.	
9th.	Returned again to camp........................	100
22nd.	This Day the Maryland Division arrived at Camp.	
27.	This Day the troops under Command of Genl. Gates Marched to Charlotte, where they built Hutts.....	
28th.	This Day had orders to hold our selves in readiness in a moments warning to March. Accordingly left our tents standing with all our sick behind and marched to twelve mile Creek, which at this place Divides No & So. Carolina; & from thence to the Hanging Rock, the Infantry remained at this place untill Col. Washington went down to Col. Ridgely's, and with the Deception of a pine knot took the garrisons	
		1621

When	Year 1780 & 1	Miles
		1621
	Consisting of one Col. one Majr. and 107 privates:— from thence returned to Camp, December the second	100
Decmbr.		
6th.	This Day Maj. Genl. Green took command of the Southern Army in room of Maj. Genl. Gates.	
17th.	March'd to Charlotte	13
21st.	March'd to Biggon Ferry on Catawba River.........	15
22nd.	Crossed the Ferry and March'd...................	5
23rd.	March'd	16
24th.	March'd	13
25th.	March'd to Pacolet.............................	8
1781.		
Jan. 1st.		
11th.	March'd	10
16th.	March'd to the Cowpens........................	12
17th.	Defeated Tarlton.	
18th.	March'd for the Catawba River and arrived the 23rd.	100
Febr.		
1st.	March'd to Col. Locke..........................	30
2nd.	Marched and crossed the Yadkin River............	12
4th.	March'd this Night.............................	13
5th.	March'd this Day...............................	16
6th.	March'd to Guilford............................	18
8th.	March'd this Night.............................	5
14th.	Crossed the Dan River at Ewings Ferry............	80
15th.	March'd and crossed the Banisster River...........	7
17th.	March'd and Recrossed.........................	6
20th.	Crossed the Dan River..........................	9
21st.	Marched	5
22nd.	Marched to Dobbins............................	12
23	March'd	12
24	March'd	12
25	March'd to Hilsborough and Returned; in all........	21
March		
4th.	We came up with the Enemy at the Allamance......	60
		2233

When	Year 1781	Miles
March		2233
5th.	Marched this Night to the old Regulation ground and attack'd the advanc'd picquet. Brought off one of their Centinells & returned to Camp by morning...	24
6th.	This Day we arrived near the South Branch of Haw River	36
7th.	This Day the Enemy made a movement and were within a mile of our Camp before they were Discovered. We Crossed the South branch of Haw River Leaving a Party of militia on the other Side to oppose the Enemy; A brisk fire Shortly commenced in which the militia were obliged to give way.	
	Marched this Day...............................	21
8th.	Marched this Day to Troublesome Creek..........	12
9th.	Marched this Day & encamped on the Ground where the British Lay, having crossed Troublesome & Haw River	10
10th.	This Day my Company & one from Virginia were ordered to remain with Col. Washington to Act as a Legion. The rest of the Infantry joined their respective Regiments, marched.....................	7
11th.	Marched this Day towards Guilford Courthouse......	5
12th.	Col. Lee's Light Horse took 30 prisoners and brought them to the Gen'l on our march.................	5
13th.	Marched this Day...............................	7
14th.	Marched within 3 miles West of G. Court house.....	8
15th.	This day commenced the Action at Guilford Court House between Genls. Green & Cornwallis, in which many were Killed & wounded on both sides, Genl. Green Drew off his Army with the loss of his artillery.	
	Marched this Day...............................	16
		2360

When.	Year 1781	Miles
March		2360
16th.	Marched to James Saunders Farm, near to the Iron works where our Army Lay, on Troublesome Creek	3
19th.	Marched to Simmons's Farm.....................	6
20th.	Marched this Day about........................	7
21st.	Marched towards Deep River....................	21
22nd.	Marched near the Little Allamance River..........	5
23rd.	Marched	4
24th.	Do	7
25th.	This Day was Executed by hanging a Certain Solomon Slocum being a Spy from the Enemy Likewise a Deserte₁ from the 2nd. M. Regt.	
	Marched	17
26th.	Marched to Brooks Farm, near Wilcoxs Iron works..	10
27th.	Marched this Day..............................	10
28th.	Marched and Crossed Deep River at Ramseys Mill, on the bridge the British made for themselves. This Day we expected a Genl. Action to have commenced but his Lordship thought it most prudent to decline it, by a speedy march to Cross Creek.............	14
29th.	Marched	3
30th.	Marched towards the Gulph Mill on Deep River.....	4
31st.	Marched this Day..............................	14
April		
1st.	Marched	3
3rd.	Marched up the River..........................	9
7th.	Marched towards the Buffaloe Ford and encamped on Brush Creek	18
8th.	Marched to Spinks Farm........................	16
9th.	Marched to Cottons Farm.......................	15
		2546

When.	Year 1781	Miles
April		2546
10th.	Marched & Crossed Little River about 2 miles......	20
11th.	This day Crossed the River Pee Dee at Colston's Ferry	15
13th.	This day Crossed Rocky River....................	3
14th.	Marched Near Mays Saw Mill....................	18
15	Marched this day about.........................	2
16	This Day marched near Andersons Cross Roads......	17
17th.	Marched to Big Lynches Creek...................	16
18th.	Marched to Little Lynches Creek.................	12
19	Marched within 4 miles of Camden, took Eleven of the Enemy prisoners	15
	This evening Genl. Green gave me orders if possible to take possession of Logtown, which was in full view of Camden & if I could take it, to mentain it untill further orders, Leaving Camp about 8 at night, arrived before the town between 9 & 10 and about 12 OClock got full possession of the place, A scattering firing was kept up all night, And at sun rise next morning, had a smart schirmage, Beat in the Enemy, About two hours afterwards had the Very agreeable Sight of the advance of the Army...............	3
20th.	This day Col. Washington with my Infantry went Westerly round Camden, Burnt a House in one of the Enemys Redoubts on the Wateree River; took 40 horses & 50 Head of cattle & returned to Camp	4
		2671

When	Year 1781	Miles
April		2671
22nd.	Moved Southerly Round the town................	10
23rd.	Marched back to our old ground..................	⌐6
25th.	The enemy sallyed out and drove us back..........	7
27th.	Marched to Ridgley's Mill.......................	10
29th.	Marched this Night.............................	6
30th.	Moved our Encampment.........................	1
May		
1st.	This day there was five Desserters Hanged that was taken in the Action of the 25th of April.	
3rd.	Marched and crossed the Wateree.................	11
4th.	March'd to the Ferry and took the Redoubt, and burn'd the Block House on the South side of the Wateree, then Return'd to the Army at the 25 mile Creek....	16
7th.	Marched this day..............................	9
8th.	The Enemy moved over the River and was within two miles of us before we knew of them being out when our Vadet Came in and inform'd us. We then Drew up in order of battle and lay their in Sight of other untill Evening when both Armys Drew off and we marched	4
10th.	At Night was sent out with a party of the Horse to Surprise a party of Tories and Marched 18 miles, but not Coming up with, we altered our Rout and March'd for Camden hearing that it was Evacuated, and Reached there the next Day being in all.......	29
12th.	March'd to Mr. Randels Mill....................	12
13th.	March'd to Mr. Westons........................	18
15th.	March'd this day..............................	18
16th.	March'd this day..............................	6
18th.	Marched and Crossed the Broad River..............	15
		2849

When	Year 1781	Miles
May		2849
19th.	This day was executed three Deserters from our Army, who were taken at Fort Granby near Fridays Ferry, on the Congree. Marched.....................	25
20th.	Marched this Day..............................	17
21st.	Was ordered with Col. Washington's Horse to Surprise a party of tories under command of Col. Young; Coming up to the place found it evacuated, the Horse left me, with expectation to Come up with them, while I moved on at Leisure. The Tories taking us for some of them selves come out of a Swamp in our Rear, & being undeceived took one of my men prisoners; upon which A firing Commenced, but they being on horse back pushed off with the Loss of one man Killed & one Horse taken, A Short time Afterwards the Horse joined me, and before Dark killed 4 more taking 6 Prisoners; Marched this Day....	23
22nd.	This Day Crossed the River Saluda. Surprised a party of Tories within sight of Ninety Six, Killed four, Spent the Day in reconoitering the Garrisson, which was commanded by Col. Cruger. Marched.......	9
	At Night were employed in raising a three Gun Battery, about 130 yards from their works and under a Scatering Fire from the Enemy all night.	
		2923

When	Year 1781	Miles
May		2923
24	This Day opened our first Battery on the Enemys Star Redoubt.	
26th.	Received express from Col. Lee that he had taken two redoubts at Augusta in Georgia; making 70 of them prisoners & Killed about 40; taking a Quantity of stores, Rum etc.	
June		
5th.	This Day Augusta was Captured by Col. Lee making all the Garrison prisoners of war consisting of 165 British & the like Number of Tories, the whole being under the Command of Col. Brown.	
18th.	This Day the Garrison of 96 was attacked on two Quarters Viz:—the Star Redoubt by the main army, and Homes's by Col. Lee's Infantry, with mine, with the assistance of three 6 pounders Commanded by Col. Harrison. Our Redoubt held out about an hour, then left it in our full possession; the other being so verry strong, & the officers who commanded in their Ditch being wounded with the greatest part of the men Killed and wounded, were obliged to give over the attempt.	
20th.	Raised the siege from Ninety Six; Lord Rodden being within 25 miles of us, with 2000 men this Day Marched towards Charlotte....................	14
		2937

When	Year 1781	Miles
June		2937
25th.	Marched this Day..............................	8
22nd.	Marched this Day..............................	16
23rd.	Marched this Night and Crossed the Innoree River...	15
24th.	Marched this Day Crossed the Tiger and Broad River	21
25th.	Recrossed the Broad River and Marched...........	6
26th.	Marched this Day to the Tiger River.............	7
28th.	Marched and Crossed the Inoree River...........	12
29th.	Marched this Day..............................	9
30th.	Marched this Day..............................	20
July		
1st.	Marched this Day..............................	6
2nd.	Marched this Day and Cross'd the Broad River......	17
3rd.	Marched this Day and encamped at Capt. Howells...	16
4th.	Marched this Day..............................	9
5th.	Marched this Day and Cross'd the Congree at Mc. Cord's Ferry	32
6th.	Marched this Day down the Santee River..........	13
7th.	Marched this day and Cross'd the Congaree and was ordered back towards Orangebourgh.............	25
8th.	Marched this Day and encamped at Doughey's Farm..	25
9th.	Marched this Day to Col. Middleton..............	10
10th.	Marched this day and join'd the Army at Beaver Creek	7
11th.	Marched this day towards Orangebourgh..........	10
12th.	Marched to the Enemys Lines, and within 4 miles of Orangeburgh sent out parties to draw them out; but all to no purpose, Col. Cruger being within one days march of Lord Rodden, Genl. Green thought it prudent to withdraw his army, and march towards McCords Ferry	15
13th.	Marched this day near Brown's Mill..............	11
14th.	This day Crossed the Congaree River at McCords Ferry & encamped on Mr. Simmons Farm 7 miles from ye River...............................	20
		3268

When	Year 1781	Miles
July		3268
23rd.	Marched with Col. Washington's Cavelry to the Fork of Wateree & Congaree Rivers encamped on Mr. Dawson's Farm (very sickly place)...............	8
27th.	Marched to McCords Ferry on ye Congaree........	1
29th.	Marched to Mr. Lightwood's Farm, up ye Congaree..	6
Augst.		
3rd.	This day the Enemy's Horse took possession of Mc-Cord's Ferry with one Large Boat and Negro, on the News of which our Horse, and foot, marched down to the Ferry, and remained there untill Evening; and marched back to the ground we left in the morning..	12
4th.	Marched crossed the Wateree, encamped on Lambert's Farm	13
6th.	Marched and encamped on Mr. Yore's Farm.........	4
7th.	Marched and encamped on Capt. Ritcheson's Farm....	8
24th.	Marched this morning towards Camden up the river..	20
25.	Marched this day to Camden....................	18
26th.	Crossed the Wateree River passed the Army and Halted at Colonel's Creek.........................:...	18
27th.	This Day arrived at Capt. Howells on ye Congaree...	18
28.	This day joined Col. Washington's Horse..........	5
	At Mr. Culpepers on ye Bank of the River; about Evening were informed the Enemy this morning left Col. Thompson's on their way towards Charles Town.	
31st.	Marched to Howell's Ferry on the River where the Army had crossed. This Day the Genl. received information the Enemy had marched from the Center Swamp on their rout for Town, which Occasioned the Horse and my Infantry to return to the place we left in the morning.........................	12
		3411

When	Year 1781	Miles
Sept.		3411
4th.	Crossed the Congree River at Culpeper's Ferry, and Encamped on Mr. Johnstown's Farm.............	15
5th.	Marched and Encamped with the main Army at Everett's Creek 6 miles Below Col. Thompson's........	14
6th.	Marched to Midway Swamp.....................	6
7th.	Marched this Day within seven miles of the Eutaw Springs, where Lay Col. Stewart with the British Army Consisting of 2,000 men..................	20
8th.	This morning our Army was in motion before Daybreak, with a determination of Fighting the British Army.	

We marched in the following order of Battle Viz. The South & North Carolina Militia in front, Commanded by Genls. Marion & Pickens, having Col. Lees horse, & Infantry on their right Flank, and the State Horse, and mounted Infantry on their left. The Second line was Composed of North Carolina regulars, Virginians, & Marylanders, having two three Pounders, between the N. Carolinians, & Virginians, and two six Pounders, between the Virginians & Marylanders. Col. Washington's Horse, with my Infantry were the Corps De Reserve In this order we marched Down to Action, Coming within 3 miles of the Enemy's

| | | 3466 |

When	Year 1781	Miles
Sept. 8th.	Encampment, we overtook a Rooting Party of 60 men Coming in with Potatoes, most of whom were either Killed, wounded or taken. We met with no further opposition, untill we arrived within one mile of their Encampment, where we met their front line, which soon brought the Action general, we Drove their first, and Second Lines, took upwards of 500 prisoners. The Enemy took shelter in a large Brick House, and a hollowway in rear of the House. At this time our men were so far spent for want of water, and our Continental Officers suffering much in the Action, rendered it advisable to Genl. Green to Draw off his Army, with the Loss of two 6 pounders, Majr. Edmund of the Virginians, with a Small party of men joined me in the British Encampment, keeping up the fire for A small space of time. Found our Army had withdrawn from the Field, made it necessary for us Likewise to withdrawn. We brought off one of the Enemys three Pounders, which with much difficulty was performed through a thick wood for near four miles, without the assistance of but one Horse, We got to the Encamping Ground which we left in the morning about two In the evening..............	3466
		14
		3480

Return of Killed, Wounded & Missing in the Action of
the 8th. Sept'r. at the Eutaw Springs.

Continental	Lt. Col.	Majr.	Capts.	Lieuts.	Serjts.	R & file
Killed	1		6	4	4	94
Wounded	2		7	19	24	202
Missing					1	31
Total	3		13	23	29	327
South Carolina State Troops						
Killed		1		2	4	6
Wounded	2		4	4	7	26
Missing						
Total	2	1	4	6	11	32
South Carolina Militia						
Killed						2
Wounded			1	2		24
Total			1	2		26
N. C. Militia						
Killed						6
Wounded						31
Missing						8
						45
Total in the Army	5	1	18	31	40	430

430
40
31
18
1
5
———
Total 525

When	Year 1781	Miles
Sept.		3480
10th.	Received information that the Enemy had left the Eutaw Springs the Evening before, on the Road to Monks Corner, the Genl. persued them to Mr. Martins, within 12 miles of the Corner..............	20
12th.	Return'd as far back as Whistleing George's.........	6
13th.	Marched to the Widow Floods, on ye Santee River..	14
14th.	Marched with the Army to the road leading to Lawrence's Ferry on the Santee, and Separated from them; they being bound for the High hills of Santee, and we for the Congaree Encamped on Mr. Caldwells Farm at the half way Swamp..............	19
15th.	Marched up the Congaree to Mr. Kelly's Farm.......	20
16th.	Marched to Mr. Patrick's Farm..................	13
17th.	Crossed the Congaree at Mr. Patricks & marched up to Mr. Culpepers and from thence to Col. Gooden's Farm	10
19th.	Marched this morning a little after sun rise joined Col. Washingtons Horse, & Encamped one mile below them on Mr. Pierce's Farm....................	11
27th.	Went to Head Quarters (on the High Hills of Santee) for Docts. Medecine for my men.	
	And returned the 30th, Inst.....................	40
Octbr.		
5th.	Took the Ague and fever.	
6th.	Marched to Mr. Simmons Farm on the Wateree......	10
9th.	By invitation from Mr. Danl. Huger, went in Compy with Lnt. Vaughen to his house..................	6
		3649

When	Year 1781	Miles
Octbr.		3649
27th.	Received Intilligence of the Surrender of Lord Cornwallaces whole Army to this Excellency Genl. Washington In York Town Virginia on the 17th Inst.	
Novembr.		
5th.	Left Mr. Huger's and returned to Camp at Simons's Farm	6
6th.	This morning began our march for Col. Goodens Mill on the Congaree river, Halted on Mr. Pierce's Farm	12
7th.	Marched this Day to New Market.	8
8th.	Marched this Day to Col. Goodens Mill............	8
18th.	Marched for Head Quarters which was at the High Hills of Santee, got this night to Mr. Danl. Hugier's	130
19th.	Crossed Wateree river arrived at Head Quarters......	10
20th.	Drew Cloathing for my men, and returned back to Mr. Hugier's	10
21st.	Returned to Col. Gooden's Mill....................	30
22nd.	This day was ordered to March by the way of Howell's Ferry to Col. Thompsons and there to join the Army, the troops moved, But I went to Capt. Howells having the Ague & Fever where I staid untill the 27th, Inst. being better, I set out for Col. Thompson's	
27th.	where I arrived this Night......................	30
28th.	Marched with the Army to Brown's Mill..........	10
29th.	Marched this day to Orangeburgh.................	16
Dec.		
1st.	Marched this day to Youngs Farm................	14
3rd.	Marched this day to 4 hole bridge on 4 hole Creek...	26
		3859

When	Year 1781 & 2	Miles
Dec.		3859
13th.	This Day arrived (at the 4 hole Bridge to relieve me) Capt. Moore of the S. Carolina State troops with 60 rank & file.	
14th.	Marched this day to Mr. Rumps................	8
15th.	Marched this day to Fergussons Saw Mills on the River Edisto	2
16th.	This day we arrived at Camp at Round O.........	10
18th.	This day I received orders to mount in Company with the Virginians near Stono, on Edisto river, and to be under the Command of Col. Lawrence. Accordingly crossed Edisto river at Parker's Ferry 14 miles from the Round O, and encamped three miles on the South side on Capt. Sanders Farm...................	17
20th.	March about two miles below Sandy Hill and encamped on Mr. Fergusson's Land.....................	6
1782. Jany.		
1st.	I went this day up to Head Quarters and got Liberty to retire to the Delaware State on Furlough.......	23
2 & 3rd.	Returned again to Camp which was moved to Spring Garden	25
4th.	This day began my march for the Delaware and got to the round O..............................	25
6th.	Left the round O and two hours before day arrived at Orangeburgh	50
7th.	Crossed the Congree River & staid all night at Mrs. Weston's	33
8th.	This day got to Mr. Randle's Mill..............	18
9th.	Lay at Camden this Evening....................	9
10th.	Lay within 6 miles of the Hanging Rock..........	20
11th.	Lay this Night at Majr. Crawfords in the Waxaws..	30
12th.	Lay this Night at Mr. Robt. Phillips's within 2 miles of Charlotte................................	30
13th.	Got to Hezekiah Alexanders, Esqr..............	4
14th.	Staid at Mr. Pattens near Fifers................	18
16.	Arrived at Salsbury..........................	22
		4219

When	Year 1782	Miles
January		4219
17th.	Left Salsbury & on the 19th Inst. Arrived at Guilford Court house..................................	54
	From thence went to the Revd. Mr. Caldwell's and	3
	from thence to Mr. Robt. Rankin's and from thence	3
	to Mr. Alexander Gray's......................	8
Febry.		
26th.	Arrived at Mr. Robt. Gray's 12 miles N. E. of Hilsborough	45
March		
3rd.	Returned to Mr. Alexander Gray's in Company with two of Mr. Robt. Gray's Daughters—And returned the third of March...........................	90
4th.	I had the very agreeable sight of Lt. Anderson and Ens. Platt at my Quarters.	
11th.	Left Mr. Gray's in Compy with Capt. Jaquett, Lts. Campbell, Anderson, Ens. Platt, and Doctr. Hartley (from South Carolina) remained all night at Genl. Parson's—Granville County....................	20
12th.	Lay this night at Robt. Gillispes..................	29
13th.	The next morning Crossed the Roanoke Stoped at Mr. Deloanes, who is termed a Col. in that County, & no doubt thinks himself a Gentleman, but shall leave the readers to Judge whether or not, When they are informed by this that after Genl. Sinclier had remained at his House one night, the next morning had to pay three guineas, after being invited there.	
		4401

When	Year 1782	Miles
		4401
	In a few Weeks afterwards Col. O. H. Williams called at the same house, but could not get Quarters. And some days afterwards I called there not knowing his Character, shared the same fate with those before me, and indeed he turned my waggon off the Plantation without my knowledge, I requested only the floor to lay on which was refused me, & rather than Quarrel with one of the first rank in the famous State of Virginia, chose to Lay in the Woods. Marched this day	25
March		
14th.	Marched this day to Commissary Lambs............	30
15th.	Marched this day to Denwidie Court house..........	25
16th.	Marched to Petersburgh and Stayed at Mrs. Spencers	18
17th.	Capt. Jaquett, Doctr. Hartley, and the Waggon went round by land.	
	Lts. Campbell, Anderson, & Platt with myself went on Board a Vessel at the Broad Way, Bound to the Head of Elk.	
18th.	Weighed Anchor about one OClock & on the 25th put into Pianketanck, which is 210 miles from Petersburgh	210
	And in this place our Vessel was taken by a small Vessel from New York called "Hook-in-Sneevy."	
		4709

When	Year 1782	Miles
		4709
	We made our escape by a small Boat and marched to Capt. Lockleys Ferry on Rapahanock River, Virginia	15
27th.	March'd to Notingham Court House at this place there was a Genl. Field Day of Muster, here we got a Boat destined for the Head of Elk Comm'd. by Capt. Brewer, went on board in Coan River, landed this morning at the Mouth of Sd. River. Lodged all night at Mr. Crawley's........................	16
28th.	Made sail at Night with a fair wind got near Petuxen River but by a head wind were beat back into Coan River Sailed this Night......................	30
April 1st.	Being Easter Monday set out on foot for Yocommico River Crossed over the Potowmack in Mr. Mithaney's Boat Landed at pine point marched about 3 miles Lodged at the Revd. Mr. Sebastian's........	22
2nd.	This day Crossed Petuxen River at Junifers Ferry Lodged at Mr. M. Summervills................	25
3rd.	March'd this Day to Mr. Smiths in Annarundle County Maryland	20
4th.	This Day Crossed the South River at Browns Ferry Quartered at Mr. Middleton's in Annapolis........	25
5th.	Crossed the Severn River at the Town Quartered at Mr. Poes D. Q. M. Genl.....................	30
7th.	Took a passage on board the Pacquett Commanded by Capt. Simpson & arrived at Newark about 8 OClock in the Evening...............................	90
	Total of Marches From the 13th of April 1780 untill the 7th of April 1782........................	4982
	Omitted one nights march to the old regulating ground	24
		5006

COPIES

No. 1.

Summons to Majr Lgenl Lincoln, 10th April, 1780, with his Answer of the Same Date.

Sir Henry Clinton, K. B, General and Commander in Chief of his Majesties forces, in the Colonies, laying on the Atlantic, from Nova Scotia, etc., etc., etc., and Vice Admiral Arbuthnot, Commander in Chief of his Majestys Ships in North America etc., etc., etc., Regretting the effusion of blood, and the Distress which must now Commence, deem it Consonant to Humanity to warn the Town and Garrison of Charles Town of the Havock & Desolation with which they are threatened from the formidable force surrounding by Land & Sea.

An Alterative is offered at this Hour to the Inhabitants of saving their lives & Property (Contained in the Town) or of abiding by the fatal Consequences of a Cannonade and storm. Should the place in a fatal Security, or its Commander in a Wanton Indifference to the fate of its inhabitants delay the Surrender; or should Publick Stores or Shiping be Destroyed, the resentment of an exasperated Soldery may intervene, but the mild & Compasionate Terms never be renewed.

The respective Commanders who hereby summons the town, do not apprehend so rash a part as that further resistance will be taken; but rather that the gates will be opened, and themselves received with a degree of Confidence which will forbode farther Reconciliation.

No. 2.

HEAD QUARTERS, Charlestown, April 10th, 1780.

Gentlemen

I have received your Summons of this Date—Sixty days have passed since it has been known that your intentions Against this Town were Hostile, in which, time has been afforded to abandon it, but duty and inclination point to the propriety of Supporting it to the last extremety.

> I have the Honour
> to be Your Excellencys
> Humble Sert.
> (Signed)   B. LINCOLN

Major General Lincoln, to Sir Henry Clinton, K. B, Proposing Articles of Capitulation, with Sir Henry Clinton's Answer, And the Articles of Capitulation.

No. 3.

Charlestown, April 21st., 1780.

Sir

I am willing to enter into the Consideration of terms of Capitulation—if such can be obtained as are Honourable for the Army, & Safe for the Inhabitants. I have to propose A Cessation of Hostilities for six hours, for the purpose of digesting such Articles,

> I have the Honour to be
> Your Excellencies obt. Sert.
> (Signed)   B. LINCOLN

His Excellency Sir H. Clinton.

No. 4.

CAMP BEFORE CHARLESTOWN, April 21st., 1780.

Sir

Admiral Arbuthnot who Commands the fleet, should have been addressed jointly with me on this Occation. As I wish to Communicate with him, and as I give my consent to a Cessation of Hostilities, for six hours; I desire an Aid de Camp may pass to the ships with a letter & my request that the Battery on James Island may desist firing.

I have the Honour to be etc.,

(Signed) H. CLINTON.

Majr Genl Lincoln.

No. 5.

Articles of Capitulation proposed by Major General Lincoln.

Art. 1st. That all acts of Hostilities & works shall cease between the Naval & land forces of Great Britain and America, in this State, Until the Articles of Capitulation shall be agreed on, Signed & executed, or Collectively Rejected.

Art. 2nd. That the town, Forts, & Fortifications Belonging to them shall be surrendered to the Commander in Chief of the British Forces, Such as they now Stand.

Art. 3. That the several troops garrisoning the town & Forts, including the French & American Sailors, the French Invalids, the North Carolina & South Carolina Militia, & such of the Charles Town Militia as may choose to have this place, shall have thirty six hours to withdraw to Lampriers, after the Capitulation has been accepted & Signed on both sides and that those troops shall retire with the usual Honours of War & Carry off during that time their Arms, Field Artillery, Amunition, Baggage, & such of their stores as they may be able to Transport.

Art. 4. That after the expiration of the thirty six hours mentioned in the preceeding Article, the British Troops before the Town shall take possession of it, And those at Wappetau shall proceed to Fort Moultrie.

Art. 5. That the American Army thus collected at Lamprier's shall have ten days from the expiration of the thirty six hours before mentioned, to march whereever Genl Lincoln shall think proper to the Eastward of Cooper River, without any movement being made by the British troops, or part of them out of town, on Fort Moultrie.

Art. 6. That the sick and wounded of the American, & French Hospitals, with their Medecines, Stores, the Surgeons, and Director Genl shall remain in the Town, and be supplied with the necessaries requisite, untill provisions can be made for their removal, which will be as speedily as possible.

Art. 7. That no soldier shall be encouraged to Desert, or permitted to enlist on either side.

Art. 8. That the French Consul, his House, papers and other moveable property, shall be protected untouched, and a proper time granted him for retiring to any place that may afterwards be agreed upon between him and the Commander in Chief of the British Forces.

Art. 9. That the Continental Ships of War, Providence, Boston & Ranger, now in this Harbour, with the French ship of War the Adventure, shall have liberty to proceed to Sea, with the necessary stores on board and go unmolested, the three former to Philadelphia and the latter to Cape Fran-Cois, with the French Invalids mentioned in Art. 3.

Art. 10. The Citizens shall be protected in their Persons, & Properties.

Art. 11. That twelve months be allowed such as do not choose to continue under the British Government, to dispose of their effects, real and Personal in the State, without any molestation whatever; or to remove such part thereof as they choose, as well as themselves & Famelies, and during that time, they or any of them may have it at their option to reside occationally in Town or Country.

Art. 12. That the same protection to their Persons, and Properties, and the same time for the removal of their effects, be given to the Subjects of France and Spain Residing amongst us, as are required for the Citizens in the preceeding Articles.

Dated at Charlestown 21 April 1780

(Signed) B. LINCOLN

No. 6.

Sir Henery Clinton and Vice Admiral Arbuthnot to Major General Lincoln.

CAMP BEFORE CHARLESTOWN April 21st, 1780.

Sir

We have in answer to your third Article (for we cannot proceed further) to refer you to our former offer, as terms which although you cannot claim, we yet Consent to grant.

These however must be accepted immediately, and responsible Hostages of the rank of Field Officers must be sent us as Securities that the Custom of War on these Occasions are strictly adhered to; that no person of the Garrison or Inhabitant be permitted to go out, nothing to be removed or destroyed, & no ship or Vessel pass from the Town.

All dependent posts are to be included in the Surrender, and the Hostages to be answerable for these as for the Town.

Your answer is expected at 10 OClock, at which hour Hostilities will Commence again, unless our Offers are Closed with.

(Signed) H. CLINTON
M. T. ARBUTHNOT

No. 7.

CAMP BEFORE CHARLES TOWN, May 8th, 1780.

Sir

Circumstanced as I now am with respect to the place invested, Humanity only can induce me to lay within your reach the terms I had determined should not again be pre-offered.

The fall of Fort Sullivan, the Destruction (on the 6th. Inst,) of what remained of your Cavelry, the Critical period to which our approaches against the Town have brought us, mark this as the term of your hopes of Succour, (Could you ever have framed any) and as an hour, beyond which, Resistance is temerity.

By this last Summons therefore I throw to your Charge whatever vindictive Severity, exasperated Soldiers may inflict on the Unhappy People, whom you devote by persevering in a fruitless Defence.

I shall expect your answer untill Eight OClock, When Hostilities will Commence again, Unless the Town be surrendred, etc, etc.,

(Signed)   H. CLINTON

Major General Lincoln

No. 8.

CHARLES TOWN May 8th 1780.

Sir

Your letter to me of this date is now under consideration there are so many different Interests to be Consulted, that I have to propose that Hostilities do not again Commence till twelve.

(Signed)   B. LINCOLN

His Excallency Sr. H. Clinton.

No. 9.

May 8th 1780.

Sir

As more time has been expended in Consulting the different Interests than I supposed there would be, I have to request that the truce may be continued untill Four OClock.

(Signed) B. LINCOLN.

His Excellency Sr. H. Clinton.

No. 10.

May 8th 1780.

Sir

I consent that Hostilities shall not again Commence before the Hour of twelve as you desire.

I have the Honour to be

Sir

(Signed) H. CLINTON

Major General Lincoln.

No. 11.

Articles of Capitulation proposed by Major General Lincoln.

Art. 1st. That all acts of Hostilities and Work shall cease between the Besiegers & Besieged, Untill the Articles of Capitulation shall be agreed on, Signed, & executed, or collectively rejected.

Art. 2nd. The Town & fortifications shall be Surrendred to the Commander in Chief of the British Forces, such as they now Stand.

Art. 3. The Continental troops & Sailors, with their Baggage shall be conducted to a place to be agreed on, where they will remain Prisoners of War, Untill exchanged.—While Prisoners, they shall be supplied with good & wholesome provisions, in such Quantity as is served out to the troops of his Britanic Majesty.

Art. 4th.   The Militia now in Garrison shall be permitted to return to their respective homes, and be secured in their Persons & Property.

Art. 5th.   The sick & wounded shall be continued under the care of their own Surgeons, and be supplied with Medicines, and such necessaries as are allowed to the British Hospitals.

Art. 6th.   The officers of the Army & Navy shall keep their Horses, swords, Pistols & Baggage, which shall not be searched, and retain their Servants.

Art. 7th.   The Garrisons shall at an hour appointed, march out with Shouldred arms, Drums beating, and Colours flying, to a place agreed on, where they will pile their Arms.

Art. 8th.   That the French Consul, his House, Papers, and other moveable property, shall be protected & untouched, and a proper time granted to him for retiring to any place that may afterwards be agreed on between him & the Commander in Chief of the British Forces.

Art. 9th.   That the Citizens shall be protected in their Persons & Properties.

Art. 10th.   That a twelve months time be allowed all such as do not choose to continue under the British Government; to dispose of their effects, real & personal in the State, without any molestation whatever, or to remove such part thereof as they Choose, as well as themselves & families; and that during that time, they, or any of them, may have it at their option to reside occationaly in Town or Country.

Art. 11th. That the same protection to their persons & Properties, & the same time for the removal of their effects, be given to the subjects of France & Spain, as are required for the Citizens in the preceeding articles.

Art. 12th. That a Vessel be permitted to go to Philadelphia with the Genls despatches, which are not to be opened:

(Signed)   B. LINCOLN

Charlestown May 8th 1780.

No. 12.

May 8th 1780

Sir

As I wish to Communicate with the Admiral upon the subject of your last letter, I have to desire that an Aid-de-Camp may be permitted to pass to the Fleet for that purpose.

I have the Honour to be etc., etc.,

(Signed)   H. CLINTON

Maj Genl Lincoln.

No. 13.

May 8th 1780

Sir

In order to give the Articles of Capitulation which you have proposed a due consideration, I propose that the Cessation of Hostilities shall Continue untill tomorrow morning at Eight OClock, and that in the mean time every thing shall Continue in its present Situation, if you accede to this, you will please to give me immediate Information of it.

I am

Sir etc.,

(Signed)   H. CLINTON

Maj Genl Lincoln.

No. 14

Sir   May 8th 1780

I accede to your proposal, that Hostilities shall cease untill tomorrow morning, Eight OClock, and that in the mean time all works shall continue in their present State.

(Signed)   B. Lincoln.

His Excellency Sir H. Clinton.

No. 15.

Sir   May 8th 8 OClock P. M.

Your answer to my letter proposing the Continuation of the truce untill to morning at Eight OClock, only accedes to the Cessation of Hostilities, & that in the mean time all works shall Continue in their present State; but my proposition was that untill that time everything should Continue in its present Situation; & my meaning was, that there should be an attempt made to remove any of the troops, or destroy any of the Ships, Stores or other Effects whatever, now in the Town or Harbour.

If your idea is the Same, I must request you will express your Self more explicitly.

I am
Sir etc.,
(Signed)   H. Clinton

No. 16.

Sir   May 8th 1780

In Agreeing that the truce should be Continued untill Eight OClock tomorrow morning, & all works remain as they were,

I meant to accede to your proposal that everything should Continue in its present Situation, which I again assent to.

(Signed)   B. Lincoln

His Excellency Sir H. Clinton

No. 17.

Articles of Capitulation, as proposed By Major General Lincoln, and Answered by their Excellencies General Sir Henery Clinton, K. B. And Vice Admiral Arbuthnot.

Art. 1st.   All acts of Hostilities and work shall cease untill the Articles of Capitulation are finally agreed to or rejected.

Art. 2nd.   The Town & Fortifications, with the Shipping at the Wharves, Artillery and all Public Stores whatsoever, shall be surrendered in their present State to the Commanders of the investing Forces.   Proper Officers shall attend from the respective Departments to receive them.

Art. 3rd.   Granted.

Art. 4th.   The militia now in Garrison shall be permitted to return to their respective homes, as Prisoners upon Parole; which Parole, so long as they observe it, shall secure them from being molested in their Property by the British Troops.

Art. 5th.   Granted.

Art. 6th.   Granted; except with respect to their Horses, which will not be allowed to go out of town, but may be disposed of by a Person left from each Corps for that purpose.

Art. 7th.   The whole Garrison shall at an hour to be appointed, march out of the Town to the ground Between the Works of the place & the Canal, where they will deposit their arms.   The Drums are not to beat A British march, or Colours to be uncased.

Art. 8th. Agreed; with this restriction, that he is to consider himself as a prisoner on Parole.

Art. 9th. All Civil Officers, & the Citizens who have Borne Arms during the Siege, must be Prisoners on Parole; and with respect to their property in the City, shall have the same terms as are granted to the militia. And all other persons now in the Town, not described in this, or other Article, are notwithstanding understood to be Prisoners on Parole.

Art. 10th. The Discussion of this Article, of Course, cannot possibly be entered into at present.

Art. 11th. The Subjects of France & Spain shall have the same terms as are granted to the French Consul.

Art. 12th. Granted; and a proper Vessel with a flag will be provided for that purpose.

All Public papers & records must be carefully preserved, & faithfully delivered, to such persons as shall be appointed to receive them.

(Signed)   H. CLINTON
M. T. ARBUTHNOT

Camp before Charlestown
   May 9th 1780.

No. 18.

May 9th 1780.

Sir

In reply to your Answers on the Articles of Capitulation, I must remark that in their present State they are inadmissable, and have to propose that these now sent may be acceded to.

If any further explaination should be necessary, I have to purpose also, that two or three Gentlemen be appointed to meet & Confer on the subject.

I have the Honour to be etc.,

(Signed) B. Lincoln.

His Excellency Sr. H. Clinton.

Alterations of Articles of Capitulation, proposed by Major Genl Lincoln.

Art. 2nd. The Town & Fortifications, with the Shipping at the Wharves, (excepting those which are private property) and all public stores, shall be surrendered in their present State to the Commander in Chief of the British Forces.

Art. 4th. The militia now in Garrison, shall be permitted to return to their respective Homes, with their Baggage, Unmolested, & not be considered as Prisoners of War.

Art. 6th. Such of the Officers as may be unwilling to dispose of their Horses, may keep them.

Art. 7th. This article to stand as at first proposed, the Drums not Beating A British march.

Art. 8th. The French Consul never having borne Arms, and acting in a Civil Capacity is not to be Considered as a prisoner of War.

Art. 9th. The Citizens & all other persons, now in Town, who are Inhabitants of this State, shall be secured in their persons & properties, both in Town and Country, and not be considered Prisoners of War.

Art. 10th. This Article to Stand as at first proposed. The persons who may Claim the previledge therein expressed, giving their Parole that they will not act against the British Government untill they are exchanged.

Art. 11. This Article to Stand as at first proposed, with the same restrictions as are mentioned in Art. 10th.

In order to prevent disputes, it is to be understood, that all officers of the Continental Army, who are Citizens of this State, be entitled to all the Benefits of Citizens with regard to the security of their Property.

All publick records now in Town, will be delivered to such persons as may be appointed to receive them.

(Signed)   B. LINCOLN.

Done at Charlestown May 9th 1780.

No. 19.

Sir   May 9th 1780

No other motives but those of Forbearance and Compassion induced us to renew offers of Terms you certainly had no Claim to.

The alterations you propose are all Utterly inadmissable. Hostilities will in Consequence Commence Afresh at Eight OClock.

(Signed)   H. CLINTON
M. T. ARBUTHNOT

Majr Genl Lincoln.

No. 20.

Sir   Charlestown May 11th 1780.

The same motives of humanity, which inclined you to pro-pose Articles of Capitulation to this Garrison, Induced me to offer those I had the honour of Sending you on the 8th Inst. They then appeared to me such as I might proffer, And you receive with honour to both parties your exceptions to them, as they principally concerned the militia and Citizens, I then conceived were such as Could not be concerned with; but a recent application from those People, Wherein they express a Willingness to Comply with them, and a wish on my part to lessen as much as may be, the Distresses of war to Individuals. lead me now to offer you my acceptance of them.

I have the Honour to be Sir etc.,

(Signed)   B. Lincoln.

No. 21.

Camp before Charlestown May 10th 1780.

Sir

When you rejected the favourable terms which were dictated by an earnest desire to Prevent the effusion of Blood, and interposed Articles that were wholly unadmissable, both the Admiral and my Self were of opinion that the Surrender of the Town at Discretion was the only Condition that should be afterwards attended to; but as the motives which then Induced them, are still prevalent, I now Inform you that the terms then offered will still be granted.

A copy of the Articles shall be sent for your Ratification as soon as they Can be prepared, and immediately after they are exchanged, a Detachment of Granadiers will be sent to take possession of the Horn Work apposite your main gate, every arrangement which may Conduce to good order in Occupying the Town, shall be settled before noon tomorrow, and at that time your Garrison shall march out.

I have the honour to be Sir
Your most obt. & Humbl. Sert.

(Signed)   H. Clinton

Majr Genl Lincoln.

Part II

A BOOK OF GENERAL ORDERS
FOR THE YEAR 1777

Kept by

Captain Robert Kirkwood

"Capt. Robt. Kirkwood's Book of General Orders for the year 1777 with a Journal of Marches performed by the Delaware Regt for sd year, in the last part of the Book."

(March 1st 1777)

Proceedings of a Reigmental Court Martial held at Hel' Co. this 1st day of March 1777 (for the trying of a certain James Pemberton charged with stealing a piece of check linnen) whereof Capt. Enoch Anderson is President.

$$\text{Lt.} \left.\begin{array}{} \\ \end{array}\right\} \text{Members} \left\{\begin{array}{} \text{Ens. Hyat} \\ \text{Ens. Jordan} \end{array}\right.$$
Parvis

All members being present.

Court adjourned untill 2 OClock P. M. all members present,

The Prisoner being called the question being put guilty or not guilty (Prisoner) pleads not guilty.

EVIDENCE—James Moones, being called & sworn, sayeth gt.

Prisoner had a piece of check, which he endeavoured to conceal under his coat, but Mr. Jordan ordered him to come back the road he was going which was towards Wilmington he moving it from the fore part to the back part of his coat he the sd Moones, saw the check; and told him to hide it under the snow, for he would be detected with it.

The Prisoner being asked if the above oath were true or not he replyed that he had nothing with him that he was affraid of being detected with, & being asked again if he had the check, sd. he had none but an old check shirt

EVIDENCE—Hugh Coffel, being sworn sayeth gt. he the sd. Pemberton had a quantity of check which appeared to be new with fringes or thrumbs on it, as is common from the loom.

EVIDENCE—Cornelius Grimes being sworn sayeth that the prisoner told him he took a check shirt with him to Wilmington. From circumstances which appear after ye evidence being called & duly examined the court are of opinion that James Pemberton is guilty of the charge laid against him, and do sentence him to receive thirty nine lashes on his bare back well laid on with the cat o nine tails; & also to make restitution for the linen. The commanding officer approves of the sentence, & orders the punishment to be put in execution this evening.

HEAD QUARTERS, Princeton March 27th 1777
Genl Orders

The General is very sorry there should be so much foundation for the frequent complaints of the sodery, respecting their pay and cloathing, he is very sensible of these difficulties and promises them everything in his power to have them speedily redressed.

The officers of the different Corps, are for this purpose immedietely to make out their pay rolls & returns for the necessaries, and despatch them by proper persons, who will procure them without delay.

March 28th 1777
Genl Orders

The detachments from the 3rd 4th & 10th Pennsylvania Batt. are to form one Corps and be under the immediet Command of Major Larmer, the Adj't or one appointed for that duty to give in the returns of the Whole. Morning Reports are to be punctually given in at 10 OClock

Genl Orders   29th March 1777

All the Carpenters belonging to the Different Corps are to parade at Head Quarters at eight OClock to morrow morning. Additional wages will be given to good workmen.

Publick worship will be performed by the Revd. Dr. Witherspoon tomorrow at the Meetinghouse, all the Troops are to attend precisely at 11 OClock. The officers to see the men parade exactly at that time, in neat & proper order and be examplary in their attendance.

HEAD QUARTERS Princeton 30th March 1777

Genl Orders

All the Troops in Camp to Parade to morrow morning at guard Mounting. James Robinson, & Matt. Jones, under sentence of Death for Desertion are to be Executed to morrow between the hours of 10 & 11 OClock Major Larmer's Detachment from ye 3rd, 8th & 9th Virgr. Regt. & Capt. Scheirs Independant Company to hold themselves in readiness to march immediately after Execution tomorrow.

Princeton March 30th 1777

The Court met according to Orders, Proceeds

Col. Shreeves   President

Capt.	Lowery		Cap.	Dillen
do.	Christy		do.	MClellan
do.	Anderson	Members	Lt.	Vananglin
Lt.	Helms		do.	Lane
do.	Appelton		do.	MBride
do.	Conn		do.	Rhea

Geo. Hofman Judge Advocate *Pro Tempore* Nicholas Luke a Soldier Brought Before the Court Martial For Desertion,

The Prisoner pleads guilty

The Court Considering him, Sentence him to Receive 50 Lashes, on his bare back well laid on wt ye Cat o' nine Tails.

Isaac Pain Soldier, brought before the Court for Desertion, Prisoner pleads not guilty

EVIDENCE—Lt. Reynolds The Court finds the prisoner guilty And do Sentence him to Receive 15 Lashes & to be Discharged from the Service.

William Watson Brought before the Court for mutiny & Drawing his Bayonet on Lt. Bowman the Court Sentence him to receive 400 Lashes

(March 30th 1777)

Moses Joab a Soldier Brought before the Court for taking of a waggon and Horses the Prisoner pleads guilty. And Sentence him to Receive 100 Lashes & have 3 Dollars stop't out of his Wages to be paid to the waggoner.

James Bartley a Soldier Brought before the Court for Stealing and Selling a Shirt, the Prisoner pleads not guilty. The Court finds him guilty. And do Sentence him to Receive 100 Lashes.

Hopewell Jewell Brought before the Court for Stealing and imbezeling a Continental Mare, the Court finds him guilty, and do Sentence him to Receive 100 Lashes; s'd Jewell is to Receive 25 pr. Day untill he has got the 100 Lashes. Should the Mare be brought before Monday night he then Receives the whole at once.

Jno Bryan A Soldier on Suspicion of Desertion James Murphy for persuaiding Jno Bryan to Enlist with Ens. Carpenter knowing that he Before was Inlisted. the Court Sentence Bryan to Receive 100 Lashes & Murphy to Receive 50 Lashes.

Samuel M Murry brought before the Court for getting Drunk & Stealing 1 pair Shoes. No Evidence appears for Stealing is therefore Sentenc'd to Receive 15 Lashes for getting Drunk.

Andrew McCoy A Suttler brought before the Court for fraud & Extortion, the Court finds him guilty & Sentence him to Receive 100 Lashes & be drummed out of the Camp & never permitted to Sell any more.

The Above Sentence has been approv'd of by the Genl.

Apl 9th 1777

The Officers of the Differrent detachment are to Attend at Mr. Days Quarters Adjst to the 2nd Virgi. Regt for orders and Details at 2 OClock Presisely.

Apl 10th 1777

1 C, 1 L, 2 S, 2 C, 25 P of the 11th Regt with three days Provisions to parade at head Quarters to morrow morning at 6 OClock.

Apl 15th 1777

1 C, 1 L, 2 S, 2 C, 30 P of the Delaware Detachment with three Days Provisions to march to the Enemys Lines Tomorrow morning & Relieve Capt. Hines now on Scout.

Genl orders from Morriston Apl 25 1777 Colns and Commanding Officers of Corps must Cause their Reigmental pay Masters to make up their Pay abstracts to the first of this month, & order them to attend at the Paymaster Generals for the Money.

Proper attention to genl orders of this nature Issued the 21st Last month would not only have moved the Complaint of the Soldiers for want of their pay to frequently made to the Commander in Chief, but would have saved them much trouble in Settling their Account for money drawn uppon Acct. and the most punctual obedience must be paid to this order no Execuse for delay will Admitted.

They are also to make Returns of the medicins and Instruments in their Possession to the Director General at Head Quarters on Monday next.

The Adjut Genl will transmit you Copies of this to gentn Concerned.

Apl 26 1777

A Court of Enquiry to Set Tomorrow at 9 OClock at Major Taylors Quarters.

Major Taylor to Preside.

	Members	
Light Horse	1 C	0 L
Col. Antl	1 C	1 L
9th V. Reigt	0 C	0 L
D. B.	0 C	1 L

Apl 30th 1777

Procedings of A Court Martial held at princeton

Members present

C. Anderson ⎫
Lt. Wilds   ⎬ members ⎰ Lt. Wyat
Lt. Purvis ⎭   ⎱ Ens. Campbell

Saml McMurry A Soldier brought before the Court for getting Drunk & neglect of Duty.

Prisoner being Called pleads guilty The Court after Considering the nature of the offence & bad tendency of Drunkenness Sentence him to Receive 50 Lashes on his bare back.

HEAD QUARTERS Princeton May 4th 1777

The Following orders Came from his Ecellency this Morning and is to be Perticularly Observed By the Officers in this Division of the Army.

Every Corps must put their Arms in the best firing order and compleatly furnished With Amunition the Commanding Officers will see this done, as they will Answer for the Least neglect of this Important duty.

The Qr M. Genl to Furnish them with tents and proper Convenniencies to Carry them, that they may be Ready to move with the Troops at Shortest notice.

The Genl Laments the necessity he is Laid under of Repeating his orders by which the Officers were forbid to Ride About the Country This Absenting themselves from their Duty—if any Sudden Call for Offensive or Defensive measures Should be made during their Absence, they assuredly will be Brought to Severe Acct.

The Major Genrls will Publish those Orders at their Respective posts, for which purpose the Adjt Generals will furnish them wt Copies.

The Commanding Officer of Companies or Detachments are Immediately to make out five Muster Rolls of Each Company or Detachment Printed forms of muster Rolls may be had by Applying to the deputy Muster Master Gen. at Head Quarters, Col. Hazen's Reg't to Parade for muster at 10 OClock on Tuesday morning and the other Troops in Princeton at three in the Afternoon. Those at Kingston will parade on Wednesday forenoon at 10 OClock and then at Rocky hill at 3 P. M. on the same day.

(May 4th 1777)

Every Soldier whose Absence is not Accounted for on the Muster Rols Must without fail appear on the parade—The Rolls to be made out Alphabetically & the non effectives to be placed After the Effectives.

Proceedings of A Court Martial of the Line May 1st 1777 Capt. M Connell Prisident.

Capt. Anderson ⎫
Lt. Gilbert ⎭ members ⎰ Lt. Hoops
⎱ Lt. Tallott

Francis Dougherty of Capt. Dorseys Comp. tried for being insolent & Drunkness sentenced to Receive 50 Lashes.

Thomas Donaldson of Capt. Nevin's Company tried for being Drunk on his post Sentenced to Receive 150 Lashes.

Patrick Ferrel of Capt. M Connell's Company for being Drunk and Attempting to desert Sentenced to Receive 200 Lashes.

The Genrl Approves of the Sentence and orders them to be put in Execution to Morrow at the Releiving of the Guards.

Timothy Collins, and William Man, are forgiven for their Crimes and ordered to Join their Reigt.

HEAD QUARTERS May 4 1777

The Genl again orders that the whole of the Troops turn out and are on the Parade at the beating of the Ravalie and the Officers Are to Maneuver them untill Sun Rise the Commanding Officers of Corps must Remember for to have all their men Provided with three Days Provision Ready Cook'd The Genl Perticulary forbids the Commanding officers of guards not to suffer any of the guards to be Absent from their guards Either day or Night untill properly Relieved it is with surprise the Genl hears it is A Common Practice when at the Advanced Posts of the Enemy.

Any Officers Commanding guards who shall suffer any of their Officers or men to be Absent untill Properly Relieved may Depend on his being Arrested.

Officer of the Day Col. Stone a Subaltern from the Artilery to Visit the Barracks & Hospital to Morrow.

The Genl Positively forbids any Person whatever found firing or Discharging his Arms near the Camp, Every Officer or Non Commissioned officer who finds any person guilty of that Malicious Practice Must Immediatly tye them up & give them 20 Lashes without Tryal.

The Artilery Must Parade on the Grand Parade, Every Morning at the Break of Day and Fire a morning gun at which time all the Drums in Camp Must beat the Reivelie all the Drums & fifes in Camp Must attend with the Drum Major of Col. Antles Reigt. to beat the troop Retreat & Tatto

Such who do not Attend, the Drum Major Must Confine them & they Shall be punished.

The Following order came from his Exellency to day is to be perticularly observed by the Officers in this Department.

It having been observed that no truth of Adhering to A former order, but the Contrairey some officers make A Practice of Riding Continental Horses as well as them Belonging to the Inhabitants in the Neighbourhood of the Army.

The Commander in Cheif posittively Declares that if any Off, in the Returns will Dare to Presume to Ride any Horse Either Publick or Private, Without Leave first obtain'd from the proper Off, if a Publick Horse, or from the Owner if Private property; Shall Immediatly be Brought to tryal by A Genl Court Martial.

HEAD QUARTERS May 15th 1777

As few Vices are Attended with more pernicious Consequences in Civil life, so there are none more fatal in A Military one than that of Gaming which often brings Disgrace, & Ruin upon Offs & Injury and Punishment on Soldiers, & Reports Prevailing which it is to be feared are too well founded that this pernicious Vice has Shead its banefull influence in the Army and in perticular to the Prejudice of the Recruiting Service the Commander in Cheif in the most pointed & Explicat terms forbids all Offs & Soldiers Playing at Cards or Dice or any other games except that of Exercise for Diversions it being impossible if the practice be Allowed at all to Descriminate between Innocent play for Amusement And Criminal Gaming for Pecunary Sordid purposes.

Offs attentive to their Duty will find Abundant Imployment in training and Dissipling their Men, providing for them and Seeing that they appear Neat & Clean and Soldier like, nor will any thing Redound more to their Honour, Afford more Solid Amusement or better Answer the End of their Appoint- ment than to devote the Vacant Moments they may have to the Study of Military Authors.

The Commanding Off. of every Corps are Strictly enjoined to have the orders frequently Read and Strongly impressed upon the minds of them under his Command, Any Off. or Soldier or other person belonging to or following the Army Whether in Camp, in Quarters, or on the Recruiting Service, or Else where presuming under any pretence to Disobey this order Shall be tryed by A Genl Court Martial.

The Genl Offs in each Division of the Army are to pay the Strictest attention to the Due execution thereof.

The Adjt. Genl is to transmit Copies of this order to the Different parts of the Army also to Cause the Same to be immediatly Published in the Gazzet of Each State for the Information of Offs Dispersed on the Recruiting Service.

Field Off. of the day tomorrow Major Forrest An Off. from Col. Adam's Reigt, to visit the Barracks to Morrow.

The Genl Court martial now Setting is fully Disolved.

HEAD QUARTERS 16th May 1777

A Genl Court Martial to Sit to Morrow, morning at 9 OClock at the Meeting House.

Col. Hall Prisident

Col. Antle	1 C	2 L
Col. Hall	1 C	1 L
Col. Stone	2 C	2 L
Col. Adams	1 C	2 L
	5 C	7 L

The Commissary When there is no vegitables to be had is to Deliver flower to the Soldiers in Liew of their Rations of Rum.

Feild Off, of the Day tomorrow Major Stewart

An Off. from Col. Antles Rigt to Visit the Barracks and Hospital.

1 C, 1 L, 2 S, 2 C, 30 P from Col. Stones Detachment to Parade with three Days Provisions to Morrow Morning to Relieve the Scout.

HEAD QUARTERS 17th May 1777

Field Off. of the day Col. Woodford An Officer to Visit the Barracks from Col. Adams.

HEAD QUARTERS 18th May 1777

Feild Off. of the Day Col. Stone.

The Adjutant of the Congress' own Reigt to attend at Head Quarters tomorrow, to Act as Adjt. of the Day. A Court of Inquiry to Sit Tomorrow morning at 10 OClock. Col. Adams to Sit as President A Capt. from each Reigt to Attend as members this Court to Inquire into the Charges Against Daniel Williams & Ferguson McClain, Confin'd on Suspicion of Having held Correspondence with the Enemy, and Acting unfriendly to America; the Offs of the Several Corps are desired to see that Proper Returns are made of the Waggons and tents that are Necessary for their Respective Reigts, & the Deputy QrGl is to Supply them Immediately one tent only to be allowed for Six men. The QrMGenl of the Several Reigts to make Return of what Amunition may be Wanting to Compleat each man to 24 Rounds.

HEAD QUARTERS at Princeton 19th May 1777

Feild Off. of the Day Col. Stone.

Col. Adams to furnish the Adjt. of the day The Offs of the Several guards are Desired if one Wm. Delawin Should appear with A pass from his Exellency Genl Washington to go unto Brunswick that they cause him to be Sent to the Genls Quarters Near the Colledge.

The Court of Inquiry appointed to Sit yesterday Are also appointed to Inquire unto the Conduct of Capt. Ewing in the Scrimage with the Enemy on Thursday last, Capt. Heron and all other Witnesses to Attend at 12 OClock this Day and wait the Courts order.

Col. Adams to be Immediately furneshed with A Coppy of this order, And Capt. Ewing with Another.

The Genl intreats the Offs of the Several Reigts to Improve Every Oppertunity for Menouvering & Desciplining their Troops and he further Requests them to be perticularly Carefull to have the Rolls Called twice A day. As Nothing more Conducive to the health of Soldiers than their being kept neat & clean, the Genl Requests the Offs to be Attentive to them, & to Confine Such as will not (after being Admonished) pay proper attention to their Dress and Appearance.

The Morning Reports to be made in future at 8 OClock, The Feild Off. day is to be regularly relieved by the Field Off. of the Succeeding day, at the time of the Guards being paraded, where both of them are Requested to Attend in future.

The troop is to beat at 8 OClock the long Roll is to beat in each Reigt at half past Seven at which time the Parade for Guards & Fatagus are to parade Ready to march to the Grand parade as Soon as the Troops begin to beat. The Adjts of the Several Reigts are to March their parties on & Deliver them over to the Adjt of the present day, who is to Deliver them over to the Adjt of the Preceiding. The Off. of Fatague, when Such as is appointed is to attend on the Parade to take Charge of the fateague party. A Subl. & 20 men for fatague Tomorrow.

All the Field Offs are Desired to attend at head Quarters this Evening at 6 OClock except those on Duty, the Adjt to attend orderly time at Eleven OClock each Day.

HEAD QUARTERS Prince Town May 20th 1777

Field Officer of the day Major Stuart, Adjt of the day Col. Antill. The Troops at each part to turn out at Revellee' beating and assemble on the Grand parade and remain there till the sun rises up, All the Officers are Desired to attend the Parade with, their Troops. The Drum & Fife Majors of the 3 Reigts Stationed at Princeton, and one Drummer from each of those Reigts to Attend at Head Quarters this Afternoon at 4 OClock to receive Some orders from the Genls Aid de Camps, the Qrms of the Reigts Stationed at Princeton are to attend at head Quarters at 5 OClock this Afternoon all non Commissioned Offs and Soldiers are Strictly forbid to hold any Correspondence or Conversation with the British Soldiers in and about this town, all Commissioned Offs are Directed to order under Confinement, any non Commissioned Off. or Soldier which they may discover conversing with Such British Soldiers.

The Adjuts are in future to have the Parole and Countersign delivered out to give at orderly time Seal'd up, which they are not to open till Tattoo beating, & then Send it to the offs Commanding the guard, in their Respective Departments, Should any Sentry Desert his post, After the CounterSign is given, the Commanding Off. is to Alter the Counter Sign in the Departments, notice of which is to be immediatly Sent to

Head Quarters, The Sutlers in and about Princeton to make Returns to the Adjt Qm. Genl of their Names and the manner of appointment As soon as possible. Col. Hall Commanding at Rock'y hill is ordered to Send And relieve Col. Stone's Scouting Party, Consisting 1 Capt. 2 Subs 2 Serjts 2 Corps & Forty Privates, this Evening at 6 OClock they to provide themselves with 4 days Provision.

HEAD QUARTERS 21st May 1777

Field Off. of the Day Major Howard, Adjt of the Day from Col. Adams, Patrick McCallaster of Capt. Kirkwood's Comp. of the Delaware Reigt Sentenced by a Genl Court Martial to Receive 50 Lashes for Stealing a Rifle & Selling the Same, the Genl approves of the Sentence, & orders it to be put in execution at the head of the Reigt tomorrow morning at Guard Mounting.

Jas Collins of the 2nd Maryland Reigt Sentenced by the Court to Receive 100 Lashes for Desertion. the Genl Approves the Sentence & orders it to be put in Execution at the head of the Reigt to morrow morning at 8 OClock, Peter Robinson of Capt. Herons Comp. Col. Hazens Reigt, tryed for Leaving his post & for Desertion, Sentenced to Receive 100 Lashes for each offence, the Genl approves the Sentence, & orders the Execution tomorrow morning at 8 OClock at the head of the Reigt.

Hanna Taylor tryed for persuaiding the Soldiers to Desert, found not guilty the Genl orders her immediatly Released.

John Chard 2nd Maryland Reigt tried at the Same Court for Sleeping on his post Sentenced to Receive 100 Lashes well laid on, the Genl Approves the Sentence, & orders it to be executed at the head of the Reigt tomorrow morning at 8

OClock the Court Martial to Sit again to morrow morning at 9 OClock to try Such persons as may be brought before them.

Fergusson M'Clain trued at a Court of enquiry on Suspicion of being an enemy to his Country.

The Court finding no evidence against him, the Genl orders his immediat Release.

A Return of the Drums & fifes wanting in the Several Reigts are to be made immediately.

HEAD QUARTERS May 22nd 1777

Feild Off. of the Day Major Taylor.

Adjut. of the Day Col. Adams Adjt.

A Weekly Return of All the troops in this Department to be made at Head Quarters on Saterday at orderly time.

The Court of Inquiry Already apponted are to enquire into the Conduct of Mary Quin Confin'd on Suspicion of being an Enemy to her Country, Also into the Conduct of Daniel Williams, & John Jakel taken up going to the Enemy, all Witnesses to attend tomorrow morning at nine OClock.

HEAD QUARTERS 23rd May 1777

Feild off. of the Day

Adjt of the Day

Barbara Bowie tryed by A Genl Court Martial for Persuaiding the Soldiers to Desert & found not guilty.

The Genl Approves the Sentence & orders her Release.

(May 23rd 1777)

Hugh Wallace of Col. Hazen's Reigt tryed for Desertion, from that Reigt & Joining in Another of the Maryland Reigts into which he had previously Inlisted. The Court Adjudge him to refund the money he Rec'd of the Off. in Col. Hazen's Reigt though the Genl Supposes the Court must have had some Mittigating Evidence before them, in favor of the Prisoner, beside what accompanies the Sentence to Induce them to Pass so faivourable A Sentence Yet he finds himself oblidged to Disaprove it on account of its Incertainty, & orders the Prisoner to Remain for further Consideration, the Genl orders for the future the Judge Advocate to take down in writing the whole Evidences & furnish him with A Coppy at the time he Received the Proceedings of the Court Martial.

The Court finding no evidence against Danl Williams John Jakel, Danl McGuire, & James Robinson, the Genl orders their immediet Release.

The Genl Cannot forbear expressing his astonishment at the number of prisoners, Dailey confined in this Department as those Prisoners as well as the Rest of the Soldery are possessed of Rational faculties, He desires them Seriously to Reflect on the Differrence that Soldiers Situation—who Consious of Doing his duty Fears no Punishment & Reasonably expects favour, Countenance and prefirment, and that of a Soldier whose Constant beheavour Exposes him to the Censure of his Country, the Resentment of his Offs, and the Several Punishments by Sentence of Court Martials: punishment not only hard to endure, but must in their Consequences make them infamous among their fellow Country men forever After, it is truly astonishing that Considerations of the Sort Should have escaped the Lowest Soldier and what is yet more Surprising is that there Should be persons in the American Army so Lost to every principal of virtue, & Since of his own Happiness as to Attempt Desertion to an Enemy Already Destressed by famine and worn out with fatigue, and who Dailey live in

fearfull expectation of feeling the Weight of American Resentment, that this is the Situation of the British Army at present
all the prisoners and Deserters agree. And the wreched Regulars now among them with tears Confess it to their friends
when among them. while all Europe is arming in favour of
the Americans, while volunteers from all the States in Europe
are coming into venture their Lives in favour of American
freedom and while the Enemy Acknowledges that they have
no prospect of Conquering this Country, what can Induce
Persons to Desert to Such A Wreched Enemy, who have distinguished themselves by their Cruelty to the misguided Soldiers who have Deserted to them, as by their inhumanity to
the Inhabitants of this State who have fallen into their Power.

The Sentence of A Genl Court Martial ordering Richd
Burrest of Col. Hazen's Reigt to be Shot for Desertion is
approved the time for execution will be fixed in future orders.

The Bakers in the Several Reigts to Attend the Commissary
to morrow morning at Eight OClock and Receive his orders.

HEAD QUARTERS 24 May 1777

Field Off. of the Day to Morrow Col. Antill.
Adjt. of the Day Col. Antills Adjt.

The Commander in Cheif positlively Directs that all offs.
Stationed at out posts do not Come to Morristown but when
their Business Absolutely Requires it, and in that case that
they Return to their posts with all possible expedition.

Thos. Mullen Esqr. is appointed Brigade Major to Brigadr
Genl Debarre & is to be respected & obey'd as Such, A number
of Horses having been Drawn from the QrM. Gnl for per-

ticular Services & not Returned when the Business was performed, all Offs of Regts & others in possession of Horses Belonging to or hired by the States, are immedietly to return to the QrM. Genl his Deputy or Assistants in the Districts they may be at, the Genl Offs are to order Returns to be made of any publick horses imployed in their families that the States of the Horses Belonging to the Army may be known.

Valantine Peers Esqr. is appointed Brigade Major to Brigadier Genl Weeden & is to be Respected and Obey'd as Such, Lewis Woodruff Esqr. is appointed deputy Muster Master Cols & Commanding Offs of Regts and Corps must Cause their Reigmental Paymasters to make up their pay Abstracts to the 30th day of April or exclusive, & order them to attend to the paymaster Genls office for the money, they must be examined & Signed by their Respective Commanding Offs & Brigadiers who Will Diligently Compare them with the dailey & weekly Reigmental Returns & Certify them, the Company Abstracts must be Deliver'd into the paymaster Genl with the Regtl abstracts that the great and necessary purpose of Adjusting the Rank of all the Offs in the American Army may be effected with all expedition his exellency the Commander in Cheif, is pleas'd to order that the Feild Offs of each Continental Batt. do immediatly examine into the present Rank and hear their pretentions thereto, of all the Capts & Subalterns, Settle them where they Can to the Satisfaction of all the Gentlemen Concerned and make a full & fair Report of all their proceedings to the Brigadier commanding their Brigade; & that the Brigadiers with the Assistance of the field Offs of their Brigade do upon the reports of such, proceed to Adjust the Rank of all their Offs in the Seperate Brigades and make a full and fair Report of their proceedings. To the Major Genl Com-

manding their Divisions that Should there be any instance of
Dissatisfaction in the Offs they Candidly inumerate by such
Feild Offs and parties Complaining with all their attending
Circumstances & Report it to their respective Brigades Who
Shall Call before them all parties interested enquiring into
their Claims (& if it Cannot be settled with Satisfaction)
make A Special & Particular Report to their Major Genl upon
receipt of which Several Reports; A board of Offs will take
a Dispationate Comparative view of the whole & Determine
the Rank in the Army, untill which time it is expected the
Service will not be injured, in Disputes about Rank, but that
every Off. will by an emolous Discharge of his Duty recommend him Self to his Country, & to the promotion he ranks
himself intitled to.

HEAD QUARTERS Princeton 25th May 1777

Feild Off. of the Day Majr Forrest.
Adjt of the Day Col. Adam's Adjt.

All the Troops Stationed at Princeton except those on
guard & fatague to Parade for Exercise to morrow 10 OClock
forenoon, The Sentence Against Hugh Wallace being ex-
plained to the Genls Satisfaction the Genl Approves the Sentence and orders that as Soon as he refunds the Money Recd
of Col. Hazen's Off. or of the Off. with whome he Stands
Inlisted in the Maryland Regt will become Responsible for it;
the Said Wallace be Released from his Confinement and return
to his Duty in the Maryland Regt.

The Qrm. to See the Bridge near Kingston mended as Soon
as possible.

HEAD QUARTERS May 26th 1777

Feild Off. of the Day Majr Stewart.
Adjt of the Day Col. Antles adjt.

The Genl Court Martial to Sit to morrow morning at 9 OClock to try Such matters as may be brought before them. The Court of Inquiry to Sit at the Same time to Inquire into A Complaint against Capt. McConnel, for withholding the Bounty money from Jas Irwing also to Inquire into the Conduct of Ens. Hook Accused of Embezling Stores, the Court Martial to try the Complaint of Capt. Herons against Capt. Ewings for misbehaving before the Enemy—The troops at Rockey hill and Kingston to parade at Kingston to morrow three OClock afternoon for Exercise.

As Catridges are now arrived the QrMasters are to make an Immediet Return and Draw what is wanting to Compleat each man to 24 Rounds all firing is forbid without Special orders.

All the Armourers and Smiths in the Several Regts to appear at Head Quarters to morrow morning 9 OClock.

The Genl is Surprised that there has not been more attention Paid to the orders of the 21st Inst. Relative to A Return of the Drums and fifes Wanting in the Several Regts.

The Genl Strictly Injoins it upon all Offs of guards and other Offs that when A Considerable firing of Cannon or Musketry is heard, they give him immediate notice of it; the Adjt of the Day is to furnish the Captains of the Main Guard with the Countersign.

HEAD QURTS Princeton 27th May 1777
Off. of the Day Major Stewart.
Adjt of the Day Col. Adams.

Genl orders, all the Carpenters & Wheelrights at Princeton to parade at Head Qurts to morrow morning at 9 OClock. A Scouting party Consisting of one Capt. one Subl. two Serjts two Corpls & 36 privates ordered out of Col. Stones Regt to Relieve A Scouting party at the Quaker Meeting house on Brunswick Road, to be on the ground to morrow morning at 9 OClock to try Lt. Sanford for Neglect of Duty & Lt. Hanson for the Same Offence the Genl expects in future when any Off. puts another in Arrest they will immedietly Report it at Head Quarters with A Coppy of the Charge Similar to that which he leaves with the Off. arrested, the Genl Strictly enjoins it upon all offs to use their utmost endeavours to apprehend all persons who Shall be found Discharging their piece in and about the Camp that they may be punished. The Court of enquiry that was Ordered to Sit upon Capt. M Connell is a mistake, so it appears that James Irving was not Inlisted with Capt. M Connel but with Capt. Burns; Majr Taylor to Sit as President of the Court of Inquiry to day in the Room of Lt. Col. Adams who is Sick.

The guard to be furnished with one Subl. only; as nothing Can be attended with worse consequences than the Issuing out a Wrong Countersign. The Genl orders that in Case any Such thing Should again happen that the Off. of the Day, put in arrest the Off. who has given it out. As frequent Complaints has been made of the Remisness & Ignorance of the Kingston guards, the Genl Desires those Offs acquainted with Camp Duty to instruct the younger Offs in that Department, that an end may be put to Such Complaints and the Duty done in a Soldier Like manner.

Princeton 28th May 1777

Reigmental Orders

A Reigmental Court Martial to be held this Day at 9 OClock for the Tryal of Several Prisoners of the Delaware Reigt Commanded by Col. David Hall; Whereof Capt. Robt Kirkwood is president.

Lt. Queenault ⎫
Lt. Bratten ⎬ members ⎰ Lt. Duff
             ⎭   ⎱ Ens. Horsman

The Court Adjourned to 9 OClock Thursday morning 29th May.

HEAD QRTS Princeton 29th May 1777

Feild Off. of the Day Col. Woodford.
Adjt. of the Day Col. Antle's Adjt.

Wm. Applegate tryed by Genl Court Martial for Desertion no Evidence appearing to the Court against him the Genl orders him to be Released; Alxr Cook tryed by the Same Court for Desertion; the Court finds that he inlisted in another Regt through ignorance and not with any evil Design, & that he has always behaved as A good Soldier, and Adjudge that twenty Shillings be Stopped out of his Wages, for the use of the Sick in the Regt to which he Belongs, and that he do Duty in Col. Hazens Regt till his proper officer (of the 7th Pensulvania Regt apply for him.

James Duffy tryed at the Same Court for Desertion the Court finding no evidence against him, the Genl orders his Release, & that he Joines Capt. Tories Company.

Alaxander Graham tried by the Same Court for Desertion, the Court finding no evidence Against him orders him to Join Capt. Tories Company till Capt. Wilson is present; the Genl orders him to be released from the guard house & that he Continue in Capt. Tories Company till Capt. Wilson is present.

The troops at Princeton to Assembel for exercise to morrow morning at 10 OClock at the Grand parade, to have Wooden knockers instead of flints, all the guns to be Drawn that may be Loaded; As nothing in War is so essentially Necessary as the instructing Troops in the Loading and firing motions, & in the Different Manuevres, the Genl Desires all the Offs to pay perticular attention to these essential points & not to let too much time be spent upon the unessensial parts of the Manuel Exercise which in time of Action can be but of little use.

The Genl Strictly orders that no Horses be turned into any persons inclosure but by order of the Qrm. G, Forrage MrGl Waggon Mr G, or their Deputies or assistants.

The Genl Desires that in future all Soldiers for Small offences be Confin'd in Qrtr guards, and tryed by Reigmental Court Martials, also in future one Subl. at least is to be with every fatague party.

Head Quarters 29th May 1777

Feild Off. of the Day, to morrow Lt. Col. Antle.
Adjt. of the Day Col. Adam's Adjt.

The Court of Inquiry now Sitting to inquire into the Complaint against Mary Quin, and Elizabeth Brewer Confined on Suspicion of being an enemy to their Country.

Head Quarters 29th May 1777

Proceedings of a Genl Court Martial held this day by the Delaware Regt Commanded by Col. David Hall for the Tryal of the undermentioned Prisoners belonging to s'd Regt Whereof Capt. Robt Kirkwood is Prisident.

$$\left.\begin{array}{l}\text{Lt. Queenault} \\ \text{Lt. Brattan}\end{array}\right\} \text{members} \left\{\begin{array}{l}\text{Lt. Duff} \\ \text{Ens. Hosman}\end{array}\right.$$

Saml McMurry of Capt. Andersons Copany Confin'd 10th May by Lt. Col. Antle for being Drunk.

Prisoner being Call'd pleads not guilty, and no evidence appearing against him this Court is of Opinion that he ought to be Released from his confinement, therefore orders him to Join his Company.

George Connoly, a Soldier in the Same Company Confin'd 27th May by Serjt Murphy for Drunkeness & on Suspicion of Theft.

EVIDENCE—James Bennet a Soldier in the Same Company, being duly Sworn deposeth that he told him that he had found A pocket book with about twenty pounds in it, that he Could now give him A treat, & Shewed him an eight Dollar bill, & he Saw Some other bils in his hand.

The Prisoner on his Defence Sayeth that he had but A four Dollar bill that he Recd of his Capt. and further Sayeth that he had an eight Dollar Bill between him and his Comrade.

From Circumstances wich appear after the evidence was duely Examined, the Court are of opinion the Prisoner is guilty of the Crimes Laid against him, and do Sentence him to 25 Lashes well Laid on for being drunk & 150 lashes well laid on for theift; and what pay may be Due him to the 1st May, stopt and 25/c pr month after that time untill he Refunds the Sum of Twenty pound twelve Shillings & Sixpence.

Richard Garret a Soldier in the Same Compy Confin'd 27th May by Serjt Murphy for Drunkeness.

The Prisoner being Calld pleads not guilty.

EVIDENCE—Serjt Murphy being Duly Sworn deposeth that the prisoner was drunk and he thought unfit for Duty, but that he is a Quiet harmless fellow when Sober, & that he never Saw him drunk before.

Prisoner in his Defence Saith, that being ordered on A party with Capt. Anderson, and on his Return from the party, was put on guard and on fatague till with in Some few hours before he was Confin'd and therefore Left it to the Court to Judge if he had time to get Drunk, from Circumstances that appears after the evidence was called and Duely examined, the Court are of opinion that the prisoner is guilty of the Crime of Drunkeness, but taking into Consideration the Character he bears when Sober, & that he is not apt to be in Liquor, and being the first time he has been Confin'd for any fault Do acquit him, on Conditions that he promises to do the Like no More.

HEAD QUARTERS Princeton 30th May 1777

Feild Off. of the Day Majr Howard.

Adjt. of the day Col. Antles Adjt.

Lt. Sanford Tryed by A Genl Court Martial for behaving Unlike A Gentleman and an Off. to Capt. O'Hara, the Court find him not guilty of the Charge, the Genl approves the Sentence and orders that he Return to his duty.

The troops at Kingston & Rocky hill to Assembel to Morrow three OClock afternoon; the Soldiers are to have wooden knockers instead of flints.

HEAD QUARTERS Princeton 31st May 1777

Feild Off. of the Day Col. Gunby.
Adjt. of the Day Col. Adam's Adjt.

The Court Martial Whereof Col. Hall is President to Sit on Monday Morning 9 OClock to try Capt. Longstreet, who is Arrested by Majr Taylor, for making use of Impertinent & Abusefull Language to him, unbecoming an Off. or Soldier.

A Return to be made Immediatly of all the Catridges on hand, the Off. Commanding the Several Regts are to See that their arms & accoutriments are in good order and fit for Action.

The QrMaster is once more Requested to furnish the Several Regts with their Quoto of Waggons Immediatly.

HEAD QUARTERS Princeton June 1st 1777

Feild Off. of the Day Lt. Col. Ramsey.
Adjt. of the Day Col. Antle's Adjt.

Capt. Ewing tryed by A Genl Court Martial for Misbehaving before the Enemy, the Court are of opinion that the Charge has Some foundation as he did not Act in Conjunction with Capt. Heron According to his agreement, or give him notice when he went off—but as the Circumstance of his not being made Acquainted with the Signal agree'd on Between Capt. Longstreet, & Capt. Heron and his former good Conduct Appeard in mittigation of the offence the Court Sentence him to be Reprimanded by the Genl in presence of Capt. Heron—The Genl Approves the Sentence & orders him and Capt. Heron to Attend at Head Quarters, or as Soon as Capt. Heron Returns, all the Soldiers to furnish themselves to Day with two Days Provisions Ready Dressed & hold themselves to march on the Shortest notice.

The QrMaster & Commissary to Acquaint themselves every day with the Genl orders, & Send Some person to take them off and take the Countersign.

After orders will be issued this Day at 5 OClock P. M. All Adjts and others whose business it is to take off orders to attend punctually.

The Off. of the Day by no means to go the Grand Rounds without a Serjt and proper escort when Gr. Rounds are to be performed on Horseback, it is usual for him to take Some officers of the Regt to which he belongs & A Serjt with him on horseback.

HEAD QUARTERS Princeton June 2nd 1777

Parole Washington C. S. Stephens.

> Feild Off. of the Day tomorrow Col. Stone.
> Adjt. of the Day Col. Gunby's Adjt.

The Genl Court Martial whereof Col. Hall is Prisident that was to Sit to Day is to Sit tomorrow morning 9 OClock.

Col. Stone to Send A party Consisting of 1 C, 1 L, 2 S, 2 C, 36 P to Releive a Scouting party on Brunswick Road at or near the Quaker Meeting house to be on the ground tomorrow morning at 9 OClock well equip't with five Days Provisions.

Col. Stone to give them their Necessary orders.

HEAD QUARTERS June 3rd Princeton 1777

Feild off. of the Day to morrow Majr Forrest, Adjt. of the Day Col. Harzen's

HEAD QUARTERS Princeton June 4th 1777

Feild Off. of the Day Majr Stewart.
Adjt. of the Day tomorrow Col. Hazen's Adjt.

The Adjt. in future to take of orders themselves unless when Sick or Absent from their Regt. And then A Subaltern must take the orders.

———————

HEAD QUARTERS Princeton June 5th 1777

Feild Off. of the Day to morrow Majr Stewart.
Adjt. of the Day Col. Hazen's Adjt.

The Court Martial Whereof Col. Hall is President is Adjourned. A Genl Court Martial to Sit at ten OClock this Morning to try Deserters Col. Gunby President, Col. Hazen to furnish Out of his Regt only for to day 4 C, 4 L. Col. Gunbys Regt to furnish 1 C, 1 L, the Del. Reigt to furnish 1 C, 1 L. The Troops at Princeton to furnish A party to Relieve A Scouting party on the Brunswick Road at or near the Quaquer Meeting house, to be on the ground tomorrow morning 9 OClock the Party to Consist of 1 C, 3 L, 4 S, 4 C, 100 P Well equipt with five Days provisions.

A party to be Sent from the 3 Regts at Princeton to Relieve Capt. Heron at Cranbury to Consist of 1 C, 1 L, 4 S, 4 C, 60 P.

A Genl Court Martial to Sit to morrow morning at 9 OClock to try Such matters a Shall be laid before them, Col. Gunby President.

Col. Hall to furnish 1 C, 1 L as members; Col. Stones to Summon from the 3 Regts under his Command 2 C, 3 L as members of Sd Court. Col. Hazen to furnish from his Regt

2 C, 2 L Col. Gunby to furnish 1 C, 1 L and the D. Regt 1 L all to be members of the Genl Court Martial. The Genl flattered himself that tenderness to all Soldiers under his Command, and A Proper attention to this Comfort, when Join'd With due Consideration of the Justice of the Cause we are engaged in, would Strongly operate to Prevent Desertions; but finding Some Soldiers are deaf to all calls of Justice & Reason, & void of these gratefull feelings which every Soldier Should possess, when treated with tenderness & Humanity, he finds himself under the Disagreeable Necessaty, to punish Deserters with the greatest Rigour, therefore orders that Richd Burress be Shot on the Publick parade between the hours of ten in the forenoon & two in the Afternoon tomorrow.

That the Court Martials in future try Persons for Desertion before they proceed to any other Business, that they may be punished as Soon as possible; he further orders the Offs Commanding the Scouting parties, & out parties that if any of their party attempt to Desert and are Retaken that they Cause them Instantly to be hanged or Shot on the Spot, he further orders that when any of our out Guards Discover any Soldier attempting to Desert to the Enemy that they Immedietly fire on them & kill them on the ground. Every Soldier who may in future be Discovered near our advanc'd lines without A pass in Writing Shall be Deem'd Deserters, & punished as Such without further evidence; that no plea of Ignorance of orders may be offered in excuse. The Genl orders that all orders be Read at the head of the Companies at Roll Calling in the Evening & at the head of the Companies in the morning at Roll Calling, and that every Capt. of a guard, or picket, or Scouting party Shall Before he Dismisses his party Cause all orders Issued while he was on Duty to be Distinctly Read to them, Copy of these orders to be immedietly Communicated to the Offs Commanding at the out posts & to the Commanding offs at Cranbery. The Genl Court Martial that is to Sit tomorrow is to try Lt. Price who is under arrest for Neglect of Duty when on guard.

HEAD QUARTERS Princeton 6th June 1777 P Hancock, C L Trumbull

> Feild Off. of the Day tomorrow Col. Hall.
> Adjt. of the Day to morrow Col. Harzen's Adjt.

James Irving tried by A Genl Court Martial for Deserting, found guilty, the Court Sentence him to receive 100 Lashes on his Bare back. Thos. Larkin tried by a Genl Court Martial, being Charged with an Intention to Desert. Upon a full examination the Court think proper to Acquit him, the Genl approves the Sentence And orders him to be immedietly Released from his Confinement And to go in his Regt.

HEAD QUARTERS Princeton 7th June 1777 Parl. Arnold C S Scott

> Field Off. of the Day tomorrow Lt. Col. Woolford.
> Adjt. of the Day Col. Hazens Adjt.

Robt Buckannon is appointed Judge advocate unto this Division untill further orders. The Genl Directs that all the pay Rolls be made up untill the 30th of April agreeable to former orders, the Pay Drawn and all the men paid off immedietly; Francis Ward and Henery Barrier, both tried by a Genl Court Martial for attempting to Desert to the enemy the Court finds them guilty and Sentence them to Suffer Death, his Exellency Genl Washington has Approv'd the Sentence the time of execution will be notified in future orders.

The following Regts are of Genl De Boris Brigade; Col. Hazens, 2nd Maryland, Col. Price, 4th do. Col. Hall, 6th do. Col. Williams, Genl De Bore is to take Command of his Brigade & march those Regts at Princeton to Kingston & take possession of Kingston, Rockey hill & Scudders mill, he is to furnish the Picquet at the 7 Mile Tavren, also the guards at Greggs tavren, all the other troops Belonging to the Division of the Army are to march to Princeton; & take up the ground of Encampment; the Troops to prepare to Day and to March to Morrow at 9 OClock.

A Corporal & 4 Men to be Sent Dailey from the Main guard to Obdikes hill to guard the Beacon the Corporal to take his orders from Head Quarters, the Main guard to furnish A Sentry at the Beacon at Princeton daily.

HEAD QUARTERS Princeton June 8th 1777

Feild Off. of the Day Col. Antill.
Adjt. of the Day Col. Ramseys Adjt.

Lt. Price tryed by a Genl Court Martial for neglect of Duty when on guard, found guilty and Sentenced to be Reprimanded By the Genl in prisence of Col. Stone is also required to Attend Wm. Steel & Thomas Jonston of Capt. Henerys Company 5th Maryland Regt, tried by the Same Court for Attempting to Desert & Sentenced to Receive 100 Lashes each the Genl Approves the Sentence & orders them to be put in execution to morrow morning at guard Mounting. Col. Stone to take command of Genl Smallwoods Brigade till further orders, he is to appoint Some Suitable person to Act as Brigade Major, no light horse is to Stand Sentry on our advanced posts, but Remain in the Rear Ready to give intilligence of the Enemys movement if necessary all the Mecanicks of Genl Smallwoods Brigade to attend upon the Assistant QrMaster General tomorrow morning at 8 OClock to Receive his orders.

The Court of Inquiry Whereof Majr Taylor is president is Disolved; The troops at princeton to furnish A Scouting party Consisting of 1 C, 2 L, 4 S, 4 C, 100 P to releive A Scouting party on ˙Brunswick Road at or near the Quaker Meeting house to have five Days Provision to be well equipt & to be on the ground tomorrow morning at 9 OClock.

HEAD QUARTERS 9th June 1777 P. Crambery C S Philada.

> Feild Off. of the Day Col. Ramsey.
> Adjt. of the day tomorrow Col. Ramseys Adjt.

The Genl Court Martial Whereof Col. Gunby's President to Sit to morrow morning to try Capt. Ewing for breach of Genl orders. Major Sherburn to furnish the Court with A Coppy of the Sentence of the Court martial Against him As also with A Coppy of Gnl orders of the 7th Inst. respecting Capt. Ewings Attendance at Head Quarters, Major Sherburn & Capt Heron to Attend the Court as Witnesses to prove Capt. Ewings non Attendance; the guard at the 7 Mile tavren is to be by no means Commanded by A Subaltern, the Genl is much Surprised to hear that after express orders was given for a Capt. & fifty men that so unsoldierly a manner Should be gone into as to Send A Subl. to Command 50 men which is properly A Capt. guard, the Main guard to consist for the future of 1 C, 2 L, 4 S, 4 C, 58 P the Several Regts to have Qr. Guards established which is to furnish the Necessary Sentries for the Field Off.; as Catridges are now at hand the Soldiers amunition to be immedietly Compleated each Brigade to furnish a field off. of the Day to visit their Respective Separate guards.

Brigade Orders June 9th

Genl Smallwoods Brigade Consisting of the 1st 3rd & 7th Maryland Regt & D R to be on the parade every morning at Revellie Beating in the field in the front of the encampment every Off. to be on the field with their Regts agreeable to Genl orders, morning reports to be made from each Regt & Deliver'd to Col. Stone at his encampment, every Soldier for guard to be dress'd neat and Clean & head powdered each Regt to Draw what Catridges are Necessary to Compleat each man with 24 Rounds.

Head Quarters 10th June 1777

The Commissary to pick out of any Company at Princeton any Baker or Bakers that he thinks Necessary to Carry on the Baking Business for this Brigade.

It is Suppos'd that a number of Deserters now coming out are employ'd by the enemy as Spies, the Genl Strictly orders that no off. or Soldier except those that have them immedietly in Charge, Shall attempt to Speak to or hold any Conversation with them; the parties having them in Charge Shall bring them immedietly to head quarters all offs are requested immedietly to Confine every non Commissioned off. or Soldier who Shall be Seen gathering Round or holding any Conversation with any Deserter that they may be punished for breach of Genl orders.

Brigade Orders June 10th

Field off. of the Day tomorrow Majr Sterrit.

Adjt. of the day tomorrow 3rd Maryland Regt Adjt.

The Adjt, of the Day is to See the Different guards march in proper time to Releive the main guard & to Receive the Countersign & deliver it to the offs of the guard   Each Regt to parade precisely at half past three P. M.

Head Quarters Princeton 11th 1777

Off. of the Day tomorrow Majr Forrest.

Adjt. of the Day to-morrow 1st Maryland Regt.

The troops at Princeton to parade to day precisely at half past 3, OClock in the afternoon.

James Whight, & Jonathan Wright of Col. Harzens Regt tryed by A Genl Court Martial for Suffering a prisoner to escape, the Court find them not guilty; the Genl approves the Sentence & orders them to be Releas'd.

James Cox of Col. Hazens Regt tried by the Same Court for Attempting to Desert to the Enemy & Sentenc'd to Receive 100 Lashes on the Bare back & be Confin'd During the War, the Genl Approves the Sentence, & that he Receive the 100 Lashes to Morrow morning at guard mounting, that Col. Hazen Discharge him from his Regt & Send him to Philada with a Coppy of the orders that he may be Confin'd in Such place as the Commanding off. Shall Direct.

Mary Quin try'd by the Same Court, for acting as an Enemy to her Country, no Evidence appearing the Genl orders her to be Releas'd. Elizabeth Brewer try'd by the Same Court & found guilty of acting as a Spy in the Service of the Enemy, do Sentence her to be Confin'd During the War, the Genl Approves the Sentence & orders her to be Sent to Morrow in Company with James Cox to Philada with a Coppy of her Sentence & to be there Confin'd in Such place as the Commanding off. Shall direct during the War. Genl De Bores Brigade to furnish A Scouting party to Consist of 1 C, 2 L, 4 S, 4 C, 60 P to Releive the Princeton Scouting party on the Brunswick Road at or near the Quaquer Meeting house, to be on the ground tomorrow morning at 9 OClock with 5 Days Provision & well equipt.

Field Off. of the Day Majr Forrest.
Adjt. of the Day 1st M. Regt.

Head Quarters Princeton June 12th 1777

All the Paymasters in their Divisions are ordre'd to attend at the Paymaster Genl at Middle Brook to Morrow morning at 10 OClock presisely each to take paper with them to take A Coppy of the pay Roll formed agreeable to the New establishment; those Regts who are Destitute for Paymasters are to Send Some Carefull off. for that purpose those offs Commanding the Different Brigades are Desired to See that their men are Supplied with amunition Immedietly and that their arms are in good order, & for their Men to be Ready at a Moments warning to march, & by no means for Off. or Soldier to absent himself from Camp & the Waggons Belonging to the Different Regts are not to be out of the Way but to keep with their Respective Regts. The Sick are to be Removed to Trenton Immedietly, the Court Martial of which Col. Gunby's president is Disolved All the troops in the Division to have three Days provision Cooked Immedietly.

BRIGADE ORDERS

All the Muskets that are Charged are to immedietly drawn and the Muskets to be Cleaned & put in the best order for Action, the Offs Commanding Comps are to See this done, the Brigade to parade this afternoon at 4 OClock to Examin their Arms, Returns to be made immedietly for Catridges & flints, the Provision to be Drawn immedietly to furnish each man with 3 Days the Offs and Soldiers of this Brigade to have their Baggage Packed up & Ready to put into the Baggage Waggons at a moments warning the Commanding Offs to See their Sick Removed.

The QrMaster to provide waggons for that purpose; in Case of any alarm immedietly the Waggons to be guarded by those Soldiers that are Lame or Muskets may be out of order as to Render them unfit for action. No Soldier as Able Bodied to Bare arms & those Muskets that is out of Repair to be detain'd.

Field Off., for tomorrow Majr Sterrett.
Adjt. for tomorrow Jas. Lucas.

HEAD QUARTERS Princeton 13th June 1777

All the Troops to have their tents Struck Immedietly and their Baggage Waggons Loaded and be Ready to March by 3 OClock in the Afternoon, All the guards about Princeton Kingston and Senders Mills to be Call'd in, the Prisoners to move on their Respective guards.

BRIGADE ORDERS

Provision to be Immedietly Drawn to furnish each man with 3 Days, and to be immedietly Cook'd. Field Officer of

the Day to morrow Col. Gunby, Adjt. of the Day from the
3rd Regt Col. Stone is Surprised that each Regt has not furnished the Artilery with the number of men ordr'd for that
purpose The Commanding Off. of each Regt is to order 2
men the best Qualified to Serve in the Artilery Immedietly
to Join Capt. Stewell.

Flemington 18th June 1777

The Genl orders that all the troops be immedietly furnished
with 3 days Provision to have it Cook'd Dirictly & that no
Soldier make any plea after the 3 Days is expired, that he has
no provisions As the Genl is Determined None Shall be Drawn
till that time is Expired, the troops to hold themselves in Readiness to march at A Moments Warning with their Knapsacks,
Blankets & provisions.   Proper guards to be left with tents &
Baggage Composed of those persons who are least able to
undergo a March the Weomen who are left at the other Side
of Corrells ferry & the men who are left to guard the Baggage to be Brought forwards immedietly to this Camp the
QrMaster to furnish each Brigade immedietly for the future.
An orderly Serjeant from each Brigade to attend at Head
Quarters Daily A Main guard consisting of one Capt. 1 Sub.
2 Serjts & 36 Privates to be established immedietly for the
tryal of Such persons as may be Brought before them.

Col. Hazen President; Six Captains & Six Subalterns to
be furnished from each Brigade to Sit as Members; John
Powell Esqr. is appointed Brigade Major to Genl Smallwood
& is to be Considered as Such.

Brigade Orders 18th June

Each Regt of Genl Smallwood's Brigade to have their baggage pack'd up & parade in the Road immedietly, and march

to the place of encampment, the loads to be all Drawn & the arms to be put in the best order; The Brigade to parade at 6 this afternoon, the Commanding Off. of each Regt to examine their Armes, The 3rd Maryland Regt to occupy the Barns & where Col. Gunby is now Quarter'd the Catridges to be examined & those that may be wet to have others put in their Room, any Catridges that may be wanting may be had by Sending their Returns to Col. Stone.

Flemington June 19th 1777

Genl Orders

The troops to parade immediately & march to Prospect hill the Baggage to be left at Flemington, under the Command of Major Vaughen.

BRIGADE ORDERS June 19th

All the Troops to parade this evening on the brow of the hill for Scout.

Delaware Regt 1 Capt. 40 Privates & 2 Subalterns.

REGIMENTAL ORDERS Rockey hill June 20 1777

A Court Martial to set immedietly for the tryal of Sundry prisoners: Whereof Capt. Robt. Kirkwood is President, Lt. MKennon, Lt. Qenocualt, Lt. Bratton and Ens. Skillington Members.

Proceedings of the Above Court Martial.

Pr order of Col. David Hall, for the tryal of Sundry prisoners Belonging to the Delaware Regt. Members as Above.

Robt. Hoskins Joseph Brown William Black John Lays John Randam William Skinner Belonging to Capt. Thomas Holand's Compy.

(left margin, rotated) Mountain which is 10 Miles & from thence to Rocky hill which is 8 Miles.

Confin'd by Col. David Hall for plundering A house of an Inhabitant of the United States near prospect hill, The above prisoners being brought Before the Court pleads guilty.

The Court after Duly Considering the Offense do Sentence John Random to receive 75 Lashes on the bare back 50 for the Above offence, & 25 for lying Before the Court, Robt. Hoskins, Joseph Brown Wm. Black John Lays, to receive 50 each on their bare backs.

Wm. Skinner to receive 39 Lashes, & the whole of them to have half a months pay each Stop'd out of their pay for the use of the Sick Soldiers of the Regt.   Sign'd

ROBT. KIRKWOOD
Capt. DR president

The Above Sentence is approv'd of, & order'd to be put in execution this Evening at parading time Except, Wm. Skinner who on Acct. of his Youth is ommitted.

DAVID HALL
Col. DR

HEAD QUARTERS Sampton June 23rd 1777
Genl Orders

Field Off. of the day from Genl Smallwood's Bridage.
Field Off. of the day tomorrow from Genl Debres Brigade.

Adjt. of the Day from Genl Debores Bridage, an orderly Serjt to be sent from each Brigade to Genl Sullivans Head Quarters, A Picquet to be established Consisting of 2 C, 2 L, 4 S, 4 C, 100 P. A main guard of 1 C, 1 L, 2 S, 2 C, 36 P, guard for Genl Sullivan to be taken from Col. Hazen's Regt of Genl Debores Brigade to consist of 1 L, 2 S, 2 C, 24 P to be a standing guard until further orders, Genl Debores Quota for guard is 2 C, 3 L, 6 S, 6 C, 100 P, Col. Stones Quota is 1 C, 1 L, 2 S, 2 C, 60 P. Adjt of the Division for tomorrow from Col. Stones Brigade, the Brigade Major to see the Picquets posted in Rotation, except when the business of the Brigade requires their immediet attendance, & then the Adjt of the Day must see it done, and who is to attend the parading of all guards The Genl is inform'd that the Soldiers under his Command have of late made it their business to plunder the inhabitants in their march thr'o the Country he therefore Desires the Offs Commanding Regts in the Several Brigades under his command to find out those Soldiers who have been guilty of that Scandelous practice, and immedietly Confine them, in order that they meet with Punishment Aduquet to their crimes, & for the future to take such methods as will prevent the like again.

> From Rockey hill we march to Brunswick which is 12 Miles and from thence to Sampton which is 6 Miles where our Regt Lay at a Saw Mill where we had prepar'd our Selves for an attack.

HEAD QUARTERS Middle Brook 26 June 1777
Genl Orders

The Troops are all to be compleated with 3 days provisions, one of fresh and two of Salt if to be had, & to hold themselves in readiness to march at A moments Warning; The Troops will lodge themselves in the best manner they can this night, near the gaps of the mountain from every gap proper picquets ought to be posted and patroles sent out During the night all the Troops are to Draw Spirits if it is to be had at the Commissaries at Old Head Quarters.

HEAD QUARTERS Lincoln Hill June 29th 1777

Genl Orders

Major Genl for tomorrow.....Green.

Brigadier ....Muhlenburgh.

Field Off. ....Col. Spotswood.

Brigade Major ....Swain.

The QrMaster Gen. is to make a proper Destribution of Waggons among the Brigades and Corps of the Army, and in proportion to their Respective numbers, to ascertain which, he will Apply to the Adgt. Genl.

DIVISION ORDERS

The Picquest to parade as usual A Corporal and four men of Genl Smallwood's Brigade to Relieve the same number of Genl Debores to morrow morning at Genl Sullivans Old Quarters.

Parole Manchester   Countersign $\begin{cases} \text{Milton} \\ \text{Medford} \end{cases}$

REGIMENTAL ORDERS June 29th 1777.

Proceedings of a Regimental Court Martial held at Lincoln Hill by order of Col. David Hall, for the trial of Sundry

From Sampton to Lincoln Mountain 9 Miles N. N. W.
Brunswick which is 3 Miles, that was our next march.

Prisoners Belonging to the Delaware Regiment Whereof Capt. Nathaniel Mitchel is president.

| Lt. Corse | | Lt. Queenoucalt |
| Lt. MKennon | members | Ens. Skillington. |

Serjt Johnston Confin'd by Col. Hall for Insolence and Breach of Orders;

The Prisoner Being brought before the Court Pleads Ignorance and Saith that being rais'd from his Sleep he was Quite Stupified and knew not to whom he Spoak neither what he Said.

The Court after due Consideration of the Nature of the offence are of opinion, that he Should ask Pardon for his offence, and be Reprimanded by the Col.

Serjt Stenson Confin'd by Majr Vaughen for Insolence and breach of orders.

The Prisoner being brought Before the Court pleads not Guilty. EVIDENCE — Major Vaughen being Duely Sworn Deposeth, that as he was Walking by the QrMaster & the prisoner, he heard the Prisoner Say, after the QrMaster had ordered him to make a provision Return; that he thought there was no Necessity of making one as he has already given in one, & likewise when the Major ordered him to go immedietly & make one he went away Grumbling And Saying that it was better not to be a Serjt in this Regt then be one, upon which the Major Ask'd him what he Said he turning Short about Said thats what I Say repeating what he Said before.

EVIDENCE—QrMaster Trussum being Duely Sworn deposeth and Says the same against the Prisoner as the Major except that he Absolutely refus'd to make out A Return when order'd.

The Prisoner in his Defence saith that he did not Absolutely Refuse to make out A Return but that he Told the QrMaster that he had already made out one and Delivered it him the Day before.

The Court after Due Consideration of the Offence, do Sentence him to be reduced to the Rank And Serve as A Private Centinel.

Patrick Davis A Soldier in Capt. Learmoths Compy Confin'd by Lt. Morris of the 7th Maryland Regt for Behaving in an Insolent manner to him.

The Prisoner Pleads not guilty. EVIDENCE—Lt. Morris being Duely Sworn Deposeth that the prisoner Came up to their Baggage waggons, & took gun & immedietly hallow'd out that the Centry was asleep upon hearing this he went to the waggons & Saw the Centry at the other Side of the Waggon doing his Duty, he order'd the Prisoner to go to his Regt or else he would Confine him, at which the Prisoner told him he might do his worst, for he did not Regard him, upon which he Confin'd him.

EVIDENCE — Edward Murray A Soldier in 7th M. Regt Being duely Sworn deposeth, that when the prisoner was in Confinement & going to the guard house he Damm'd the Off. that Confin'd him for A son of a Bitch & Said if he was at Liberty, he Could knock fifty Such down the hill.

The Prisoner although he pleads not guilty yet Can make no Defence for himself.

The Court order him 100 Lashes on the bare Back well laid on by the Drummers of the Regt.

The Sentence is approv'd off and order'd to be put in execution to morrow evening on the parade.

DAVID HALL
Col. DR.

MIDDLE BROOK HEAD QUARTERS 30th June 1777

Genl Orders

Major Genl for to morrow Sullivan.

Brigadier Debore, Field Offs Cols. Matthews & Willis Brigade Major Mullen, A Special Court Martial to set tomorrow morning at 9 OClock at the Usual Quarters, for the trial of Major Stewart of 2nd M. Regt. Col. David Hall is appointed president of this Court All Commissioned Offs who have in their Corps any non Commissioned Offs or Soldiers orriginally Inlisted in the Regt lately Commissioned by Col. Smallwood are on Demand to Deliver them to Col. Stone who now Commands the Same Regt upon his making it appear that they were so inlisted. A Large Horesmans tent mark'd I. H. Stone first M. Regt together with 4 Common tents, taken from a Waggon on the march from Quible Town and put into another, whoever has them are to send them to Col. Stone without Delay.

DIVISION ORDERS.

Adjt. for the Day tomorrow from Genl Smalwood's Brigade, the Picquet as Usual, Major Powell to attend at Head Quarters tomorrow for orders, & for the Parole & Countersign and Leave them at Genl Sullivan's Quarters An orderly Sergt from each Brigade to attend dailey. A Return of the Brigade to be made immetietly.

Lincoln Mountain July 1st 1777

Regimental Orders

That an Off. of each Company constantly attend the Drawing of Provisions for their Respective Companies and take Care that no unsound Provision be delivered to them.

That George Reynolds is appointed to act as Qr Maters Serjeant to the Regt & to be obeyed as Such.

That the Weomen belonging to the Regt be paraded tomorrow morning & to undergo an Examination from the Serjeon of the Regt at his tent, except those that are married, & the husbands of those to undergo said examination in their Stead, all those that do not attent to be immedietly Drum'd out of the Regt.

Lincoln Mountain July 2nd 1777

Division Orders

Field Off. of the Day tomorrow from Col. Stone.
Brigade, Adjt. of the Day from Genl Debores Brigade.

All the Troops to hold themsleves in Readiness to march at a moments Warning, the Troops to Draw 3 Days Provisions, one of which at least must be cook'd.

The Soldiers who are not Compleat with Ammunition are to draw it immedietly, the QR Masters & Commissaries to have their waggons in Readiness to move their Stores at A Moments Warning. The Brigade Majrs to take orders at Head Quarters in Rotation.

MIDDLE BROOK HEAD QUARTERS 2nd July 1777

Major Genl for tomorrow...Lord Sterling.
Brigadier Genl   do   ...Woolford.
Field Offs .... Lt. Col. Palmer Majr Byard.
Brigade Major .... Day.

Lincoln Mountain 2nd July 1777

Proceedings of A Regimental Court Martial of the Delaware Regt held by order of Col. David Hall this day.

Capt. John Patten President.

Lt. Duff   ⎫   ⎧ Ens. Hosman
Ens. MClean   ⎬ members ⎨ Ens. Skillington

Abram Meers of Capt. Kirkwood's Compy of Sd Regt brought before the Court, for Stricking and abusing A Drummer for doing his Duty Prisoner Pleads not guilty. EVIDENCE —Thos. Clark Drummer being duely Sworn deposeth & Saith, that he went into the tent where the prisoner was at Breakfast with whome he mest the prisoner ask'd him if he did not want some Breakfast he Replied yes & thank him too, the Prisoner then said he did not Deserve any for whiping A man so hard & farther Said if he ever whip'd him so hard, and he met him in a bye place, he would give him A knock that he would not be aware of, & after abusing him gave the Deponent a stroake in the Side which almost Deprived him of his breath. Thomas Tool at the Request of the Prisoner being called before the Court & duly qualified, sayeth that the afores'd Thos. Clark went into the Prisoners Tent, & the Prisoner asked him if he did not want some Victuals upon which the said Clark answer'd Yes on which the Prisoner said are you not a Man that meses by your self, if so go & get your own Victuals to eat, upon which the said Clark made up of very provoking Language to the Prisoner, the Prisoner said he did not know how to whip or else he would not have abus'd the man so that he whipp'd yesterday the Drummer answer'd, he was oblig'd to do his Duty & that perhaps some day or other he might fall into his hands & then he would know whether he understood whipping or not.

Christopher Willet at the request of the Prisoner being brought before the Court and duely Qualified Saieth that he was imployed in cutting up meat in order to Cook, when Clark came in to the tent, & that the prisoner bantred him about his whiping & told him to be more moderate in whiping & not to whip as if he was in A passion or else he would get the ill will of the whole Compy upon which the Drummer seem'd to be angry but the Deponent says he could not Recollect the words the Drummer Said.

Charles Hamelton A Corporal in Capt. Kirkwood's Compy at the request of the Prisoner being brought before the Court & Sworn, sayeth being at the Prisoners tent doore heard the Drummer and Prisoner using Reproachfull language to each other he likewise saieth he heard the Drummer daring the Prisoner to Strike him.

The Court having Duely Considered the evidence for and against the prisoner are of opinion that he is guilty of a breach of the first Article of War, Sect. 7th & do Sentence him to ask pardon of the party offended in the Presence of his Commanding Off.

Patrick Davis a Soldier in Capt. Learmonths Compy Confin'd by Adjt. Lucas for a buseing Serjt Jordan in his duty, Pleads not guilty; Serjt Jordan Being Brought before the Court & duely Qualified deposeth & Saieth, that the Prisoner yesterday Evening ask'd him for a Screw to Draw his Load, the Deponent told him to go to the Serjts tent where he would get one out of his Catridge box, upon which the prisoner went & ask'd for the Screw but not getting it immedietly he Call'd for the Deponent to come & get it for him & abus'd him, saying if he did not come & get it for him he would fire off the Load, upon which the Sd Jordan told him if he would fire his gun off it would be nothing to him, but that the punishment would fall on himself, the Prisoner Came like wise this morning to Serjts Jordan's tent where he was making out a Provision Return, and ask'd him if he had Return'd him fit for Duty, upon which Serjt Jordan told him he had by order of Lt. MKennon the prisoner Replied if he (the Sd Jordan) had receiv'd what he had he would not be fit for duty & abused him; the Serjt Desir'd him to go off peaceably; the Prisoner threatened to Shake him, & the Adjt. overhearing him ordered that he Should be Confin'd Serjt Cox of Capt. Learmonths Compy being Duely Sworn Sayeth that the prisoner having asked Serjt Jordan if he had Returned him fit for Duty the Serjt Replied Yes, upon which the Prisoner us'd Reproachfull words to him after he had Desired him to go to his tent & make no Desturbance.

The Court having Duely Considered the Evidence are of opinion that he is guilty of A Breach of the 5th Article of War 18th Sect. & do sentence him to receive 50 Lashes on the bare back well laid on with the Cat o' nine tails.

The Sentence is Approv'd off and order'd to be put in execution to morrow evening on the parade.

DAVID HALL
Col. DR.

BRIGADE ORDERS HEAD QUARTERS July 4th 1777

The troops of Genl Smallwoods Brigade to Refresh themselves have their Cloath's wash'd and provisions Cook'd.

A Genl Return to be made tomorrow morning by 8 OClock that Buckets &c. may be Drawn for each Regt also the number of Arms wanting and Canteens, also all the Baggage Horses to be Shod to morrow, to expediate which each Regt will order their Smiths to parade & be Ready to go to work early in the morning, each Regt will furnish waggons, & their QRMaster to go to Morristown for what ever may be wanting.

to Morristown from Lincoln hill is 18 Miles from thence to pompton 12 Miles which was our next march.

REGIMENTAL ORDERS July 5th 1777

The Offs of the Regt are once more Requested to attend morning and evening Parade, and an Off. of each Compy to attend whilst the Sert calls over the Roll & to see that none of the men are absent it is expected that no off. signs A report of his Compy without first examining of it.

Within 6 Miles of Pompton 5th July 1777

Brigade Orders

Col. Gunby's Regt to take the front Delaware next 1st Maryland Regt next, 3rd M. Regt in the Rear the front to march verry slow, the Artilery in front, the Baggage in ye Rear, the Baggage Waggons of each Regt to follow agreeable to orders of March, 1 C, 2 S, 2 C, 20 P as a Rear Guard, the Off. Commanding these, is not to Suffer any Soldier to Straggle or Stay behind, and Soldier Staying unnecessarily will be confin'd and punished, no Off. to Quit his Division without Leave from commanding Off. of ye Compy at every Convenient place the Brigade will be halted to get water, so that it will prevent the Soldiers much fatigue & prevent their staying in the rear & doing great damage to the inhabitants if they are kept with their Regt the waggons to be Loaded Immedietly.

HEAD QUARTERS Pompton July 6th.

Division Orders

Field Off. of the Day tomorrow from Genl. Debores Brigade, Field Off. of the Bouns to night from Col. Stones, Adjt. of the Day tomorrow from Genl. Debores; A Special Court Martial Sit to morrow, to try Such Offs as are under arrest in the Division.

1 S, 2 L, 2 C, 20 P to be posted as A Picquet on the Road Leading to Haverstraw—1 S, 2 L, 2 C, 20 P to be posted as A Picquet leading to Rivers—1 S, 2 L, 2 C, 20 P to be posted as A Picquet from the Brigade the Troops Came over —1 S, 1 C, 8 P order'd as A guard to the Amunition the Detail is as follows.

From Genl. De Bores Brigade 1 S, 3 L, 3 C, 42 P from Col. Stones do.   2 " 4 " 4 " 26
    3 " 7 " 7 " 68

A Main guard to be established to morrow morning to Consist of 1 S, 1 L, 1 C, 22 P from Genl. Debores Brigade.

    1 " 1 " 1 " 14 from Col. Stones   do.

The Brigade Majors to meet in the morning to fix A proper place for the guard house where the Main guard is established, its to furnish the Necessary guard for the amunition, the Picquet to be continued in the same manner or as Above Described until further orders.

Col. Price is appointed of the Court, Martial which is to sit tomorrow morning, the Court to meet at 9 OClock.

2 Capts, 2 Subs. from Genl. DeBores Brigade ⎫ to sit as
3   do.   3   do. from Genl. Smallwoods do. ⎬
members of this Court Martial.

HEAD QUARTERS July 6th 1777

Division Orders

Field Off. of the Day to morrow from Col. Stones Brigade Adjt of the Day to morrow from . . . . do. . . . . . .

The Commanding off. of each Regt are to be punctual in Sending in their Returns of their Respective Brigades from which the Brigadeers are to send A Weekly Return to the Majr Genl of the Division every Saturday. A Forrage guard Consisting of 1 S, 1 C, 12 P to be taken in Rotation from the two Brigades, the Serjt to apply to Majr Sherriff for orders.

AFTER ORDERS

A Court of Inquiry to Sit this afternoon at 5 OClock to Inquire into the Conduct of the Surjeons of the Genl Hospital Respecting the Reception of the Sick of this Division. Col. Gunby President.

3 Capts, 3 Subs. from Genl Debores Brigade ⎫ to sit as
3 do.   3 do.   from Genl. Smallwoods do.   ⎬ members.

HEAD QUARTERS Princeton July 7th 1777

Division Orders

> Field Off. of the Day tomorrow from Genl. De Bores Brigade.
> Adjt of the Day from Genl. De Bores Brigade.

Twelve hunderd Men well Officer'd to be selected from the two Brigades with Six Days provisions & to hold themselves in Readiness to march at a moments warning, they are to take with them only their Knapsackes and Blankets, the Commanding Off. to See that their arms & Accoutriments are in good order, two Days Provisions to be Cook'd immedietly.

HEAD QUARTERS July 8th 1777

Division Orders

> Field Off. of the Day tomorrow from Col. Stones
> Brigade.

> Adjt of the Day tomorrow from Col. Stones Brigade.

The Commanding Offs of Regts are to see that Necessaries are provid'd for their Sick, & proper bills kept and presented to the Genl that he may order payment; as little Spirits remain on hand for this Division, the Commissary is not issue any more only to fatigue parties & Scouting parties till further orders, the troops to parade at 4 OClock this afternoon for Exercise.

A Genl Court Martial to Sit tomorrow morning to try such matters as may be brought before them.

Ensign James Arrested by Capt. Ridgely for neglect of Duty and Disobedience of orders, try'd by a Genl Court Martial whereof Col. Gunby was President, the Court were of opinion that Ens. James is not guilty of the charge Exhibited against him & think he ought to be Releas'd immedietly. The Genl approves the Sentence and orders him to be Released Accordingly.

Lt. Lee arrested by Majr Taylor for Disobedience of Orders the Court are of opinion that Mr. Lee is guilty of a Breach of Major Taylors Orders, & that he ought to be Reprimanded By the Commanding Off. of the Regt in presence of the Offs belonging to the Regt, the Genl approves of the Sentence and orders it to take place to morrow morning.

Lt. Erskine Arrested by Genl. De Bores, ought to be acquited from his arrest for Stricking A Waggoner, the Court having examined the evidence & finding nothing against him the Genl approves the Sentence, & orders him to be acquitted from his arrest immedietly.

It is Required that Genl DeBores Brigade Majr make a Return of the Strength of that Brigade to Head Quarters as soon as possible.

Brigade Orders July 8th 1777

Col. Stone orders each Regt in Genl Smallwood's Brigade to have Necessary houses Dug immedietly in the rear of the encampment, as near the River as possible the men to be ordered to do their occations there and no where else.

Camp At Pompton July 8th 1777

Proceedings of the Regimental Court Martial held this Day By order of Col. David Hall of the Delaware Regt for the trial of Such Prisoners as may be Brought Before them. belonging to said Regt.

Cord Hazord Capt. President.

Lt. M Kennon ⎫   ⎰ Lt. Duff
Lt. Queenoucalt ⎭   ⎱ Ens. Bennett

Wm. Kelly A Soldier in Capt. Kirkwood's Compy Confin'd by Lt. Duvall of the 2nd Maryland Regt for Desobeying of Orders, & insulting said Officer.

Prisoner being brought before the Court pleads guilty; Evidence—Lt. Duvall being duely Sworn Deposeth and Saieth, that the prisoner came to where he was on guard, over a bridge Beyond the Genls Quarters he was hal'd by the Centry, who would not let him pass without a permit, that the prisoner Curs'd & Swore, & used verry insulting Language to the Said Off., & would not Return when he bid him, upon which he Confin'd him.

The Court having duely consider'd the Evidence do find the prisoner guilty of A breach of the 5th Article of the 7th Section and do Sentence him to Receive 100 Lashes on the Bare back, well laid on by the Drummers of the Regt.

> CORD HAZORD
> *Capt. President*

The Sentence is approve'd off and order'd to be put in Execution tomorrow evening at guard Mounting.

> DAVID HALL
> *Col. D R.*

HEAD QUARTERS Pompton 9th July

Division Orders

The Division to be in Readiness to strike their tents, pack up their Baggage, and to march at A moments Warning for Peaks Kiln Genl Debores Brigade to march in front, proceeded by the Light horse an advance guard and the artilery, the Baggage of the Brigade to them Col. Stones advance Guard is to follow, then his artilery, then his Brigade, after which the Baggage, the rear guard of each Brigade is to Consist 1 Capt. & fifty men attended by 4 light horse, they are by no means to Suffer any officer or Soldier to stragle from the Brigade, or fall in the rear, when the Division is on the march if any accident Should befall the Waggons, or any of them, A Lighthorseman is to be Despached to the front to Desire a halt till the Waggons are Repaired, if any person is sick or lame on the road he is not to fall back without A permit from his Officer any Soldier found from his Division without permit in writing, is to Receive 39 lashes on the Spot, and Off. and Six light Horsemen to be sent to Col. Stone four of which to be with the Rear Guard; the Division to halt every 4 or 5 miles that the men

From pompton to the Clove being a vally Containing about 20 Acres of tillable Land is 14 Miles.

may have an oppertunity to refresh, the Commanders of Brigade to Correspond with each other & agree upon the best place of halting, & the time for Beginning the march, the Sick of the Division to be left under the Care of an Off., A Surjeon and Surjeons mate, in the most Convenient place about Pompton, who are to provide necessaries for them, the Surjeon & mates of the Division to Draw for persons to remain with the sick, the Commanders of the Brigade to agree upon an Off. the Sick to be sent forwards to Peaks Kiln as soon as able to march.

CAMP AT CLOVE between 2 Mountains New York Govermen 11th July 77

Brigade Orders

Weekly Returns to be made out this Day, & Delivered to Majr Powell this evening or early tomorrow morning; no rails to be Burnt or Destroy'd any non Commissioned Off. or Soldier Offending by Destroying any property belonging to the Inhabitants may depend upon being Severly punished, A Camp Guard of 1 S, 2 L, 2 C, 18 P to be Immediatly established, proper guards to be placed on the front and left of the encampment to prevent the Soldiers from Destroying Rails &c. the Off. is to give positive orders to the Sentinals to Confine every Soldier, who may be Destroying any kind of property, the Waggon Master is positively order'd to provide forrage for the Horses immedietly, and see that they are pastur'd in the publick pastures, which he has much neglected, each Regt Will sent out a Fatugue party to cut wood for their Regiments.

N. B: This Clove is 18 Miles from ye Peaks Kiln.

July 11th 1777

Proceedings of A General Court Martial.

Lt. M Callaster of the 1st Maryland Regt tried for Leaving his Guard on the Haverstraw Road, The Court finds him guilty of the Crime alledg'd Against him & Sentence him to be Reprimanded by Col. Stone in the presence of the Offs of the Regt, to which he belongs, the Genl Approves the Sentence and orders it to be put in execution tomorrow morning at 8 OClock.

Capt. De Vernesure of the Light Horse tried by a Genl Court Martial for Disobedience of orders and insulting Col. Stone in the Execution of his Duty, The Court finds him guilty of Insulting Col. Stone and Sentence him to ask Col. Stones pardon, the Genl Approves the Sentence & orders it to be put in Execution tomorrow morning at 8 OClock.

July 12th 1777

This Day there was a Women Duct and Drum'd out of our Encampment; For giving the men the Venerial Disorder.

IN CONGRESS Sept. 16th 1777

Resolved that Eighty eight Battallions be enlisted as soon as possible to Serve During the War, and that each State furnish their respective Quotas in the following proportions viz.

New Hampshire	3	Batallions
Maschuesetts Bay	15.	do
Rhode Island	2	do
Connecticut	8	do

New York .... 4 ...... do
New Jersey .... 4 ...... do
Pensylvania .... 12 ...... do
Delaware .... 1 ...... do
Maryland .... 8 ...... do
Virginia .... 15 ...... do
North Carolina .... 9 ...... do
South Carolina .... 6 ...... do
Georgia .... 1 ...... do

Total......... 88

That 20 Dollars be given as A bounty to each non Commissioned Officer and Private Soldier, who shall Inlist During the War, unless sooner Discharged By Congress; That Congress make provision for granting Lands in the following proportions to the Offs and Soldiers who Shall so ingage in the Service & Continue therein to the Close of the War, or until Descharg'd by Congress, & to the Representatives of Such Offs and Soldiers as Shall be Slain by the Enemy; Such Lands to be provided by the United States and Whatever expense Shall be Necessary to procure Such Lands, the Said expence shall be paid and Borne by the States in the same proportion as the other Expense of the War.

To A Colonel .... 500...... Acres
A Lt. Col. .... 450...... do
A Major .... 400...... do
A Captain .... 300...... do
A Lieutenant .... 200...... do
An Ensign .... 150...... do
Each non Commissioned Officer & Soldier. 100...... do

That Appointment of all officers & filling up Vacancies (except Genl Offs) be left to the Governments of the several States and that every State provide Arms, Cloathing and every Necessary for its Quota of Troops According to the foregoing estimate, the expense of the Cloathing to be Deducted from the pay of the Soldiers as usual.

That all Offs be Commissioned by Congress That it be Recommended to the Several States that they take the most Speedy and effectual measures for enlisting their Several Quotas, that the money to be given for Bounties to be paid by the Paymaster in the Department where the Soldiers Shall inlist.

That each Soldier Receive pay and Subsistance from the time of their Enlistment.

September 18th 1776

Resolved, that if the Rations be Received by the Officers or privates in the Continintal Army in money, they be paid at the rate of Eight Ninetieth part of a Dollar pr. Ration. That the Bounty and grants of land, Offered by Congress by a Resolution of ye 16th inst. as an encouragement to the Offs and Soldiers to engage to serve in the Army of the United States during the War, Shall extend to all who are or Shall be enlisted for that term, the Bounty of ten Dollars which any of the Soldiers have Received from the Continent on an account of a former enlistment, to be Reckoned in part payment of ye twenty Dollars Offered by Said Resolution:

That no Off. in the Continintal Army is allowed to hold more than one Commission.

September 19th 1776

That the Adjts of the Regts in the Continintal Army Be allowed the pay and Rations of Captains, and have the rank of first Lieutenants.

In order to prevent the Offs and Soldiers Who shall be entitled to the Lands hereafter to be granted By the Resolution of Congress of the 16th inst, from Desposing of the Same During the War.

Resolved that this Congress will not grant Lands to any person or persons Claiming under the Assignment of an Officer or Soldier.

By Order of the Congress.

Signed   JOHN HANCOCK
                                              President

HEAD QUARTERS Ramapaugh Clove July 12th 1777

Parole Putman C: Sign M Dugall.

Those Regts who are in want of Shoes, are to have an Off. Sent to Morristown to procure them as soon as may be, and any other Articles are to be immedietly applied for, that no Delay may happen when orders are given to March.

The Court Martial Whereof Col. Price is President to Sit tomorrow at 9 OClock to try Such Prisoners as may be Brought Before them.

The Commissary to Deliver out one Gill of Rum this Day to each man in this Division.

COUNTREY MEN, and fellow Soldiers.

When I Consider the Cause, for which we have Drawn our Swords, and the Necessaty of Striking an effectual Blow, before we Sheath them again, I feel Joifull hopes arising In my mind, that in one day an opening Shall be made for the Restoration of American Liberty, and for shaking off the Infamous Yoke of British Slavery.

AMERICA is yet free, the all grasping power of Briton has not yet been Able to seize our Liberty, but it is only by Valor. As it is by Arms, that the brave Acquire Immortal fame, so it is by arms, that the sordid must defend their lives & Properties, or lose them. We are the verry men, my friends, who have hitherto set bounds to the Unmeasureable Ambition of the Britons.

In Consequence of our Inhabiting the more inaccessable parts of the Continent, to which the Shores of those Countries on the Continent are enslaved by the Britons are Invisible, We have hitherto been free from the Common Disgrace, and the Common Sufferings, We lay almost out of the Reach of fame itself. But We must not expect to enjoy this untroubled Security any longer, unless we Bestir our Selves so effectually, as to put it out of the power of the Enemy to Search out our Retreats, and Desturb our Repose. If we do not curiosity alone will Set them a Prying, and they will conclude, that there is Some what worth the Labour of Conquering, in the Interior parts of the Continent, merely because they have never Seen them. What is little known if often Coveted, because so little known. And We are not to expect, that we should escape the Ravage of the General Plunderers of mankind; by any Sentiment of Moderation in them, When Provinces, which are more Accessable, come to be Subdued, they will then force their way into those, which are harder to come at. For We See, that if A Country is thought to be powerfull in arms, the Britons attact it, Because the conquest will be Glorious; if Inconsiderable in the Military Art, Because the Victory will be easey; if Rich, they are drawn thither by the hope of plunder; if poore by the desire of fame. The East and the West, the South and the North, the face of the whole earth, is the Scene of their Military Atchievements; the World is too little for their ambition, & their Avarice. They are the only Nation ever known to be equally desirous of Conquering a poor kingdom as A Rich one. Their Supreme Joy Seems to be Ravageing, fighting, and Shedding of blood; and when they have unpeopled a Region, so that there are none Left alive able to bear arms, they Say, they have given peace to that Country. Nature itself has pecularly endeared to all men, their Wives and their Children. But it is known to you my Countrymen that here to fore Our Young Men were daily Draughted off to supply the Deficiencies in the British Army. The Wives, the Sisters, and the Doughters of the Conquered are either exposed to their Violence, or at least Corrupted by the arts of these Cruel Spoilers. The Fruits of our Industry are plundered, to make up the taxes imposed on us by oppressive Averrice. AMERICANS Sow their fields; and the greedy Britons Reap them. Our verry bodies are worn out in carrying on their Military Works; and our toils are Rewarded by them with abuse and Stripes. Those, who are born to Slavery, are bought and Maintained by their master. But this Happy Continent will pay for being enslaved, and feed those who enslave it. And our Portion of Disgrace will be the Bitterest, as the Inhabitants of America are the last, who have fallen under the galling yoke. Our native bent against tyrany is the Offence, which most sensibly irritates those Lordly Usurpers. Our Distance from the Seat of Goverment, and our natural Defence, by the Ocean render us obnoxious to their Suspicions; for the know that the Americans are born with an instinctive love of liberty; and they Conclude, that we must be naturaly led to think of taking the advantage of our Situation, to Disengage ourselves, one time or other from their oppressions.

Thus, my Countrymen and fellow Soldiers, suspected and hated, as we ever must be by the Britons, there is no prospect of our enjoying even a tolerable State of Bondage under them. Let us, then, in the name of all that is Sacred, & in defence of all that is dear to us, resolve to exert our Selves, if not for Glory, at least for Safety; if not in vindication of American honor, at least in Defence of our lives. How near were the Brigatines to shaking off the Yoke—led on too by a Women; they burnt A Roman Settlement; they attacked the Dreaded Roman Legions in their Camp had not their partial Success drawn them into a fatal security, the business was done. And shall not We, of the United States Whose territories are yet free, & whose Strength entire, Shall we not, my fellow Soldiers, attempt Some what, which may shew them foreign Ravagers, that they have more to do, than they think of, before they be masters of the whole Continent.

The Brigantines, according to Ptolemy, inhabited what is now called Yorkshire the Bishopwick of Durham, &c.

But after all, who are these mighty Britons; are they Gods; or Mortal men, like ourselves; Do we not see, that they fall into the same errors, and Weaknesses, as others; does not peace effiminate them; Does not abundance Debauch them; Does not Wantoness enervate them; Do they not even go to excess in the most unmanly vices and can you imagine, that they who are Remarkable for their Valor; What then do we Dread; Shall I tell you the verry truth, my fellow Soldiers; It is by means of our intestine Divisions, that the English have gained so great advantages over us. They turn the mismanagement of their enemies to their own praise. They boast of what they have done, & say nothing of what we might have done, had we been so wise as to Unite against them. What is this formidable British Army. Is it not Composed of a Mixture of People from Defferent Countries; some more, some less; disposed to Military Atcheivements; some more, some

less Capable of bearing fatigue and Hardship. They keep to
gether, while they are Successful. Attack them with Vigor
Distress them; you will see them move Desunited among themselves, that we are now. Can any one Imagine that English,
Irish, Hessians Hanoverians and with Shame I must add Americans, who basely lend, for a time, their limbs, and their lives,
to build up a Forreign tyranny; can one imagine that these
Will not be longer Enemies, than Slaves; or that Such an
army is held together by Sentiments of fidelity or affection;
No; the only body of union among them is fear. And whenever terror ceases to work upon the minds of that mixed Mul-
titude, they who now fear, will then hate, their tyranical Master, On our side there is every possible excitement to valour,
the British Courage is not as ours, In flamed by the thoughts
of Wives and children in danger of falling into the hands of
the Enemy. They have no parents as we have to reproach
them, if they Should Desert their infirm old age, They have
no Country here to fight for. They are a Motley Collection
of Forreigners, in a Land wholly unknown to them, cut off
from their Native Country, hemmed in by the Surrounding
Ocean and given I hope a prey into our hands, without all
possibility of escape. Let not the Sound of the British name
affright your ears. Nor let the glare of gold or silver, upon
their Armour, dazzel your eyes, It is not by gold, or Silver,
that men are either Wounded or Defended; though they are
Rendered a Richer Prey to the Conquerers. Let us boldly
attact this desunited Rabble. We shall find among them
selves a Reinforcement to our army. The Irish, who are in-
corporated into their forces, will through shame of their Country's Cause Deserted by them, Quickly leave the English, and
Come over to us. The Scotch Remembering their former
Liberty, and that it was the English who deprived them of it,

will forsake their tyrants, and join the assertors of Freedom. The Hessians who Remain in their army will follow the example of their Countrymen. And what will there then be to fear. On our Side, an Army united in the Cause of their Country, their Wives their Childres, their Aged Parents, their Liberties, their lives, at the head of this army I hope I do not offend against Modesty in Saying, there is a general Ready to exert all his Abilities, and to Hazard his life in Leading us to Victory, and to freedom.

I Conclude, my Countrymen and Fellow Soldiers, with puting you in mind, that on your Beheavour Depends your future enjoyment of peace and liberty, or your Subjection to a Tyranical Enemy, with all its Griveous Consequences. When therefore, you Come to engage—think of your Ancestors—& think of your posterity.

HEAD QUARTERS Ramapaugh Clove 13th July 1777
Division Orders

The following orders of march to be observed by the Division on their march to New Windsor, the first day the Brigade Commanded by Col. Stone to march in front, having his Baggage in the Rear, the Same Advance and Rear Guards of Horse and foot as Specified in the last marching orders, the Baggage in Genls DeBores Brigade to follow the Rear guard of Col. Stones Brigade; which is to be followed by Genl De Bores Brigade, he is to have the Same advanc'd & Rear Guards of Horse & foot as Specified in the last marching orders, & the same orders, Respecting the Halting & Refreshing the men, & to prevent their Straggling is to be observed, the Artilery of Col. Stones to march between his Advanced guard & Brigade, that of Genl DeBores, to march Between his Rear guard &

main body, the Second Day Genl De Bores to march in front
with his Baggage, and Col. Stone with his in the Rear, keeping
up the Same order of march as to guards, Artilery, Baggage,
and Troops, only changeing the front Brigade with the Artilery, Baggage &c. to the Rear, & the Rear to the front Alternately.

The whole Division to be in Readiness to march as soon as
the Weather will permit.

AFTER ORDERS 13th July 1777

Returns of the Sick in Camp to be made immedietly that
proper Offs may be appointed to see them Convey'd to Pompton, each Regt to have two Days Provisions immedietly
Cook'd for tomorrow and next day, the arms to be Cleaned,
immedietly & put in the best order for Action.

CAMP AT NEWBOROUGH 16th July 1777

Regimental Orders

That a Court Martial be held immedietly for the Trial of
Such Prisoners as may be brought before them, the Court to
Consist of: Capt. Hazzard President.

| Lt. Quenouault | } members { | Lt. Jordan |
| Ens. Bennet | | Ens. Kidd |

Sign'd David Hall Col. DR

Proceedings of the above Court.

Ellis Flowers of Capt. Hazzard Compy Confin'd by order
of Majr Vaughen for Deserting twice.

The Prisoner being Brought before the Court, Saith that being Inlisted when in Liquor; & having had liberty to go for
his Cloaths, and being over persuaded by several of his ac-

quaintance who lived in Carlisle County was the Cause of his Deserting, and that, he was unacquainted with the Consequences of Deserting.

The Court find the Prisoner guilty of a Breach of ye 1st Article of the 6 Section & do Sentence him to Receive 100 Lashes on his bare back well Laid on and Stoppage to be made out of his pay, till the expences for taking him up are paid.

James Addams of Capt. Pattens Company Confin'd by said Capt. for leaving his guard at Philada.

EVIDENCE—Serjt Davis of Capt. Hollands Compy being duely Sworn, Deposeth that the prisoner was on guard with him at Philadelphia, & that two days Before they were to march from thence, Strict orders were issued that no Soldier Should leave his post, that the prisoner informed some of the guard, that he wanted to go and have his fire lock chang'd, that he and another soldier went, the other Returned, but the Prisoner did not, that he had not seen him since till this day then he Confin'd him by order of Capt. Patten.

Prisoner Saith on his Defence that he went to see a friend in Tun Alley, was taken sick there & that Before he was able to march the guard was gone that he took A passage in a Wilmington boat, and applied to Lt. Purvis there, that he was Desirious to join his Compy but the Lt. told him A Detachment was going to Camp and that he might Stay and go with them that he had Liberty to go and see his Wife, & returned at the time limited him, was Sick there at his Return three Days, and that he did several services there as ordered him by Lt. Purvis.

The Court having duely Considered the evidence and the Prisoner Defence, do find him guilty of a Breach of the 2nd Article of the 6th Section and do Sentence him to receive 100 Lashes on his bare back well laid on.

(left margin, rotated) 18 miles Tuesday July 14th march'd from ⸺ Tanapaugh Cove⸺ within 12 Miles of new Windsor of being ⸺ Monday July 15th march'd to Newborough being 15 Miles, from thence 3 miles further up the North River then to New Windsor and opposite to Fish Kiln ferry.

The Commanding Off. Approves the Sentence & orders it to be put in exceution this afternoone when the Regiment Parades.

DAVID HALL
Col. DR

HEAD QUARTERS New borough 16th July 1777

Division Orders

The Genl Court Martial Where of Col. Price is president to sit to morrow at Sun Rise, on the other side the North River to try Lt. Seymour, & the QR Master of Capt. De Vernegour's troop of Horse Jas M Mullen alias King alias Cain McMullen confin'd on Suspicion of being an Enemy to America by Majr Powell try'd by a Genl Court Martial Whereof Col. President, the Court are of opinion that he is not guilty of the Charge, the Genl approves the Sentence and orders him to be released.

Phillip McDonald Corporal & Dennis McCalahan Private try'd by the Same Court martial for Desertion; the Court are of opinion that they are guilty of the Charge; & having Designed by sold their arms &c. and do Sentence the Corporal to be Reduced to a private Sentinal, and each to Receive 200 Lashes on the bare back well laid on, the Genl Approves the Sentence and orders it to take place to morrow at 6 OClock; Joseph Wood A Private try'd by the same Court for Stealing nine Stamp'd Handkfs, the Court are of opinion he is guilty of the theift, & do Sentence him to Receive 150 Lashes on his bare back will laid on, the Genl Approves the Sentence and orders it to take place to morrow at 6 OClock.

Col. Stone immedietly to supply the Commissary with Butchers.

AFTER ORDERS 16th 1777

The Qr. Master & Adjutants of each Regt immedietly to make out returns to Head Quarters of the Number of men and tents on hand & the number wanting to Compleat.

Lost the 15th Instant in or near the Encampment of this Division A Red morocco pocket book Containing one 30 Dollar bill, some small bills & some Accounts, which will be useless to any person except the owner, if any person has found Said book, & will Return it to Majr Morris A.D.C. or any of the Brigade Majors so as the owner may have it again, shall have 20 Dollars Reward from Andrew Taylor Deputy QR M Genl.

Wednesday 16th Inst.

A Women duck'd belonging to this Division for stealing & Insolence.

Thursday 17th

Our Brigade Cross'd the North River to Fish Kiln Landing about one mile, & from thence to Fish Kiln Town 5 Miles Distance from Sd Landing where we Encamp'd in an Orchard.

HEAD QUARTERS Fish Kiln's in Dutchess County

New York State 18th July 1777

Division Orders

A trusty Serjt. and 12 men to be Draughted from each Regt of the Division who are to act as Pioneers & to be Severally furnished with 4 handsaws, & 8 axes and that each Brigade of the Division be furnished with one Grindstone for the purpose

of keeping their Tools in proper order Lt. Seymour of the light
Dragoons tried by a Genl Court Martial for Saying (when
Capt. De Vandejour ordered him to see the mens Accoutriments was in good order) that it was the Business of the Serjeants & Corporals, the Court are of opinion unanimously that
Lt. Seymour be Released with Honor from his Arrest & Join
his troops the Genl approving the Sentence, at the same time
Requests that Officers in future will be more Carefull of arrest-
ing others without a sufficient Cause, as such Conduct will be
Attended with Serious Consequence the Commanding Officers
of Regts to examine into the Amunition of the men and Compleat them to 24 Rounds Pr man.

1 Capt., 2 Subt., 2 Serjts, 2 Corpls, 1 Drum, 1 Fife & 50
Privates to be Stationed as A Picquet at the forks of the Road
Leading to the Ferry & New York as the Genl expects to
move tomorrow he Desires the Division to hold themselves in
Readiness for that purpose, and Draw three Days Provisions
immedietly. A Main guard to Consist of 1 C, 1 S, 2 C, 24 P
who are to Collect and take care of all prisoners from Quarter
Guards of Regts who come within cognizance of a Genl Court
Martial; Field Officer of the Day from Genl De Bores Brig-
ade Adjutant of the Day from the same.

Those QR. Masters who have not made out their Returns
for tents to make them immedietly to Col. Sherriff D Qr. Mr.
General. Phillip McDonald being try'd by a Genl Court Martial & to Receive 200 Lashes, the Genl at the Request of Col.
Antill & some Faivourable Circumstances having appeared in
his faivour from steady adherance to his Duty remits the Sentence as an Encouragement to others to behave equally well, &
orders him to be Restored to his Rank & dismis'd from his
guard.

HEAD QUARTERS Fish Kiln 19th July.

Division Orders

The Several Paymasters immedietly to make out their abstracts & have them properly examined that the troops may Draw their pay as soon as possible, Should they not be able to Draw it on this Side the River, they will apply to Head Quarters for it.

Field Officer of the Day to morrow from Col. Stones Brigade. The Adjutant of the Day from ye same.

The Picquets at the forks of the Road to be properly Releived.

CAMP AT FISH KILN 19th July 1777

Regimental Orders

That A Court Martial be held immedietly for the tryal of Such Prisoners as may be brought before them, the Court to Consist of Capt. Nathaniel Mitchel President.

Lt. John Wilson ⎫ members ⎧ Lt. M Kennon
Lt. James Bratton ⎭ ⎩ Ens. Skillington

Proceedings of the Court:

John Pemberton of Capt. Kirkwood's Company Confin'd by Ens. Truelock on Suspicion of Stealing A Watch; Prisoner being brought before the Court Pleads not guilty. EVIDENCE —John Chambers being duely Sworn deposeth that when he was in the Barracks at Philada the Prisoner came frequently to his Room to see some of his Acquaintance who were there, and Seeing a Watch hanging up in the Room, the Prisoner ask'd him whose Watch that was, upon which he Reply'd that it belong'd to Joseph Purdie a Drummer in Capt. Henery's Compy, the Prisoner then asked him if he knew whether or not Purdie would Sell it, he answer'd he believed he would, the Prisoner took down the watch & opened her he farther Saith that from that time since he has never seen the Watch. EVIDENCE— Gregory Peirce being Duely Sworn Deposeth that in the Barracks at Philada he saw the prisoner have the watch in his hand, but whether he took her or not he Cannot Say.

Prisoner on his Defence saith he was in Liquor at the time he went into the Room in the Barracks & seeing the Watch took her down, & looked at her, and then put her up again.

The Court after, a Due Consideration of the matter before them, are of opinion that he is not guilty of the Charge laid against him, & that he should be immedietly Releas'd from his Confinement.

Natt. Mitchel President

Approved of & ordered that the Prisoner should be immedietly released from his Confinement.

DAVID HALL
Col. DR.

AFTER ORDERS 19th July 1777

The Genl Desires the Qr Master of each Regt to make A Return of Cloathing wanting, & send it by a trusty Off. to-morrow morning, this Officer is to receive A Letter from Genl Sullivan to Head Quarters where he will be supplied.

HEAD QUARTERS Fish Kiln 20th July 1777

The Genl Court Martial to sit tomorrow to try Barney M Manus of Col. Gunby's Regt, and others confin'd by Col. Antill's order on Suspicion of theft, the Division to march to morrow morning between day Break & Sun rise towards peeks

Kiln, about 12 or 15 Miles to the most Convenient ground, & there incamp till further orders   The Qr Masters of Regts to make a Return of the number of Waggons belonging to each Regt to the QR Master Genl of the Division; this afternoon at 4 OClock & the QR.M Genl is to proportion the number of teams agreeable to the Regulations of Congress, and those that have neglected to make their returns to the QR. M Genl are to send them in, and Draw their tents immedietly.

Monday 21st July marched from Fish Kiln to Peeks Kiln being 18 Miles we pass'd through A Continental Village where they Informed us that 23 Horses had Died that morning Being over heated by Drawing Cannon the Day before; And encamp'd on the Brow of a hill; Westchester County.   Tuesday 22nd we struck out tents and March'd 5 Miles further on the Road Leading to North Castle where we encamped on A verry stony hill.   Wednesday 23 Struck our tents and march'd 4 miles further on the same Road and encamped near the fork of the Road that Leads to Danbury.
****

HEAD QUARTERS Courtlands Mannor July 23rd 1777
Division Orders

The Genl desires Offs commanding Regts and others to be verry exact in observing the orders he gave at the arival of the Division, that no Off. leave the Camp without leave from his Superior Off. & that no soldier stray beyond the Confines of the encampment without a written Licence from the Commanding Officer of the Compy he Belongs to, the Genl is sorry to observe that the orders he issued this morning, were not so Strictly observed as they ought to have been, he therefore Requests that all Officers observe and see them executed with the greatest Punctuality, and to have the Offenders punished on the Spot: If any Soldier leave the encampment and are guilty of any outrages or unsoldier like behaviour, the Commanding Officer of the Compy, he or they belonging to will be Considered culpable, the Rolls to be Called at troop and Retreat beating, when if there be any absent they must be immedietly Sought for, & Confin'd for Disobedience of orders, the Soldiers to parade at all times Arm'd and accoutred.

Brigade Major for tomorrow Powell.

Adjutant for do Bartholmew.

The Picquet to be Relieved at 10 OClock.

HEAD QUARTERS July 24th 1777

Division Orders

Each Regt to Clear a Parade in front of their encampment and to clear their Streets of the Stones, which Stones must be thrown in the front of the Parade, a fatigue party from each Regt of 20 men under the QR. Mr. Serjants to dig necessary holes in the rear of the encampment, & close to the edge of the Woods; any Soldier &c. who shall be caught, doing his occations any where but in the holes dug for that purpose will be severely punished, the Camp Colour men to cover the excrements in the holes of their Respective Regiments every morning, & also take care that no filth, bones &c. be found within their Respective Districts, A Camp Colour man to be appointed to each Company, who together with the Pioneers will parade every morning when the Pioneers march beats, the Pioneer to cut wood for their Regts under the Inspection of an Officer, & fatigue parties to be sent from each Regt to bring in wood for the use of their Respective Regts.

AFTER ORDERS 24th July 1777

Genl Debores orders that there be 5 Capts 10 Subs 10 Serjts 10 Corps 5 Drums, 5 Fifes & 250 Privates out of each Brigade Commanded by Genl Sullivan, to be ready to march any hour the Genl chuses to call for them, they must have their Knapsacks, Blankets, and two days Provisions, every man of them must have their Arms in good order, and have their Amunition Compleated to 24 Rounds.

CAMP ON A HILL CORTLANDS MANOR 24th July 1777
Regimental Orders

The men to have their arms in good order & their Flints well fix'd in their Pieces, with lead or leather, the Serjts of each Compy to see this put in execution.

EVENING ORDERS 22nd July near Cramp Pond. (Omitted)

John Murphy of the 2nd & Daniel Brown of the 7th Maryland Regts & Canady Bay of the Delaware Regt tried by a Genl Court Martial whereof Col. Price is president for house breaking, Stealing and Beating the Inhabitants the Court are unanimously of opinion that Murphy and Brown, are guilty of the Charge & that they should suffer Death, & therefore do Sentence them to be hanged until they are dead; The Court do Sentence Canady Bay, to Receive 50 Lashes well laid on Barney M. Manus of Col. Gunby's Regt. Tried by the same Court for Marauning and absenting himself all night from Camp, the Prisoner Confessing the Crime, the Court do Sentence him to receive 100 Lashes well Laid on; The Genl Approves the above Sentence and orders the execution of

Canady Byay and Barney M. Manus to take place to morrow
at 9 OClock on the march, the time for the execution of the
other two, to be made known in future order.

July 25th 1777

This Evening our Division were ordered to parade to see
Jn Murphy & Daniel Brown Hanged, they being brought
under the gallows the Genl granted them 3 Days longer to
live.

Saturday 26th July

Struck tents and march'd to Peaks hill Landing from thence
to Kings Ferry to the North River being 14 Miles and encamp'd there.

HEAD QUARTERS Kings ferry 26th July 1777

Parole Peeks Hill C Sign Ramsey.

Brigadier Genl DeBores orders that the Division by ready
to Cross the North River to morrow morning at Day break
the Baggage to be ready at the same time, Genl Deborres
Brigade to Cross first.

His Excellency Genl Washington has ordered, that a Sufficient number of Waggons be ordered to Carry the tents, no
other Baggage to be put in them, and they must not be heavy
loaded, that nothing might hinder us of Arriving in time where
we are to go; the Commissary will Strive all means to get
hard Bread for the use of the Division on the Road. The
Waggon M. Genl to order two Waggons to be ready to march
in the Rear of each Brigade, to take in the Sick & the lame.
The remainder of the Baggage will Stay behind the Division

under the Command of 1 C, 2 L, 2 S, 2 C, 60 P, 1 D, 1 F which each Brigade will furnish an equal number, Genl Debores to furnish 1 C, 1 L, 1 S, 1 C, 1 D, 1 F, 30 P Col. Stones 1 L, 1 S, 1 C, 30 P the Capt. that Commands will strive and bring up the Baggage in the Rear of the Division, as soon as possibly he can; His Excllency Genl Washington has wrote to Genl Debores this Day, that Several Complaints, came to him of our Division Plundering the Inhabitants as they pass, Genl DeBores begs the Superiors will order their Capts not to let any of their men out of Camp without a permit in Writing. No Women to go with the Division, they are to stay with the Baggage & none of them allowed to go on the Waggons except such Weomen, as the Capt may judge is realy Sick.

CAMP NEAR KINGS FERRY 28th July 1777

Brigade Genl Debores orders the Division will be Ready to march at 2 OClock. Col. Stones in the front two Pieces of Artilery in the front with their Baggage, and after that each one Alternately, Genl Devores Requests the former order for the Waggons may be observed, each Commander of each Regt will take Care to suffer nothing to be put into the Waggons but the tents, the Rest of the Baggage will follow after the Division the Genl also Requests all the field Officers and others of the Division to take Care that the Greatest Care be observed on the march every day that no Soldier be going before to enter into the Houses, burn the fences or Commit other abuses.

Sunday being ye 27th inst. our Division Cross'd the North River and encamped 1½ Miles from the ferry on the 28th we marched 9 Miles to A place called Cackgat on ye 27th Ult the

Revd Mr. Leonard thought to have deprived himself of his life by Cutting his throat with A Rasor but Unfortunately mist his aim; the wound was so deep that his life was much despair'd of.

EVENING ORDERS 28th July 1777

The Genl Orders the Division will be in Readiness at Break of Day, Genl Devores Brigade will march in front with the Artilery belonging to them and their amunition and Baggage after marches. The Tent Waggons of each Brigade, and Ye Comp'y stores after them wich will be followed by Col. Stones Brigade, after that the Baggage of all the Division will follow with a guard of 60 men as Usual. Genl Debore Requires the last time, all the Field Offs and others of the Division take care that the greatest order in the march may be observ'd every Day; no Soldier to go on Before it is Strictly order'd that no Soldier go into the Houses or Barns to take straw or any other thing belong to the Inhabitants, It is like wise Strictly ordered upon pain of 50 Lashes to burn fences or any thing belonging to the Inhabitants; The straw will be Distributed Regularly to all Soldiers at every Camp they come to.

29th do.

Struck tents and march'd to A place Called Paramus 13 Miles distant from Carkgat Bergen County West Jersey.

CAMP PARAMUS 29th July 1777

C. Sign Gunby.

By Genl Debores orders the Division will be in Readiness at Break of Day; Col. Stones Brigade to march in front the same orders for the Waggons will be observed; the Genl Requires that the Gentlemen Offs will be exactly in the Road with their Divisions and Encamp in the order of their Compy. No Gentlemen Officers will lodge in any house Without leave from the Genl, the same Orders to be observed Respecting the Soldiers Commiting Hostilities.

30th July. Wee Struck our tents and Marched 9 Miles to A Place Called Psaic falls which place afforded two great Curiosities, the one was the Cataracks or falls which fell about 100 foot from the upper part of Sd falls to the Surface of the River; the other was A Man of 23 years of age Who Lay in a Cradle from his youth his head Being the Most Remarkable, was In my opinion, Between 22 & 24 Inshes long, his forehead about 12 Inshes broad across the Eyes with out any fall on either Side, his Body of the Common Size, his arms & hands about the Size of a Child of 7 years old, having no use of his Right arm, but Could wave the other so much as to keep the flies of his face, he had no use of his leges which was like a Child of the same age with the other he could talk both Low Dutch and english but in a verry low voice, Could Repeat the most of the Shorter Catachism by heart. from thence we Proceeded the Same Day 3 Miles Blow the Acquacanack Bridge on Sd. River in Essex County which Days march was 20 Miles.

N. B. This man whome I have Been Describing upon Seeing Some of our Weomen form'd a laugh and looked with the greatest earnestness at them and at the Same time I saw him put his left hand under the Cloaths But Shall write no more of what I saw.

July 31st. We struck our tens and march'd 2 Miles to the West of Newark where we Stop'd to Refresh at Which time there was a Court Martial held on one of the Inhabitants of the place where We encamped the night before, his crime was Perswaiding the Soldiers to Desert to the Enemy his Name was Richard Ennis, The Court found him guilty by his own Confession, and sentenced him to be hanged, which was put in execution in two hours after, being about 5 OClock P. M.

Our Division march'd from thence and left him, Hanging for his Brethern to Cut him down; We marched within one Mile of Spring Field, our Days March was about 13 Miles. Said Ennis was not cut down from where he was Hanging until the next day about 8 OClock.

———

August 1st. By Day Break Struck our tents and march'd by the way of the Scotch Plains to Quible Town which is 15 Miles.

———

August 2nd. From Quibble we Proceeded on our march to Bon brook and encamp'd one Mile West Said town which days march Consisted of 8 Miles; here we Stop'd the Remainder part of the Day to give our men an oppertunity of Cleaning their Cloaths.

Somerset County.

———

Bon brook 2nd Augst 1777

Regimental Orders

That the Offs of each Compy take perticular care that the Arms immidietly be put in good order belonging to their Respective Companies.

HEAD QRTRS Bond brook 2nd Augst 1777

Division Orders ·

Genl Deborre orders the Surjeons of the Division to make an immediet Return of all the Sick in the Respective Regts to the Deputy Qr M. General this order to be Complied with by 6, OClock this evening;

AFTER ORDERS

E. Sign Vanhorne.

The Division will Beat the Genl at ½ after four OClock & be ready to march at five,   Col. Stone's Brigade to march in front, the Same order for the Waggons & the guards will be observed. The Genl is verry thank full for the good order the Gentlemen Offs have observed on the Road, he is well Satisfied with the greatest part of the Sol-diers; but some of them last night have Robbed a man of A Hundred Dollars, he hopes that if the good and honest Sol-diers descover that Crime, they will give notice to me or to their Field Officers.

Sunday Augst 3rd. Struck tents & March'd about 7 Miles to A place Call'd Pluckanim in Somerset County from thence to Veal town in Morris County being about 8 Miles, & there encamp'd (in all 15 Miles.

CAMP NEAR VEAL TOWN 3rd Augst 1777

Division Orders

C. Sign Lee.

The Genl to Beat to morrow at 5 OClock, the Division to march at ½ past 5 Brigdr Genl De Borres Brigade in front,

the same orders for the Waggons & guards will be observed,
20 Pioneers, 10 from each Brigade Commanded by A Subn.
will march at 5, Before the Division to repair the Roads, the
Offs will take Care to Conduct them in the best order.

I. G. Hamelton A. B. Majr.

Monday 4th August 1777

Strick tents & march'd through Morris town to a Village
Called Hannover in Morris County being About 10 Miles,
there Encamp'd in A Stony Orchard; this day arrived here
Majr Genl Sullivan having been sick at the Fish Kills.

CAMP AT HANOVER 4th Augst 1777

Proceedings of A Genl Court Martial.

Jas. Carter of the 3rd Maryland Regt tryed by Said Court
on Suspicion of having Stole money from Micaia Dunn the
Court is of opinion that Jas Carter is guilty of the Charge &
do Sentence him to Receive 500 Lashes & to return to Maica
Dunn all the money found in his possission amounting to 26
Dollars 1/3rd of a Dollar, & that 35 Dollars be Stop'd out of
his pay, at the rate of 25 pr month by his commanding Offs &
to be paid to Said Dunn or his order.

The Genl approves the Sentence and orders it to be put in
exectuion to morrow morning at 9 OClock.

CAMP AT HANOVER 5th Augst 1777

Brigade Orders

A Weekly Return to be made and Delivered to Mr. Lucas
of the Delaware Regt this Day.

CAMP AT HANOVER 5th July 1777

Regimental Orders

That the Commanding Officers of Companies take Perticular care that their Arms are forthwith put in good order; That they immedietly make out their pay Rolls for the month of July; That they use their utmost diligence in preventing any Inquiry being done to the properties of the Inhabitants of this place.

HEAD QUARTERS Hanover Township Morris County

5th August 1777

Division Orders

The Court Martial Whereof Col. Price was President is Desolved, the Genl Returns them his hearty thanks for their service.

A Genl Court Martial to Sit to morrow Morning at 9 OClock, to try Ens. Farmer, for beating Thos Allen a Soldier in Col. Prices Regt also to try Adjt Edley for beating a Negro Belonging to the 3rd Maryland Regt, likewise to try Majr Mullen, Brigade Major to Genl Deborre, for Ungentleman like and unsoldier like beheaviour, and for giving Impertinent language to Genl De Borre at the Head of his troops, and for being intoxicated with Liquor, And Contemptiously tearing A Coppy of his arrest; the Court to try such other matters as may be brought Before them, & to exist till further orders. Prisident of the Court Lt. Col. Smith, 2 Captains & 4 Subalterns from Genl De borre's Brigade, 3 Captains & 3 Subalterns from Col. Stones, the Brigade Major to Notify them immedietly.

Nothing can be more pleasing to the Genl than to hear from Genl De borre, & from the other officers of the Division of the Regular and orderly Beheaviour of the Soldiers of this Division while he was absent, a continiance of Such conduct, will not only wipe of the Aspersions Cast upon this by Divisions but raise it high in the eye of the Commander in Cheif, the Army in General and the Inhabitants of the Country, in order to effect this, the Genl earnestly requests of the faithful & honest Soldiers that they use every means in their power to discover & Inform against Such persons as may in future by their Licentious Behaviour, attempt to bring infamy in this Division.

In order that the Soldiers may as much as posssible be enabled to rest themselves from their fatague, the guards to be as Small as possible, & no duty to be done but what's realy necessary.

The Field Officers of this Division are to attend at the Genls Quarters at 5 OClock this Afternoon.

The D. QrM. Genl to Regulate and assign the Waggons to Day, to the Several Regts.

HEAD QURTS Hannover August 6th 1777

Parole Lima   C. Sign Perill.

Field Officer of the Day from Genl De borres Brigade The Acting Brigade Major is to Send an Adjt of the Day to attend at Head Qrs from day to day taking the Brigades in turn.

A Court of inquiry to Sit to morrow morning at 9 OClock to inquire into A Complaint against Capt. Patten and Lt. Sewell for Beating Edward Rock of Col. Hazens Regt Col. Hall of the Delaware Regt President of the Court of inquiry, A Captain and two Subalterns of each Brigade to attend as members.

HEAD QUARTERS Hanover 7th Augst. 1777

Division Orders

> Field Officer of the day to morrow from Genl Small-
> wood Brigade, Adjutant of the Same.

An orderly Serjt from each Brigade to be Sent to Hd Qrs
daily; if any Cartridges Boxes, or Bayonett belts are Wanting,
the officers commanding the Different Regts are Desired to
Call upon the Commissary of Artilery Stores, who Shall supply
them with what they Shall want to compleat their Regts.
The Brigade Return to be made regularly every Saturday; the
Brigade Majors to call at Head Quarters for A form of A
Brigade Return; Ens. Farmer try'd by A Genl Court Martial
for Stricking A Soldier, whereof Col. Smith was president the
Court were Unanimously of opinion that Ens. Farmer was
Justifiable in Striking Thomas Allen, for his Insolence and Dis-
obedience of his orders, & that Mr. Farmer ought to be Acquitted of his Arrest with Honour, the Genl Highly Approves
the Sentence and orders Mr. Farmer ought to be Acquitted of
his Arrest with honour, the Genl highly approves the Sentence
and orders Mr. Farmer to be Released from his Arrest the
Genl also orders Thos Allen released from his Confinement.
Though the Genl would by no means encourage Officers in
Stricking Soldiers upon every Trivial occation, yet he can never
think of Countinanceing the Soldiers in giving Impertinent &
abusive language to Officers, & he desires that in future no
Officer may put another in Arrest where there is only A Suspicion of his guilt, but that instead thereof an Application may
be made for A Court of inquiry; Patrick Ivory Drum Majr &
Edward Crossgrove of the 1st Maryland Regt Accused of
Stealing, tried by the Sd Court, they arc of opinion unanimously that the are both guilty of the Charge laid against

them. And do sentence Patrick Ivory to be Reduced to A Private Drum & Receive 100 Lashes & Crossgrove 300 well laid on the bare back, the Genl approves the Sentence of both & orders it put in execution to Morrow morning at Troop beating at the head of the Regt to which they Belong.

HEAD QRTRS Hannover 8th August 1777

Division Orders

> Field Officer of the day to morrow from Genl De borres Brigade; Adjt from the Same.

The Genl Court Martial whereof Lt. Col. Smith, was President, Abm Phillips try'd by Said Court for Desertion the Court are unanimously of opinion that the Said Phillips is guilty & do Sentence him and do Sentence him to be Shot, the Genl approves the Sentence and orders it put in execution between the hours of 10 in the morning & 3 OClock to morrow Basil Dennis try'd by the Same Court for Desertion the Court are of opinion that the Said Dennis is Guilty of the Charge, but being over persuaded when in liquor by Phillips & from his General good behaviour, the Court do Sentence him to Receive 100 lashes, the Genl approves the Sentence & orders it put in execution to morrow morning at guard mounting, Wm. Wood, Geo. Phillips, & Jas Taylor try'd by the Same Court for Stealing, the Court are of opinion that James Taylor is not guilty of the Charge, & that he ought to be releas'd from his Confinement, but are of opinion that Wm Wood & Geo. Phillips are guilty, & do Sentence Phillips to receive 100 Lashes & Wood 60 well laid on, the Genl Approves the Sentence & orders it put in execution to morrow morning at guard Mounting; The Court of inquiry whereof Col. Hall was Prisident have reported that Capt. Patten who was unjustifiably accused of beating Edw. Rock of Col. Hazens Regt is in no Respect guilty of the Charge, but that the Sd Rock was unjustifiably beat, & that Lt. Sewell who Commanded the Guard did not behave out of the line of his duty, in what he did to Said Rock.

The Court having not Reported what officers were guilty of that inhumane abuse, the Genl thinks Necessary to observe, that th'o the officers who bring up the Rear of any Corps, on the March may with Propriety Strick Such Soldiers as will neglect obeying orders, or Stragle behin'd, yet this only to be adopted from the necessaty of the Case, & is by no means to be brought to Such a degree of wanton cruelty as appears by the Evidence in the Present Case, espacially when the offender does not aggravate his Crimes by giving the officer Abusive Language nothing of which appears by the evidence before the Court of inquiry, had the Soldier off'red any insult to those officers either by word or Action it would undoubtedly been compleat Justification for their Chastising him so long as his insolence continued, but this not appearing to be the Case, nothing can Justify such Conduct.

The Brigade Majors or those who act as such to attend at Head Quarters for orders Precisely at 10 OClock.

HEAD QUARTERS Hannover Augst 9th 1777

Division Orders

The Execution of Abm Phillips is suspended untill Afternon & then to be between the hours of 3 & 5 OClock at which time the Division to be under Arms, Genl De borre to appoint some person to receive one half the Saws and axes from Col. Stone, that was delivered him at Fish Kills for the use of the Pioneers,

Col. Stone is desired to give orders for the Delivery of them when apply'd for.

A Court of Inquiry to sit on Monday morning at 9 OClock, Major Adams Prisident, 3 Caps & 3 Subs. from each Brigade to form the Court, to inquire into the Complaint of Col. Wall against Commissary Durrah for Beating and abusing Patrick Burk a Soldier in Col. Halls Regt.

Saturday Augst 9th the Division Paraded about 4 OClock this afternoon & march'd in field in the Rear of our encampment to see the execution of Abm Phillips of the 2nd Maryland Regt he was Shot about 6 OClock, his crime was attempting to Desert to the Enemy but did not effect it.

CAMP HANOVER 10th Agst 1777

Brigade Orders

Col. Stone Requests the Officers & Soldiers of Genl Smallwoods Brigade, to attend Divine Service at 10 OClock, this forenoon, every Soldier to be neat and Clean & the greatest Decency to be observed.

HEAD QUARTERS Hanover August 11th 1777

Division Orders

Field Officer of the Day tomorrow from Genl Smallwood's Brigade, Adjutant of the day from ye Same The Genl thinking it necessary for the health of the Soldiers, that Genl De borres Brigade Should be Removed from their present ground of Encampment he requests of Genl Deborre to order A Convenient place as near the present Encampment as he can.

The Picquetts as in orders, with the other guards Remain till further orders.

A Genl Court Martial to Sit tomorrow morning at 9 OClock: Lt. Col. Antill President, 3 Captains & 3 Subs. from each Brigade, to form Said Court, to try Ensign Hillary for being Drunk, profane Swearing, and Behaving very indecent, also to try Such matters as may be brought Before them.

The main Guard to be augmented immedietly to 1 L, 2 S, 2 C, 33 P; The Court of Inquiry that was to sit this Morning whereof Major Adams was President is desolved. A Court of inquiry to Sit tomorrow morning at 9 OClock Lt. Col. Ramsey President; 3 Captains and 3 Subs. from each Brigade to form Said Court, to inquire into A Complaint by Col. Hall alledged against Commissary Durrah for Beating & Abusing Patt. Burk a Soldier in his Regt also to inquire into A Complaint lodged against Lt. Jordan, for taking A horse the property of Mr. Buchannon, also for abusing and Suffering him to be abused by A party under his command, & for not giving Mr. Buchannan proper Satisfaction for hay he had taking for the use of the States.

AFTER ORDER 11th Augst 1777

The Commanders of Brigades to give orders to their Qr-Masters to see that their Artilery and Waggons horses are well Shod, that when the Division is order'd to march, there might be no Excuse or Delay; & that the Brigade be in Readiness to march immedietly when notice is given.

CAMP HANOVER August 11th 1777
Regimental Orders

That the officers of the Regt are once more Requested punctually to attend parade & to take Particular Care that their men are present that no non Commissioned officer or Soldier presuming to appear on parade when In Camp with uncomb'd hair or unshaven, the Officers are Desired to take Care that this order be punctually observed. That as nothing is more Conduceive to the Healthiness of A Camp than Cleanliness, they are therefore whilst in Camp to keep themselves as neat and clean as their cloathing will allow; upon pain of being Court Martial'd. Returns to be made out immedietly of what Cloathing may be wanting for each Company.

Proceedings of A Regimental Court Martial held by orders of Col. David Hall for the tryal of Such Prisoners as may be Brought before them belonging to the Delaware Regiment.

Thomas Holland Capt. President.

Lt. Wilson }
Ens. Hosman } members { Ens. M Clane
{ Ens. J Lidd

Saml M Murry of Capt. Andersons Company Confin'd by Lt. Queenouault for being Drunk & offering to Sell A Razor belonging to Jno Purnell of Said Company, EVIDENCE—Wm Guttrie of Capt. Andersons Compy declared that he Saw the Prisoner offer the Razor for Sale to A Soldier, went up and told him not to buy the Razor for it was not his own the prisoner Said it was, on which Guttrie took him to Lt. Quenouault.

EVIDENCE—Jno Purnell Saith that he was Sick and had leave to put his knapsack in the Waggon, but when he Came to Camp could not find it, but on hearing that A Razor was offer'd for Sale, he went to the Lieut for leave to Search the rest of his things when he found Some of them in the prisoners Knapsack; The Prisoner told him he did not know he was come from Morriston that he knew they ware his and intended to take care of them for him.

PRISONERS DEFINCE—Saith that when the Waggon came to Camp, the things were all loose & toss'd about, & having lost all his things was looking for them, when he found his Knapsack with Purnels things in it, But who put them there he could not tell, but said he would take Care of them for him.

EVIDENCE FOR THE PRISONER—Fredrick Vanlip, saith that he Saw the Prisoner take up the Knapsack and look'd at the things, and Said they Belong'd to Jno. Purnell & that he would take Care of them for him; Prisoner further Saith that he has A Razor of the Same Mark & make as Jno. Purnells, & that he did not offer the Razor for Sale intending to Defraud any Person:

The Court having taking the whole into consideration are of opinion the Prisoner did not intend any Defraud, but that he is guilty of the unpardonable Crime of Being Drunk, & order him to be Severly reprimanded.

THOS HOLLAND
Capt. President

The Sentence of the Court Approv'd and order'd to be put in Execution by Lt. Jordan.

DAVD HALL
Col. D R

Monday 11th August. Brigadier Genl Smallwood Arrived here at Camp and took Command of our Brigade Consisting of the Delaware Regt 1st 3rd & 7th Maryland Regts.

Tuesday August 12th. Struck tents About 9 OClock in the morning & march'd about one mile and encamp'd near A Grist & Saw Mills.

HEAD QUARTERS Hannover 12th August 1777

Division Orders

> Field officer of the Day tomorrow from Genl Deborres
> Brigade,
> Adjt of the Day from the Same.

The Genl having obtaned licence from the Commander in Cheif, & in consequence thereof granted A Pardon to John Murphy & Daniel Brown he Sincerely hopes that this act of Lenity may not serve to incourage that Spirit of Disorder and Licentiousness which has always Prevailed too much in this Division, he wishes it may Shew the Soldiers the Advantage of A good Character; And the good opinion of their officer which was the real foundation for the Lenity Shown them Unhappy Persons, he trusts the future Conduct of those unhappy men, will wipe off the Stain brought upon them by their Inconsiderate Conduct, and he Strictly forbids the Soldiers to Cast any kind of Reflections, or upbraid them for the Crime for which they have Received A General Pardon.

Captain Seward to Join General Smallwoods Brigade, leaving Such officers and men to Command the Artilery of Genl Deborres Brigade as he Shall think proper; The Paymasters to make out their Abstracts to the 1st of August immedietly, till which time (Genl Washington who is on his march towards us; has ordered this Division to be paid up.

HEAD QUARTERS Hanover 13th Augst 1777

Division Orders

> Feild officer of the Day tomorrow from Genl Small-
> woods Brigade,
>
> Adjt of the Day from the Same.

The Genl is much Surprised that the orders of the 11th
inst. is not complied with (Respecting the Court Martial
whereof Lt. Col. Antill is president) the President having attended at Several times, & could not proceed to Business for
want of members to form Said Court. The Brigade Major
to See the Court form'd Agreeable to Genl orders immidietly
Brigade Major Powell for the Day tomorrow an orderly Serjeant in future to be Sent by the Brigade Major of the Day to
attend upon Such Court as may be Setting agreeable to Genl
orders.

Hannover 13th August 1777

Brigade Orders

The Commandants of Regts in Genl Smallwoods Brigade,
are Requested immidietly to furnish Returns of their Regts,
and Render lists of Such arms & Accoutrements, Cloathing
&c. as may be wanting in order that the Same may be procured, to put the Regts in the most formidable & Comfortable
Situation; and as the Ground for the Encampment was yesterday Regularly laid off the Genl can't avoid observing that
it would have been much more pleasing; had the officers attended to, and had their tents more Regularly pitch'd which
it is expected will be better attended to in future; as it will
not only contribute to the Beauty of the encampment, but also
to the health and Disclipine of the Soldiers;

The Adjutants are Required to Draw one Camp Colour man out of each Company in their Respective Regts, who are to act and do no other Duty for the space of one week, after which they will be Releived, and the QrMasters are Required to assemble every morning at gun fireing, & direct them to Clean and Sweep the Streets of all nausances, throwing the Same into the pits and Covering the filth therein with fresh dirt every morning, all Cooking, washing, &c. are expressly forbid within the limits of the Encampment, which must be performed at A Proper Distance in front and on the Flanks thereof, & the latter to prevent trash and filth in the Encampment, & within the tents of the Soldiers. A Visiting officer from each Regt must be daily appointed to inspect within the limits of his Regiment and Direct the Removal thereof. The Brigade Compleatly Arm'd & Accoutred must Parade in front of the Encampment at troop & Retreat Beating, tis expected the Officers in General will on those occations make A point of attending in their proper posts; Officers will attend to and Direct their men to Shave & Shift twice A Week, & also inspect their Arms, Accoutriments, & Provision, & their mode of Cooking verry frequently, & that they do not load their muskets without orders, and unless the Cleaning their arms is attended to, they will be apt to bend their gun Barrels, any Soldier without leave in Writing from his officer, found Straggling above one mile from the Encampment will be Liable to be taken up and punished as a Deserter; Sobriety, good order, & Diligence are earnestly recommended.

CAMP AT HANNOVER August 14th 1777

Proceedings of a Regimental Court Martial held by order of Major Vaughen for the trial of Dennis Maanna of Capt. Hollands Company; Confin'd by said Capt. for theft.

Robt. Kirkwood Capt. President.

Lt. Queenouault ⎫
Lt. Brattan ⎬ members ⎧ Lt. Duff
⎭ ⎨ Ens. Bennett

EVIDENCE—Prisoner being brought before the Court pleads not guilty; John Tappan an Inhabitant of this place being duely Sworn Deposeth that when he went into the Room he Saw none but a Girl and the Prisoner in it the Girl went into another Room and said She had lost A Handkf A Soldier Saw a Handkff hanging out of the Prisoners pocket and Informed the Landlady of it, the Prisoner Said he had not got it, Upon which the Soldier Shewing the Prisoner the end of it, Saying there it is, he deliver'd it up, the girl Said She saw it before but was afraid of Speaking about it. Prisoner on his defence Saith that he went into the tavern & got a gill of gin, that he Saw A Handkff on the Chair & took it up & held it in his hand, & put it by accident in his pocket & forgot it, upon being accused of taking Said Handkff denied it, having forgot he had it, & further Said he had no pockets but one in his Breeches, upon opening of which he found it, & delivered it to the Girl.

The Court are unanimously of opinion that Dennis Maanna is not only guilty of the Charge laid against him, but of lying before the Court, and do Sentence him to Receive 75 Lashes for the first Crime & 25 for the last, on his bare back well Laid on with the Cat o nine tails; which Sentence is approv'd of by Majr Vaughen & ordered to be put in execution this Evening. _____

HEAD QRTRS 14th August 1777

Division Orders

Field Officer of the tomorrow from Genl Deborres Brigade, Brigade Major & Adjt. of the day from the Same The Amaz-

ing neglect of the Field officers of the day in not making any
Report for Some days past, Oblidges the Genl to order expressly that the Field officer of the day, make his report every
day before 12 OClock & that each officer of the Guards, make
his Report to the officer of the Day before 10 OClock The
form of the Report for the Feild officer of the Day was given
out at Princeton & must be now followed, the name of the
Feild officer of the day to be Returned to Head Qurtrs By the
Brigade Major of the Brigade he belongs to as soon as he is
appointed, the Brigade Majors to return & the names of the
members of Court martials & Courts of Inquiry to the Respective Presidents as soon as appointed and warn'd that they
may be able to Report those members who neglect to attend,
A Strict & Regular Attention to the Duties of the Camp is
expected, as much as though the Enemy were at hand, good
officers will Readily see the necessaty of this, those who cannot
at present observe it, may gain knowledge from the conduct of
others.

Hanover 15th August 1777

Brigade Orders

The Brigadier General in pursuance of an order recv'd from
Major Genl Sullivan, requires from the Commandants of Regts
in his Brigade, Returns of their Sick lodg'd in the Several Hospital that a proper offr may be Despatched, to bring in Such
as may be recov'ed fit for Duty, and also Returns of such as
may have been imprisoned, that they may be brought in, tried
punished & Returned to their Respective Regts which now
want their aid its expected such Returns will be immedietly
furnished.

Head Quarters 15th August 1777

Division Orders

Field officer of the Day tomorrow from Genl Smallwoods Brigade, Brigade Majr & Adjt. of the day from the Same.

The Genl expecting speedely to Receive orders to march orders that that no artilery nor Waggon & Horses be sent out of Camp on any Buisness whatever: the QrMasters to see that they are Shod and kept in good order, for marching on the first notice.

Ens. Hilery tried by A Genl Court Martial Whereof Lt. Col. Antill is President, for Drunkness, profane Swareing, &c. the Court are of opinion that he receive a private Reprimand from the Commanding officer of the Brigade, he be Immediately Dismissd The Genl Approves the Sentence of the Court and orders it put in Execution to morrow morning at 7 OClock. Patrick Camery a Waggoner in the Continental army tryed by the same Court for theft the Court find him Guilty, & Sentence him to Receive 100 lashes upon the bare back, at such time & place as the Comm. of the Division Shall think proper to order, the Genl. Approves the Sentence of sd Court & orders it put in Execution to morrow morning 9 OClock The Adjt. of the Day for the Division to see the Sentence of sd Court put in Execution.

After Orders 15 August 1777

The Genl Court martial whereof Lt. Coll Antill was President is disolv'd.

A Genl Court Martial to sit to morrow morning at 9 OClock, Coll Gunby President, 3 Capts & 3 Subalterns from each Brigade, to try Pamabre for Confineing James McCoy Contrary to Genl Orders, After being Acquainted therewith, Also to try any other matters that may be brought before them.

HEAD QUARTERS Hanover 16th August 1777

Division Orders

> Feild officer of the Day tomorrow from Col. Deborres
> Brigade, Brigade Major from the same.

The Court Martial Whereof Col. Gunby's President is not to Sit till further orders, the Court of Inquiry Whereof Lt. Col. Ramsey is President, have Reported that Commissary Durrah is by no means Justifiable in Beating the Soldier Belonging to Col. Halls Regt they think A Private Reprimand from the Genl will answer every purpose of Calling a Court martial. The Genl approves of the Report of Said Court of Inquiry, to which Court Commissary Durrah has Submitted.

The Genl forbides the Soldiers entering the Mill Belonging to Mr. Ford or to Conscern with the flood Gates as he is Determin'd in future to bring Such Offenders to A Severe puneshment.

HEAD QRTRS Hannover 17th August 1777

Division Orders

> Feild offr of the Day to morrow from Genl Small-
> woods Brigade, Brigade Major from the Same.

A Return of all the ordinance Stores belonging to the Artilery to be made to Head Quarters as Soon as possible by the Commanding Officer of the Artilery, At A General Court Martial held at Hanover the 6th Inst Major Mullen was tried for giving insolent and Abusive Languague to Genl Deborre at ye Head of his Brigade, & for being frequently Intoxicated with Liquor, of which Charge the Court found him guilty & Sentenced him to be Cashierd, the Commander in Chief approved the Sentence, & orders it to take place Immedietly.

Those Regts which are yet in want of tents to make returns to the QrM.Genl to morrow morning by 8 OClock   The

Brigade Major to Call on the QrMasters for A Return of all the tents & Marquees that are publick property & upon the Adjts for a Return of all the men & Weomen in their Respective Regts, from which they are to make A Genl Return of each Brigade in the following manner Viz.

In one Collumn the number of Feild officers 2ndly the Serjts 4thly Privates including Drums, Fifes as also Waggoners & Weomen, then they are to State the number of tents in their Respective Brigades, & Set forth the number wanting upon the following Calculations, Viz A tent to each Feild officer, one to two Commissioned & Staff officers, one to 4 Serjts & one to 6 Privates including Corporals, as Well as Waggoners weomen &c. The Deputy QrM. Genl after Receiving the Returns is to attend with them at Head Quarters before he Delivers out the tents.

The Paymaster of the Several Regts to attend at Head Quarters this afternoon at 5 OClock.

HEAD QUARTERS Hannover 18th August 1777

Division Orders

> Feild officer of the Day tomorrow from Genl Deborres Brigade,
> Brigade Major from the Same.

HEAD QRTRS Roxborough 9th August

General Orders

By his Excellency the Commander in Cheif; The Waggon Master General and all those acting in the Department under him, are for the future to govern themselves Agreeable to the rules and Regulations of the Army, conformable to all General orders, & Division and Brigade orders Respectivily, & those attach'd to Brigades to be Subject to the Verbal orders of the Feild officers, of the Brigades appointed to the Charge and Direction of the line of march for the day; For any offence they are to be Confin'd to their Quarters and tried by Such Court Martial as Shall be appointed to hear and Determine the Same, If any Officer in the Department misbehaves either in the march, or to the Brigadier or Major General of the Brigade or Division, either of whome may order the Person to Confine himself to his Qrs Provision being made to keep Waggon masters to their Duty every officer is positively forbid to put any of them under guard or into the Provost, & there doing it will assuredly Subject them to be tried by A Court martial for Desobedience of orders; The names of the Waggon masters General appointed to Divisions to be inserted in the Division orders & these Officers are to have Recourse to Genl orders for the better Regulations of their Conduct; The Paymasters to make out their Abstracts up to the first of July which they are to Carry in and Receive their money also to lodge their abstracts for the month of July with the Paymaster General; The Regimental QrMasters are to make Returns to the D. QMr General of this Division of the Stores in these Respective Regts, and that with the utmost exactness in every article, the Returns to be given in at 5 OClock to morrow morning P. M. Capt. Parmelee of Col. Hazens Regt put in Arrest for Confineing James MKay contrary to Genl orders after being made acquainted there with, the Genl upon examination that Capt. Parmelee had no Settled Design of Disobeying orders, or Desputing his Authority And that the part Capt. Parmelee acted proceeded only from Mistake, the Genl Discharges him from his arrest.

The Commissary in future to Deliver all guards & Fatague men one Gill of Rum pr man pr Day, and to the Rest of the Division, holding themselves in Readiness to march ½ Gill of Rum pr man A Day.

AFTER ORDERS August 18th 1777

Division Orders

The Genl orders that the Muster Rolls of those Regts that were not mustred last month by the Deputy Muster Master General, to be made out Immedietly Up to the last day of July, each Capt. or Commanding Officer of A Company or Troop is to make out 4 Rolls Writ in A fact hand, the Commissioned Officers to hold the first Place in the Roll; the non Commissioned the 2nd the present & other effective privates the 3rd And the non effective, the missing, Discharged, Deserted, and dead, the Rolls must be folded up and endorsed, so as to express the Regt Company & the time when they were taken; the Rank of the Captains Should be Signified by the figures 1, 2, 3, &c on the Back of the Rolls; As the men are to be excus'd from Duty, it is expected that every man whose absence is not Accounted for, in the Collumn of Remarks will appear before the Officer of Musters.

The Genl Court Martial Wherof Col. Gunby is President is to Sit to morrow morning at 9 OClock.

CAMP HANOVER August 19th 1777

Brigade Orders

A Brigade Court Martial to Sit at 11 OClock this morning for the tryal of Patt Davis & Dennis Cain both of the Dela-

ware Regt Confin'd by Majr Powell for Being out of Camp
after Tatoo; & Beating and abusing an Inhabitant; Capt.
Kirkwood President, A Sublt. from each Regt Members.

HEAD QUARTERS Hanover 19th August 1777

Division Orders

> Field Officer of the day tomorrow from Genl Small-
> woods Brigade.
> Brigade Major from the Same.

The Waggon Masters to Draw the tents for his Officers
Immedietly, also to see that the Waggoneers draw their tents
from their Respective Brigades to which they Belong.

19th August 1777

Brigade Orders

The Dailey Complaints of the Inhabitants residing adjacent
to and in the Neighbourhood of our encampment sufficiently
Demonstrates the Depravity of the Soldery, and I am afraid
the Inattention of the Officers to restrain Such unsoldiery and
infamous practices has give Rise to these Complaints Would
the Soldery Consider that their Reputation, & in Some Instance I might add the Safety of a Corps is founded, And Depend not less on the Strict obedience to orders, Sobriety, Hon-
esty, & temperance, these on Valour, and Discipline, which are
both promoted and increased in a more or less Immediet Degree
as those Quallifications are Cherished and Practised, they must
blush for their Conduct, which must Strongly impress them
with Resembling Sheep Stealers, & theives more than honest
brave men fighting and Struggling for the Liberties of America,

the pay & Subsistance of the Continental Army is more Liberal than the allowance made to any other Soldiers in the face of the earth, this therefore cannot be an excuse for Breaking open Peoples Houses, & Stealing their Property, burning & otherwise destroying their out houses, implements of Husbandry & Handicraft Busness, together with their fencing & Crops; The latter perhaps may Destress this verry part of the Army next Winter, as well as the poore Inhabitants who are held up as the only Sufferers, to Restrain Such horrid & Shameful Practices, Let me intreat & Conjure every officer in the Brigade, to exert collectively & individually his utmost efforts; and the Brigadier Genl most earnestly begs those honest brave Soldiers who Still have A Regard to their good name, & the Credit of the Brigade, that they will use their best endeavours to disuade from & detect their Comrades in Such infamous practices; Its with conscern the Genl finds himself oblidg'd to declare that unless such practices are Drop'd the most Riged measures will be adopted, and Examplary punishments inflicted in every instance.

Proceedings of A Brigade Court Martial held in Camp, Hanover 19th August 1777.

Robt Kirkwood Capt. President.

1st Lt. Richd Anderson 7th M. R. ⎱ members ⎰ Ens. Benjm. MClean *D R*
2nd Lt. Richd Bird 5 M. R.   ⎰   ⎱ Ens. Jno James 3 m: R

     Serjt Cain   ⎱
& Pat Davis Private ⎰ of the D R confin'd by major Powell being Brought before the Court pleads guilty; but Occationed by provocation.

Major Powell being duely Sworn, Sayeth, last night about 10 OClock Complaint was lodg'd with me against two Soldiers

who was at the house of a Mr. Dennison in this Neighbourhood, and had behav'd in a verry indecent manner In Consequence of this information, I took A Corporal & file of men
and went with my informant, to Mr. Denisons, where I found
the Prisoners each with a gun in his hand, upon inquiring
what was the matter and their Buisness there at Such a time
of night, Davis told me the man of the house had used them in
a verry gross manner, had given them much abusive language,
& had taken up his gun and threatened to Shoot them for
Damn'd Rebels, saying also that he would get enough from
Staten Island to beat our whole Brigade Mr. Denison denied
the Accusation, Said they had come to his house, in a verry
abrupt manner, that Davis Swore A young woman, that was
nursing Denisons Wife Was his Wife, and he'd be Damn'd if
he did not Sleep with her, Denison Said he offred them a bed
in his Shop, & Supper if they wanted it, but that his wife was
at the point of death, & that he Could not Suffer any other
than his famely to sleep in his house that the Prisoners then
entred his house again, Search'd it, Calld him a damn'd Tory,
& took from him two guns (the Same I found them with) they
were both Somewhat intoxicated, this was better than an hour
after Tattoo beating.

Mr. Dennison Being duely Sworn Sayeth, that the above
mentioned Prisoners came to his house just at dark, & de-
manded A Young Woman which he had in his house, & one
of them Claimd her as his wife, which girl was up stairs at the
Same time. I denied that there was any Such girl there that
Blong'd to them, upon which they took two guns of my property which was behind a Door, & went out, & swore that they
would Stand Sentrie at my Door, for I was a Tory and fired
one of the guns off.

The Court are unanimously of opinion that Serjt Cain &
Patt Davis, are guilty of the Charge, & do Sentence Serjt Cain
to be Reduced to the Ranks & Receive 50 Lashes and Patt
Davis 100 lashes, on the bare back well laid on with the Cat
oNine tails:

ROBT KIRKWOOD
President

The above Sentence approv'd, but from having heard A
favourable Character of Serjt Cain have Remitted the Latter
part of the punishment, and have thought proper to Remit 50
lashes of Patt. Davis's punishment the Remainder to be inflicted at beat of Retreat.

WM SMALLWOOD
B: General

HEAD QRTRS Hanover 20th August 1777

Division Orders

Field Officer of the Day tomorrow from Genl Deborres
Brigade, Major from the Same.

The Weekly Returns to be given in every Saturday Morning by 8 OClock.

The Brigade Major to See that the Adjutants of the Brigade
they belong to, bring in the Regimental Weekly Returns to
them every friday morning; at 8 OClock The Court martial
whereof Col. Gunby is President to Sit tomorrow morning at
9 OClock to try such matters As may be brought before them.

CAMP HANOVER 20th August 1777

Brigade Orders

The Brigadier General requires the Commandants of Regts
in his Brigade, to Select as many of their men as will be able

to Stand a march, to arm and Accouter them in the best manner & Blankets Slung, to make Returns and draw Immedietly,
& have it cook'd, three days salt provisions & hard bread if they
can possibly be furnished, their tents will be left Standing &
guarded by those, who may be two infirm for the Fatagues of
the March three days allowance of Rum is also to be drawn;
but the Genl would recommend that none be delivered out
without his further orders, the whole to hold themselves in
Readiness to march tomorrow at 11 OClock in the forenoon.

Thirsday 21st Our Brigade March'd at 11 OClock by the
Way of Bottle Hill, which is 5 miles from thence to Chattam
7 miles and there Refresh'd from thence we march'd thr'o
Spring field to Elizabeth Town point 10 miles there our men
unloaded themselves of their knapsacks & Blankets & Crossed
the River in the Greatest Silence on to Staten Island all which
we effected By day Break, from thence we proceeded towards
the East end of the Island where coming near A Guard Consisting of About 100 Men of British Troops but upon first of
us they Ran away at this place We Destroyed near 3000£ of
Stores Besides A Quantity brought off; We traveled near 20
Miles on the Island but Could not see any more of the Enemy,
About 1 OClock Came to the Bazing Star Where we all
Cross'd but 100 men who were Detain'd about Bringing over
Stock these were attacked & mostly taken Prisoners after they
had fired all their Amunition away that night the Prisoners
beat off the Guard & the greatest part of them got over the
River, the Prisoners that were taken from them were as fol-
lowes Viz:

3 Cols: viz Barton, Lawrence, & Allen, 4 Captains 6 Subalterns & 150 Privates all of the greens, then march'd to Spank

town being 7 Miles, Saturday 23d march'd to Elizabeth Town 5 Miles from thence to Springfield 7 Miles Sunday 24th march'd through Westfield to Specatria being 14 Miles, Monday 25th march'd to Brunswick being 5 Miles, Tuesday 26th march'd to Princeton being 15 Miles, & quarterd our Men in the College, Wednesday 27th the Baggage came up then pitch'd our Tents in an Old Field back of the said College. Tuesday 28th Struck tents at day break and March'd to Trenton in Hunterdon County Being 12 Miles that evening I Cross'd the River in Compy with Capt. Anderson and Marched to the Red Lyon within 13 Miles of Philadelphia 29th Marched from the Red Lyon thr'o Philada down to Wilmington & the 30th I went to my Fathers.

PENNSYLVANIA STATE HEAD QUARTERS Chester Septr 1st

Field Officer of the Day to morrow from Genl Deborres Brigade, the Commanding Officers of the Several Regts to See that their men have provisions cook'd for tomorrow those Regts that have not Drawn may draw at this place.

Genl Deborre with all the Field Officers of both Brigades to attend at Head Quarters at Senals tavern at the Post office precisely at 5 OClock this Afternoon, the troops to march for Wilmington tomorrow morning at day Break, Genl Smallwoods Brigade to march in front, the Officers are Desired to prevent the Waggons being loaded with men & Weomen, none to Ride but those Soldiers who are unable to march.

Tuesday Septr 2nd Struck tents & march'd to Wilmington in the Delaware State & encamp'd about one Mile West of the town in all 13 Miles.

HEAD QUARTERS Wilmington Septr 3rd 1777

Brigade Orders

By order of Genl Smallwood the Commanding Officer of the Different Regts in this Brigade to have Returns made out of all the plunder that was taken on Staten Island the plunder to be Collected at one place in order that there may be an equal Destribution made of the Same.

The Col. desires that the Arms & Accoutrements be put in the best of Order, & that Catridges be Drawn when wanting, no guns to be taken out of the Stocks, nor locks to be taken to pieces in Cleaning the Same The officers of the Differrent Companies to examine into the State of mens Arms every Morning at parade, Should any damage happen to any of the Arms through neglect of the Soldier that their Acctt be Charged with the Same, any Soldier that Shall Descharge his fire Arms without leave from the Commanding Officer Shall Receive 50 lashes on his bare back upon the Spot, that no Soldier be permitted to leave Camp on any pertence whatsoever without leave from their Officers; The QrMastrs of the Differrent Regts to have proper Sinks dug in the rear of their Regts And the Bushes & brush to be Cleared out of the Encampment.

Wilmington 3d Septr 1777

Division Orders

Field Officer of the Day to morrow from Genl Smallwoods Brigade.

The whole Division to be paraded in the front of the encampment at 4 o'clock precisely, the Officers commanding Regts to See their Men Clean, their hair powder'd & green boughs in their hats, the Whole to be Counted of in Divisions properly Officer'd.

Genl Smallwoods Brigade to Compleat the Genls guard, Also to furnish 1 Sub. 2 Serjts 3 Corpls & 24 men, to parade in the road on the left of the Division, at Retreat beating; Genl Deborre Brigade to furnish a main guard till further orders, Consisting of 1 Sub. 2 Serjts 3 Corpls & 24 men, the guard house to be handy to the Division also to furnish for A Picquet 1 Capt. 2 Subs 2 Serjts 3 Corpls & 40 Privates, to be paraded in the Road on the left of the Division at Retreat Beating.

Every Commanding Officer of A Company is immedietly to make out his muster Roll to the first of September; Col. Hazens Regt will parade for muster to morrow evening at 5 OClock, Coll. Halls Regt will parade for muster at 6 OClock 4 Rolls are to be made for each muster, the other two Regts Belonging to the Same Brigade to parade on friday morning Precisely at 8 OClock for Muster.

AFTER ORDERS 3d Septr 1777

The orders Respecting the parade of the Division are to be Suspended, the Division to have two days provisions Cooked their Arms in order, & Supplied with a proper Quantity of Amunition and have every thing in Readiness to move at a Moments Warning.

Proceedings of A Regimental Court Martial held at Wilmington this 4th day of Septr 1777 by order of Lt. Coll. Pope of the Delaware Regt for the tryal of Such prisoners as may be brought before them.

Capt. Anderson President

Lt. Rhodes ⎱
Lt. Wilds ⎰ members ⎰ Lt. Bratten
⎱ Lt. Brown

Emanuel Triser Confin'd by Lt. Joseph Wilds for Stealing Clothes from Johnson Fleetwood.

Emanuel Triser being brought before the Court pleads not guilty that the Clothes he was Accus'd of Stealing from Johnson Fleetwood he got out of Fredreck Reeds knapsack, who was taken prisoner on Staten Island, that Reed had Borrowed A Shirt and pair of stockings of him.

Jas Cavender being brought before the Court & duely Sworn Says that he Saw the Stockings in Fredrick Reeds knapsack, And that he heard Serjt Perry Say that he Saw Triser take the Stockings out of Reeds knapsack.

The Court having Considred the nature of the offence are of opinion that the prisoner is not guilty of the Charge laid to him, & that he be Released from his Confinement.

Wm Plowman Prisoner confin'd for being drunk on his post & fireing two Shot declaring he would be the death of Some person last night when on post, & letting no persons pass without money.

The Court are of opinion that the Crime of Wm Plowman doth not Lay before A Regimental Court Martial.

ENOCH ANDERSON
Captn presdt

The Above proceedings Approv'd.

CHAS. POPE
Lt. Coll. D R

Friday 5th Septr Struck tents & march'd about 3 miles And encamp'd in A Stubble Field about one mile Northward of Newport New Castle County.

HEAD QURTRS Wilmington 5th Septr 1777

Genl Orders

Major Genl for tomorrow...........Green
Field Officer ....Weeden
Field Officers Cols Matthews, Major Powell, Brigade
Major Porus.

The Commissary Genl of Prisoners informs the Commanding Officers of Regts and other Corps that notwithstanding the
orders heretofore Issued for that purpose, he has Received but
one Small Return of Prisoners taken by the Enemy Since his
Appointment; in Consequence of Such neglect it will be Impossible for him, in case of an exchange to pay proper Attention to the orders of the different Captures as to time, he further informs them for the future the prisoners will be exchanged according to the return hereafter made to him.

As Baggage Waggons at all times are A great incumberrence
to an Army, & would be perticularly so in the day of Battle,
they in the latter can be Driven off the Field, that the Army
may not be the least incumberred by them, it is besides A
measure which Common prudence dictates, & whenever an
Action is expected, the QrMastr Genl will immedietly wait on
the Commander in Cheif to Receive his orders Respecting them.

From every Information of the Enemys Designs and from
their Movements it is manifest their Aim is if possible to possess them Selves of Philadelphia this is their Capital object, its
what they Strove to effect; but were happily disappointed, they
made A Second Attempt at the opening of this Campaign, but
after vast preparation & expences for the purpose they abandon'd, their Design and totally evacuated the Jerseys, they are
now making their last efforts; to come up the Delaware, it
Seems was their first Intention but from the measure taken to

annoy them in the River they Judged this enterprise that way too hazardous; at length they have landed on the Eastern Shore of Maryland and advanc'd Some little way into the Country but the Genl trusts they will be again Disappointed in their views Should they put their Designs against Philadelphia or this State their all is at Stake, they will put the Contest to the event of A Single Battle, if they are overthrown they are utterly undone, the war ended, now then is the time for our most Strenious exertion, one bold Stroke will free the Land from Rapine, Devestation, & Burning; Famale Inocence from brutal Lust & Violence in every other Quarter the American Arms have of Late been Rapidly Successfull, great many of the Enemy have fallen in Battle, & Still greater numbers have been made prisoners; the Militia to the Northward have fought with A Resolution that would have done honour to old Soldiers, they have Bravely fought & Conquer'd & glory attend them & who can forbear to emulate their noble Spirits, who is without Ambition to Share with them the applause of their Countrymen and of all posterity, As the Defenders of their Liberty, & the procurers of peace and happiness, to millions in the present & future Generation, two years we have maintain'd the war & Strugled with difficulties Innumerable, but the prospect has brightned and our affairs put on A better face, now is the time to Reap the fruits of all our toil and Dangers if we behave like men this third Campaign will be our last, ours is the main army to us our Country looks for protection, the eyes of all america & all Urope, are turned upon us, as on those by whome the event of War is to be Determined and the Genl assures his Country men and fellow Soldiers that he believes the Critical & important moments is at hand, which demand their most Spirited exertion to the Field, Glory waits to Crown the brave & peace freedom & happiness will be the Rewards of Victory, animated by Motives like those Soldiers fighting in the Cause of Innocense humanity & Justice will never give way, but with undaunted Resolution press on to Conquest, & these the Genl assures himself is the part American forces now in Arms will act & those he will assure Success.

Genl Ewings Brigade of Militia will releive the men of Genl Nashes Brigade now on the Little guard on the East Side of Brandewine as soon as possible and Dailey furnish it.

CAMP NEAR NEWPORT Sepr 6th 1777.

Regimental Orders

The Commanding officers of Companies are Requested to have their men Clean & hair powder'd to morrow at 2 OClock with their Arms & Accoutrements in good order, fit to bear Inspection by the Commander in Chief, any person appearing Contrairy to this order it will be looked on to be the officers Neglect for which they will have to Acct, any Soldier absent from the parade at the above mentioned time, Shall assurèdly Suffer Agreeable to the Articles of War, unless A Reasonable excuse be given for the Same.

                                        CHAS POPE
                                          Lt. Coll. D R

HEAD QUARTERS Wilmington Sepr 6th 1777

General Orders

Parole Resolution

C. Sign Firmness & Conquest

Major Genl for tomorrow Lord Sterling.

Brigadier Scott, Field Officers Col. Parker, Major Tory Brigade Major for the day.

The Genl has no doubt but that every man who has A due Sense of the Importance of the Cause he has taken to defend And who has any Regard to his own honour & the Reputation of A Soldier, will if Called to Action will behave like one Contending for every thing valuable, but if contrary to his expectation there Shall be found any officer or Soldier so far lost to all Shame as basely to quit their posts without orders, or Shall Skulk from danger or offer to Retreat before order is given for so doing from proper authority of a Superior Officer, they are to be instantly Shot down, as a Just punishment to themselves & for an example to others, this order those in the Rear, & the Corps of Reserve are to See duely executed, to prevent the Cowardly making a Sacrifice of the brave, & by their ill example and ground less tales circulating to Cover their own Shamefull conduct, Spreading terror as they go; that this order may be well known & strongly Impressed upon the Army; the Genl positively orders the Commanding officers of every Regt to assemble his men & have it Read to them; to prevent the plea of Ignorance.

The Genl begs the favour of the Officers to be attentive to all Strange faces & Suspicious persons, which may be descover'd in Camp & if upon examination of them no good Acct can be given why they are there to carry them to the Majr Genl of the day for further examination, this as it is only A necessary precaution is to be done in a manner least offensive The Genl Officers are to meet at 5 OClock this afternoon at the Brick house by Whiteclay Creek & fix upon proper Picquets for the Security of the Camp John Lawrence and Presley Thompson Esqrs are appointed extra Aid de Camp to the Commander in Chief all orders therefore through them in Writing or otherwise are to be Regarded in the Same light as if proceeding from any other of his Aids de Camp; Notwithstanding the orders relative to house, they are Still of great Nuisances to ye Army the QrMrs of Divisions are therefore to See that they are fixed at Proper distances from Camp, & that all the ofal be well buried once a day.

The Commander in Cheif will look to these QrMrs for the Execution of this order & no excuse can be admitted for neglect of So necessary A duty.

AFTER ORDERS

Information has been given that many of the Waggons horses are Suffered to go loose in the field, the Commander in Cheif Strictly orders, that every night all the Waggon horses be put to the Waggons & there kept, & if it be necessary at any time for them to go to grass, that it be only in the day time, & then the Waggoneers must Stay with them. Constantly, that they may be Ready to tackle at the Shortest notice, the Waggon masters are Required to See this order Carefully Executed, The Enemy have Disencumberred themselves of all their Baggage that their movements may be Quick & easey; it behoves us to be alike ready for marching at a moments warning & for that Reason it is absolutely necessary, & the Commander in Cheif positively requires that both officers & men remain constantly at their Quarters. Tattoo is no longer to be beat in Camp.

TIM PICKERING
Adjt. Genl

Sepr 6th 1777

Division Orders

That the Waggon horses be fixt to the Waggons at retreat beating every night & keep them so till 9 the next morning & even then they are by no means to be Separated from the

Waggons, so as to take 5 Minutes to get them fixed, the Commanding Officers of Regts & Corps to See those orders Complied with, the Commissary of the Division to provide himself immdietly with Sufficient Waggons to move his Stores & is to be Ready to move at A moments warning, his Remaining behind the Division Shall Subject him to A Tryal by A Court Martial for breach of orders, the Artillery horses to be fixed to the pieces one hour before day each morning; A Subl. & 20 men to mount guard every night at the Bridge from 6 in the evening to 9 in the morning to examine all Strangers that are passing, & to apprehend Such as do not give Satisfactory Account of themselves; all offenders not tryable by A Regimental Court martial to be Sent to the provost guard, The picquet guard to be Releived tomorrow morning in the Same manner it was this morning, the Prisoners in the Main guard are order'd to the QrGuards of their Respective Regts And to be tried by A Regimental Court Martial, the main Guard is desolved, Walter Cox Esqr. is appointed Acting Brigade Major in Genl Smallwoods Brigade in the absence of Genl Smallwood & is to be respected & obeyed as Such.

6th Sepr 1777

Brigade Orders

The Commanding officers of Regts will be pleas'd to order Weekly Returns to be made out & deliver'd to Majr Cox immedietly that proper details may be made out.

HEAD QUARTERS Newport 7th Sepr 1777

General Orders

> Parole Cambridge C: Sign Dartmouth Granby
> Major General for tomorrow Stephens
> Brigadier Weeden, Field Officers Col. Marshal

Major Ballard, The Genl has Received A Confirmation of the Intilligence mentioned in the after orders of last night, that the Enemy has Disencumber'd themselves of all their Baggage even tents Reserving only their Blankets, & Such part of their Clothing as is Absolutely Necessary, this Indicates A Speedy and Rapid movement, & points out the necessaty of following the example & Ridding ourselves for A few days of all things we possible can dispence with as A verry Imperfect obedience has been paid to former orders on this Subject, now once more Strictly enjoins that all baggage which can be Spared Both officers & men, be immedietly pack'd up & sent off this day to the otherside Brandewine, this order having been heretofore eluded by A too Indulgent Contraction of the Genl terms on which it has been Couch'd, the Genl is oblidg'd to be more explicit & to Declare that is his Intention the Officers Should only Retain their Blankets & Great Coats & only three or four Shifts of under Cloaths, & that all the men Should besides what they have on keep only a Blanket, one Shirt a piece & Such as have great Coats, all trunks Chests & boxes either bedding or Cloaths then these mentioned, to be Sent away till the elapsing of a few days Shall determine whether the Enemy means to make an immediate attack or not, its hop'd that none will have So little Sense of propriety as to deem the measure So obvious for the good of the Army & the Service (Hardships) it would be wholly in the extream to hazzard the loss of our baggage for the Sake of a little present Convenience as loss at this time would be irrepareable this disadvantage at this time to have them to take Care of at the moment of an attack when we Should be preparing for defence, its evident that the attention of both officers & men will then be wholly engrossed for its Safety, & the enemy will have time to be upon us before we are Ready to receive them the Consequence of this will be bustle & confusion & perhaps Defeat & disgrace, the loss of our baggage & not Improbable the ruin of the army, the Commander in Cheif in A perticular manner looks to the Genl Officers for the execution of these orders in their Respective Divisions & Brigades.

The whole Army is to Draw two days provisions exclusive of today, have it Cook'd & deposited with the Regimental Qr-Master, Provided Salt provisions can be got, otherwise one days fresh Provisions to be Cooked deposited as aforesaid & two days hard Bread if to be had.

All the Horses except Capt. Lewes's Troop take post on the Right of the army, tents of the whole army are to be Struck & pack'd upon the Waggons to morrow morning an hour before day and the horses tackled, all the Corps of Horses are to be Saddled at the Same time & the Whole Army Drawn up in their Respective lines, the QrM. Genl is to Spare no pains Immedietly to provide Waggons to Carry the mens Knapsacks, that they may be perfectly light & free for Action.

No more Sick to be Sent to Concord but to Bermingham.

Sepr 7 & 8th 1777

Division Orders

The Officers for tomorrow from Gen. Smallwoods Brigade (8th) The tents of the Division to be pitch'd at 11 OClock, 100 men with 2 Capts & 4 Subalterns to be paraded near Genl

Washingtons Quarters at 10 OClock this forenoon the Command to be taken by A Lt. Coll. from Genl Deborres Brigade, they are to have with them provision & Blankets & are to ground their Arms at the place of parade & remain there untill the Field officer Repairs there.

Sepr 8th 1777

Brigade Orders

Commanding Officers in Regts in Genl Smallwoods Brigade to order two days provisions to be immedietly drawn & Cook'd, the Soldiers Arms to be put in the best order, Catridge Boxes filled with Catridges, & hold themselves in Readiness to march at a moments Warning, the Commissary of ye Brigade is ordered to furnish A Sufficient Quantity of Provision otherwise his neglect will be enquired into.

It is meant to have two days cook'd on hand.

Monday Sepr 8th 1777 (Near Newport)

Struck tents & went to work in the lines, lay there till 3 OClock Tuesday morning the 9th then March'd about 10 miles to Chadds ford & forded over & there encamped, Wednesday ye 10 march'd to gordons ford being about 4 miles there lay all night, Thursday the eleventh about 2 OClock P. M. march'd About 1½ miles to the field of Action near Jeffries at Brandewine our Regt was Sent as A flanking party on the Enemys left wing, during the engagement we were Several times exposed to the fire of the enemys Cannon & Small arms.

About Sun set retreated to Chester being 15 miles.

Friday 12th march'd through Derby to Schuylkill being 12 miles and encamp'd near the Bridge on this the River Phlada County.

HEAD QUARTERS Sepr 12th 1777

General Orders

The Commanding Officer of each Brigade is immedietly to Send off as many Officers as he Shall think necessary on the Roads leading to the place of Action Yesterday & on any other Roads where the Straglers may be found & perticularly to Wilmington to pick up all Straglers from the Army and bring them on; in doing this they Should proceed as far towards the Enemy as Shall be convenient to their own Safety, and examine every house, in the main time the troops are to march on in good order through Darby, to the Bridge towards Schuylkill & Germain town & there pitch their tents, Genl Greens Division will move last & cover the Baggage Stores. A Gil of Rum or whiskey is to be Served out to each man who has not already that allowance.

Genl Smallwoods light troops will remain at Chester to Collect all the Straglers as they come and tomorrow morning follow the Army, the Directors of the Hospitals will see that all Sick and wounded are Sent to Trentown in doing this Genl Maxwell will give them all necessary assistance, the Genl expects each Regt or Officers commanding Brigades will immedietly make the most exact Returns of their killed wounded & missing.

AFTER ORDERS

The Officers are without loss of time to See that they are Compleated with amunition, that their arms are in the best order, the inside of them washed clean & well dried, the touch holes pick'd & a good flint in each gun, the Strictest Attention is expected will be paid to this order as the officers must be Sensible that their own honour, the Safety of the Soldiers &

Success of the Cause depends absolutely upon a carefull execution of it, the Commanding officers of each Regt is to endeavour to procure Such necessaries as are wanting for his men.

An exact Return of ye State of each Regt to be made immedietly.

> Major Genl for tomorrow Stevens, Brigadier Conway.
> Field officers Coll. Lewes, Major Ball.

> Saturday ye 13th Sepr 1777

Struck tents and march'd through Germaintown & encamped about one mile on the N. W. Side of Germainton in an orchard being about 8 miles. Philada County.

PENSYLVANIA STATE HEAD QRTRS Germainton Sepr 13th 1777

General Orders

> Parole Concord—C: Sign Carlisle (Danburry)

The General with perticular Satisfaction thanks those Gallant Officers & Soldiers who on the 11th Inst bravely fought in their Countries Cause; if there are any whose Conduct Reflects Dishonour upon Soldiership and their names are not pointed out to him, he must for the present leave them to Reflect how much they have injured their Country, how unfaithfully they have proved to their fellow Soldiers but with this exortation they embrace the first opportunity which may offer to do Justice to both, & to the profession of a Soldier.

Although the event of that day from some unfortunate circumstances was not so favourable as Could be wished, the Genl has the Satisfaction to inform the Troops, that from every account that has been obtain'd the Enemies loss far exceeds, and has full Confidence that in another appeal to heaven, with the blessing of Providence, which it becomes every officer & Soldier humbly to Supplicate, we Shall prove Successfull, The Honourable Congress in Consideration of the gallant behaviour of the Troops on Thursday last, their fatague Since & from a full conviction that on every future occation they will manifest a bravery worthy of the Cause they have undertaking to defend; have been pleased to order thirty Hogsheads of Rum to be destributed among them, in Such manner as the Commander in Cheif Should Direct, he orders the Commissary Genl of Issues to deliver to each officer & Soldier 1 Gill pr day while it lasts.

The Commanding Officers of each Brigade without delay is to Send a number of Active Officers into the City & its environs to pick up & bring to Camp all Stragling Soldiers whome they may find, as well those belonging to other Brigades as their own, likewise a Serjeant from each Brigade, to the Bridge over Schuylkill to direct the Soldiers as they Cross where to find their Brigades, at Roll Calling this afternoon the men are to be Charged not to be out of Drum call of their respective Parades, under pain of death, nor officers, as they value the Service & dread Cashiering.

The QRM. Genl is to have the Waggons of each Brigade Immedietly Arranged So as to move them in their proper time, at a moments warning, the order of the Encampment at this place need not be attended too, as our Stay here will be Short, each Division is to encamp in as Compact order as possible to-night, all the Continental Troops are to be Suppli'd immedietly with forty Catridges, & the officers will see that the Soldiers carry their Spare Amunition in Such a manner as to avoid Injury & Loss; The Clothier General is ordered to Send Spare Shoes Shirts &c. to Camp, to furnish such men as are destitute, the Commanding officers therefore of Corps are to delay no time in Supplying the Absolute want of their men.

The Genl does most ardently exhort every officer to attend to the due & Speedy execution of these orders without A moments loss of time.

AFTER ORDERS Sepr 13th 1777

The following proportion of tents is Allowed the Army upon its next march Viz. 1 Soldiers tent for the Field officers 1 Do. for 4 other Commissioned officers 1 Do. for 8 Serjeants, Drummers or fifers 1 Do. for every 8 Privates.

The Brigadiers to have Returns made out And the above proportion of tents taken for their Brigades & one Waggon for every 50 tents & no more, no weomen on any pretence whatsoever to go with the army but to follow the Baggage, the Soldiers to carry their Camp kettles, which if the army Should Come to Action are to be put in the waggons with the tents, the invalids under A good Subaltern are to guard the tents of each Brigade. The Division Commissaries are directed to have A good Supply of Provisions for troops, and the QRM. Genl must without fail furnish the necessary Waggon for that purpose a Gill of Rum or other Spirits to be dealt out to every officer & Private untill further orders, the Commissaries are to make provision Accordingly.

The Army are to be Ready to march presisely at 9 OClock tomorrow morning. the Genl Officers commanding Divisions will Receive the orders of march from the QRM. Genl who will also Direct the Rout of the Baggage.

HEAD QUARTERS Germainton Sepr 14th 1777
General order for the line of March.

The troops are to march to Sweeds ford in the following order by Sub Divisions from the Right.

1st Two thirds of the Light Dragoons from which their Commanding Officer will Detach Small parties to Reconitre in front and on the flanks to A Considerable distance, 800 yards in the Rear.

2ndly A Captains Command from Genl Smallwoods Brigade.

3dly One Regt from Smallwoods Brigade 200 yds in the Rear.

4thly The Residue of his Brigade 300 yds in the Rear of that.

5thly The main Body of the Army 500 yards in the rear of that Brigade.

And in the Following order Viz.

1st General Sullivans Division.
2d Lord Sterling.
3d General Waynes.
4th The park of Artilery.
5th Genl Nash's Brigade.
6th Genl Stevens Division.
7th Genl Greens Division.

6thly The Waggons with tents, Hospital & Commissaries Stores, 7thly Rear guard of two Regts of Genl Weedens Brigade 8thly A Captains Command from these two Regts 200 yds in the rear 9thly The Remaining 3d of the Dragoons 500 yds in ye rear of the foot, 10thly A Subalterns command from the Dragoons 500 yds in their Rear, the guards in front, and near each Brigade to send out Small flanking parties in their left, the rear guards of foot & Dragoons to pick up all Straglers.

Sunday 14th September Struck tents & March'd from Germainton & Forded Schuylkill at Davis's ford, then march'd to the Sign of the Brick on the Lancaster Road Chester County & lay in the woods being about 11 miles.

HEAD QUARTERS 14th September 1777

General Orders

>   Major Genl for tomorrow. . . . Sterling.
>   Brigadier . . . . Wayne.

Officers for the Day Coll. Hendricks, Major Brawster, Major Fleury, Officers for Picquet Coll. Ogdon, and Major Flower The whole Line while it keeps unseperated is to furnish 600 men properly Officer'd for guard, each Brigade to give in proportion to their Strength, these men are to be under the immediate direction of the Major General & the Officers of the day who with the Assistance of the QRM Genl agreeable to the orders of the 10th Inst, are to See that their out guards are posted in Such A manner as most effectually to Secure the Camp, if the Differrent Avenues Should not Require the Above number, the overplus is to remain as A Picquett near the park of Artilery, & to be always Ready to reinforce every Guard, or answer every other purpose that the Major General or other officer of the Day Shall think Necessary these guards in Common are to parade at 8 OClock in the morning near the Artillery Park, but when ever the troops are to march, they are to Assemble there at least half an hour before the time appointed for the March of the Army, & from thence the Major General or other officer of the day, will order so many as he or they Shall Judge necessary to move on with the QRMaster to the place of Destination, & after the

Guards & all the Avenues to the new encampment are well
Reconitred the guards are to be posted; Such troops as have
not been Supplied with their Compliment of Catridges agreeable to the orders of the 13th Inst, are to be furnished immedietly the Troops are also to get provisions cook'd for tomorrow at least; the Clothier Genl is attending with Shoes &c.

The officers commanding Regts are to delay no time in getting their men Supplied in future when ever the men are
found for Action the Serjeants are to be plac'd in the ranks on
the flanks of the Sub Divisions, that the Benefit of their fire
may not be lost, the Brigadiers & officers Commanding Regts
are also to put some good Officer in the Rear to keep the men
in order, & if in time of Action any man who is not wounded
whether he has arms or not turns his back upon the Enemy or
attempts to run away, or to Retreat before orders are given
for it, those officers are to put him instantly to death, the man
does not deserve to live who basely flies, breaks his Sollemn
engagement & betrays his Country. Such men Belonging to
Genl Maxwells light Corps as have Returned to their Regts
are again to Join Genl Maxwell without Delay And the Officers Commanding Regts are to make dilligent Search for those
men, & See that they are Sent to Join that Corps Immedietly.

Monday 15th September march'd about 14 miles on the
Same Road pitch'd our tents in the woods at night, Chester
County.

HEAD QRTRS 15th Sepr 1777

General Orders

The Commanding Officers of each Regt is immedietly to
make an exact inspection into their mens amunition, & See

that it is Compleated to 40 Rounds A man, provision to be Drawn & Cook'd for today & to morrow the Commander in Chief expects a punctual & Instant comply with these orders.

THOS. PICKERRING
Adjt Genl

Tuesday 16th Sepr. Struck Tents Cross'd the main Road and paraded in line of Battle in A Buckwheat Field expecting the enemy in order to give them battle, began to rain verry hard & Continued all day and night, filed off to the left & march'd 11 Miles to the Yellow Springs there Stay'd all night on the Brow of a hill without tents (Chester County) Wednsday 17th march'd and Cross'd French Creek Bridge being 6 miles went 3 miles further there Stayed all night being 9 miles (no tents) Thursday 18th march'd About 3 OClock in the morning, to Reading Furnace being 12 miles & there encamp'd on the brow of an hill, Friday 19th returned back to our last encampment being 12 miles, filed off to the left and forded Schuylkill & march'd towards ye Sweeds ford 7 miles and halted in the woods at 10 OClock at night march'd through the trap to Richardsons ford being 10 miles (in all 29 miles) Philada County.

HEAD QUARTERS Richardsons ford 20th Sepr 1777

Division Orders

Field officer of the day from Coll. Hazens Brigade for to morrow from Coll. Stones do.

The Conductors of military Stores for the Division to See that there is A Sufficient Supply of Suitable Ammunition got immedietly the Commissaries is to deliver out for to day A double allowance of Fatague Rum;

The Commanders of Brigades to See that their amunition is in good order & to have it carefully examined, also to Send their Respective QRMasters out for provisions, Sufficient to Supply the present necessaty of the Division, they giving Receipts for what they Receive for that purpose, unless the Commissaries Should Supply the Same; An orderly Serjt from each Brigade to be sent immedietly to the Genls Qrtrs; Coll. Stones Brigade to furnish the Generals guard as soon as possible.

HEAD QUARTERS Richardsons ford 21st Sepr 1777

Division Orders

The General is much Surprised that through the Ignorance of Some of our Officers, a British flag has Cross'd the River and come into our encampment without being Stop'd, the General expressly orders that in future no flag from the British army, be permitted to Cross the Schuylkill on any pretence, and all officers who may hereafter permit it, Shall be punished for breach of orders;

The Commanding officers of Companies are to order the amunition of their men to be inspected into at every time the Roll is Call'd & call their men to an Acct for Such ammunition as may be wanting, the Reason of the foregoing order will readily appear when it is known that men have made A practice of Destroying their powder & throw their balls about the Street, such conduct being of the most alarming nature will enduce every officer to watch the conduct of his Soldiers respecting so important A point, The Brigade Major of Coll. Stones is immedietly to repair to the Long ford with A Subaltern from Coll. Stones Brigade and relieve the one Station'd there, & put him in arrest for permitting A Brittish flag to pass the ford into our encampment without being examin'd or Stopp'd at the post committed to his Charge.

Sunday 21st Sepr march'd about 3 in the afternoon down to the bank of the Schuylkill being about 2 miles lay under arms all night, Monday 22nd march'd 2 hours before day about 10 miles on the Reading Road Stopp'd in the woods to Refresh about 2 P. M. march'd 5 miles further and encamped in A place Called Faulkners Swamp; (in all 15 miles) Philada County. _____

NEW HANNOVER HD QRS Sepr 23rd 1777

Genl Orders

    Major Genl for tomorrow..........Sterling

    Brigadier ....Weeden

    Field Officer Coll. Duncomb, Lt. Coll. Ennis, Brigade Major Fleury; Major Stubblefield.

The Genl expects Returns of the Army to morrow morning without fail, enjoins it upon the Commanding Officers of Corps to see that they are exactly made, each Regt is to proceed to make Cattridges for its own use that they may be held in Store, Genl Knox will furnish them with materials, It is expected as the weather is cool, that the troops will never have less than two days provisions by them the necessaty of this the Genl does in the Strongest manner impress upon the officers in hopes they will exert themselves in Seeing it executed, as the Soldiers or the Service must greatly Suffer unless this is attended to; The Genl is informed the Tin Cannisters which were Serv'd out for the purpose of Carrying amunition are in Some instances employ'd to other uses he therefore positively forbids Such practices;

Jas Loyd is Appointed Volunteer A. D. C. to General Green & is to be obey'd & respected as Such, the Sick in Camp are to be Sent immedietly to the Artillery Park, or house, or Barn nearest thereto, that the Surjeons may Send them in Waggons to Reading,   A Carefull Subaltern from each Division is to go with them,   If so many are not necessary the Surjeon General will dismiss Some of them, each man is to take one days provision with him.

Wednsday 22th Sepr.   Struck tents & march'd about ½ a mile, then return'd & pitch'd tents in the Same encampment, (1 mile this day).

September 23rd 1777

Division Orders

> Field Officer of the day to morrow from Coll. Stones
> Brigade.
> Major of the Day tomorrow Cox.

A Picquett Consisting of one Field officer, four Captains, Eight Subalterns, with A proportion of non Commissioned officers and 200 Privates to be paraded at the park of Artillery every morning precisely at 8 OClock, the detail to be in proportion to each Brigade excepting the Detail of tomorrow which is to be equal—one Field Officer, 2 Capts 4 Subtns with Serjts & Corpls in proportion & 100 Privates from Coll. Hazens Brigade.

The Brigade Major for of the day for ye Division to See that the Pickett is on the Division Parade, by 7 OClock in the morning in order that he march them to the park of Artillery Agreeable to the time appointed.

HEAD QRS near Bligrove 24th Sepr 1777

General Orders

> Major Genl for to morrow Stephens.
>
> Brigadier Scott, Field Officers Col. Farmer, Lt. Col. Ford, Brigade Major Williams, Field officer for Picquett Major Bell.

Sepr 24th 1777

Division Orders

> Field Officer of the Day tomorrow from Col. Hazens Brigade.
>
> Field officer for the Reserve Picquett from Col. Stones Brigade.
>
> Major of the Day tomorrow Flury;

A Court of Inquiry to Sit tomorrow morning at 9 OClock to inquire into the Conduct of Lt. Coats of Col. Prices Regt at the Battle of Brandewine, Col. Gunby President of Said Court, 3 Capts & 3 Subs from each Brigade, to Sit as members.

HEAD QRS Sepr 25th 1777

Genl Orders

> Major Genl for tomorrow..........Sullivan.
>
> Brigadier ....Conway.
>
> Field Officers Col. Grayson, Lt. Col. Deffart.

Brigade Major Cox, for Pickett Lt. Col. Barber. A General Court Martial to Sit immedietly at the house where Genl Conway Quarters for the tryal of all prisoners, which Shall be brought Before them; Col. James Wood is appointed President of this Court one Carefull Subt from each Regt is to be Sent off to Bethlehim with Col. Biddle immedietly, to inspect the Baggage of the army, to See if it Suffers from Dampness, & if it does, to have it properly dried and put it up again, & then to See that it be well Secured, & guarded against Plunderers, these Officers are to Assemble at 3 OClock in the afternoon at the QRM. Genls Qrs the next house beyond Head Qrs. Hence forward all Brigade Returns are to be made directly to the Adjt Genl; Ordinary Weekly Returns of each Brigade to be made every Monday at orderly time. Parole Bunker hill.

C. Sign $\begin{cases} \text{Bennington.} \\ \text{Brandewine.} \end{cases}$

Division Orders   Sepr 25th 1777

Field officer of the day tomorrow from Col. Stones Brigade the Pickett in future to consist of 111 men 2 Capts & 4 Subs Col. Hazens to furnish for his part 1 Capt. 2 Subs Serjts & Corpls in proportion & 61 men, Col. Stone for his part 1 Capt. 2 Subs with a proportion of Serjeants & Corporals & 50 men, The Brigade Majors to march their own men on the Grand parade every morning.

HEAD QRTRS Postgrove Sepr 26th 1777

Genl Orders

Parole Princeton C Sign $\begin{cases} \text{Trenton.} \\ \text{Bristol.} \end{cases}$

Major General for tomorrow.........Green.
Brigadier ....Nash.
Field Officer Col. Martin of the North Carolina Troops,
Lt. Col. Pope of the Delaware Regt.
Brigade Major Scott.

Field officer of the Pickett the Lt. Col. of the 6th Pensylvania Regt the troops are to be Ready to march at 9 OClock

this morning with all Baggage Pack'd & paraded, to march off
by the Aft. all the tent Waggons to go next in the Rear of the
troops, in the order in which the troops march & then the rest
of the Waggons the leading Division (Greens) to beat a
march, & march to be followed by the other troops in their
order.

The Commander in Chief approves of the Following Sentences of A Genl Court martial held the 25th Inst whereof
Col. James Wood was President, Jno. Famdon of Col. Hartleys Regt Charg'd with Desertion to the enemy & Inlisting
with them, the Court are of opinion that the prisoner is not
guilty of inlisting with the enemy, the Court upwards of two
thirds Agreeing, do Sentence the prisoner for the Charge of
Desertion to Suffer death. James Dilworth of Col. Moylands
Regt light Dragoons Charg'd with Deserting & attempting to
go to the enemy Acquitted, & is to be Sent forwith to Join
his Regt Daniel Applegate of the 1st New Jersey Regt Charg'd
with desertion & attempting to go to the enemy Acquitted & is
forthwith to Join his Regt.

The bad & wicked practices of Plundering the Inhabitants
being Still Continued notwithstanding all former orders, some
cases in the most attrocious manner, the Commander in Chief
requires the Genl orders of the 4th Inst relative thereto, be
Solemnly read without delay by the Commanding officer of
each Regt to his men the punishment denounc'd in those orders
will be instantly inflicted on the offenders— The Genl being
informed that many Regts have but one orderly book, he in
Some measures ceases to Wonder that orders are so little
known and so frequently disobeyed untill each Company can
be furnished with one, the Officers commanding Regts are to
See that their officers & men are clearly informed of every
order which concerns them respectively, by Reading or causing

the same to be Read to them, Should this be in future a grounded plea of Ignorance of orders, the Commanding officers of Regts will Consider themselves as answerable therefore.

Friday 26th Sepr. Struck tents and forded parkaoming Creek & encamp'd on the brow of a hill near S'd Creek being 7 miles Philada County.

HEAD QURTRS 27th Sepr 1777

Genl Orders

The Genl Court Martial of which Coll. Wood is president is to Sit immedietly at the house next above Head Qrs as the troops will Rest to Day, Divine Service is to be perform'd in all the Corps that have Chaplains; one orderly Serjt from each Brigade is to attend forthwith at Head Qrs & the Brigade Majors will see that done immedietly, every day when orders have not been previously given 'for marching an orderly Serjt from each Brigade likewise to attend Genl Court Martials Such Regts who have not already made up their Catridges so as to compleat 40 Rounds a man at least are to do it this day without fail, the Commanding Officers of Regts are to See this done, & all their Spare Amunition to be mark'd and put into an Amunition Waggon, & to follow, for each Division, the men are to carry only their Cartruch Boxes full & Cannisters.

Major Genl for tomorrow Stirling.

Brigadier ——— Field Officers Col. Ogden & Major Forrest of the 3rd Maryland Regt, Brigade Major Barber, for Pickett Lyon.

HEAD QURTRS Pennysakers Sepr 28th 1777

Genl Orders

Major Genl Sullivan, Brigadier Scott, Lt. Col. Nelson, Majr Morris, Brigade Major Peears;—

The Commander in Chief has the happiness to Congratulate the Army on the Success of the American Arms to the Northward, on the 19th Inst an engagement took place between Genl Burgoins Army and the Left wing of ours under Genl Gates, the Battle began at 1 OClock, & lasted till night our troops fighting with the greatest Bravery not giving an Inch of Ground, ours is about 80 killed & 200 Wounded, the Enemy is Judged to be about 1000 killed wounded & taken prisoners; both prisoners & Deserters declare that Genl Burgoine which Commanded in person was wounded in the left Shoulder. The 62 Regt was Cut to pieces & that the enemy Suffred extreamly in every Quarter where they were engaged, Such was the order of our troops that wounded men after being drest renew'd the Action, the Commander in Cheif has further occation to Congratulate the troops, on the Success of A Detachment from the North army under Col. Brown, who attacked & Carried Several of the enemies posts, & had got possession of the old French lines at Ticonderoga, Col. Brown in those Several attacks has taken 293 of the enemy prisoners with their arms, Retaken more than 100 of our men & taken 150 Batteaus below the falls, Including 17 boats & arm'd Sloops Besides Cannon, Amunition &c.

To Celebrate this Success the Genl orders that at 4 OClock this afternoon, all the troops to be paraded and Serv'd with one Gill of Rum a man and that at the Same time there be Discharged 13 pieces of Artillery from the park; All Spare Amunition in those Divisions that have not Close Spare Waggons to Secure it in, it is to be return'd to the park of Artillery.

Monday 29th Sepr. Struck tents at 10 OClock this morning & march'd 5 miles on the Skippack Road towards Philada and encamp'd on the Right Side of the Road in the woods within 20 yds of our Alarm post, Worcester Township Philada County.

Sepr 29th 1777

Regimental Orders

The Commanding Officers of Companies are desired perticularly to examine the arms of their Respective Companies & See they are in proper order, that an officer of each Comp'y attend the Dividing of provisions for their men, that A Perticular return be made out of the names of each man as is present, & also those that are absent & upon what Duty by the Commanding officers of Companies.

HEAD QUARTERS 29th Sepr 1777

Genl Orders

> Major General for tomorrow........Green.
> Brigadier ....Conway.
> Field Officers Col. Cook, Lt. Col. Estcort, Brigade Majr Day.
> Officer for Picqett the major of the 3d Maryland Regt.

John White Esqr is appointed a volunteer Aid De Camp to Major Genl Sullivan, Lt. Col. Hendricks is appointed to the Rank of Col. of the first Virginia Regt in the Room of Col. Read Deceas'd, Major Jennings of the 13th Virginia Regt to be Lt. Col. of the 6th in the Room of Lt. Col. Hendricks, Promoted Captn Alexr Campbell of the 8th to be Major of the 13th.

The Brigadiers or Officers commanding Brigades, are to parade their Respective Brigades at 8 OClock to morrow morning & under their own Eyes, have exact returns made of the Officers & men present on the Ground, which return they are immedietly afterwards to transmit to the Adjt Genl; Such of their Officers as are absent, and not on duty or Sick they are as Speedily as possible to order to Join their Corps, and if any Such officers are taken by the Enemy they will not be exchanged.

3 Parties of 150 Men each are to parade at Sun rise at the Park of Artillery with one Days Provision Cook'd, not to have their Packs. Major Joyce Suris'd & Major Howell are to Command these parties.

HEAD QRS at Skippack 30th Sepr 1777

Genl Orders

    Major Genl for to morrow.....Lord Sterling.
    Brigadier ....Forman.
    Field Officers Lt. Col. Syms, Major Bloomfield, Brigade Major Johnston.
    Field officer for Picquett Lt. Col. Ervin.

A Flag will go to the Enemys lines to morrow morning, all persons who have anything to Send in, are to have them Ready at Head Qrs by 7 OClock in the morning; one Surjeons mate from each Division who can best be Spared is to go to Bethlehem forthwith and to bring down to the army the Medecine Chests of their Respective Divisions, 150 men from Genl Sullivans, Greens, Sterlings, & Stevens Divisions each Brigade is to be Selected this day, and a like proportion from the other Brigades, these men are always to Carry their Axes with them & to march with the Picquett when the army moves, to prepare timber & Repair the Roads; When Arrived at the New encampment, they are to cut fire wood for their Respective Brigades, the Brigade QRMaster are Constantly to go with their men & Direct them in the Buisness above mentioned, for these Services they are to be excused from all guards & other ordinary Duty; but when an Action is expected they are to Deliver their Axes to their Brigade QRMaster who are to be Accountable for the Axes of their Brigades, & Join their Several Corps, A list of their names to be given without Delay to the Brigade QRMaster by the Respective Brigade Majors.

Detail for Axmen

	Ser	Privates
Smallwoods	1	14
Deborres	1	14

HEAD QRTS 1st Octbr 1777

Genl Orders

> Major General for tomorrow........Stephens.
> Brigadier ....Nash.
> Field Officer Col. Dayton, Majr Smith 5th M. Regt.
> Do. for Picquett Major Copper; Brigade Major Williams.

The Commander in Cheif approves the following Sentences of A General Court Martial held the 28th of Sepr whereof Col. James Wood was President, Lt. Robt Gray of Col. Hazens Regt Charg'd with repeated Disobedience of orders; Acquitted.

Adjutant Kincaid Acting Brigade Major to Genl Scott Charg'd with not bringing his Picquett on the Grand parade in proper time; Acquitted.

Detail as order'd yesterday; where A Field Officer is named for Duty, when he is Sick or absent the Brigade Major to which he belongs is to warn another in his Stead.

And Report his name to the Adjt. Genl when an A. D. C are from Camp with their Major Genl the Brigade Major is to be notified thereof and are Directed to attend at Head QRs for orders at orderly time, the Brigade QRMasters are to apply to the QRM. Genl for their Quoto of Axes for the purpose mentioned in yesterdays orders, no more fences to be burnt on any pretence, if unavoidable necessaty compels us to it, leave must be first obtain'd from the Commander in Chief The Paymasters of Regts & Corps are to bring in their pay Rolls for the month of August properly examined & Certified that Warrents may be given for payment.

After Orders

The whole Army are to Strike their tents tomorrow morning at 8 OClock and get Ready to march, at 9. The march to begin; Genl Sullivans Division Leading, followed by lincolns, McDougalls, & Greens, these four the first line, then the Park of Artillery, then the 2nd line in this order—Sterlings, Nash's Stephens, Genl Sullivans to beat A march as A Sign all for marching, the beat to be Continued By the others Successfully, the whole are to encamp on the new ground, in the Same order, Genl Armstrong is at the Same time to move by the Shortest Rout to the Right of the first line, and Genls Smallwood & Forman to the left of it, on the ground, the QRMGenl will appoint the Waggons to go in the rear of the Army, in the order of the Brigades to which they Belong, all the Tent Waggons first, Regimental QRMasters are to See that Vaults be dug immedietly upon the Army's arrival on the new Ground, and any Soldier found easing himself elsewhere is instantly to be made Prisoner & punished by A Regimental Court martial. The Brigade QRMasters are without fail to See all ofal Buried every morning & are to apply to their Brigades for men for that purpose, Brigade or Regimental QRMast. failing in the duty here required of them are forthwith to be arrested.

Some person from each distinct body or brigade (of militia) is to attend dailey at Head Quarters for orders at noon Each Brigade QRMaster is to make an immediet Return of the number of Brigade Waggons in his Brigade to the QRMGenl.

An Officer from each Brigade is to remain till the troops have march'd & then to make Search for, & bring on all Stragglers.

October 2nd. Struck tents at 8 OClock this morning And March'd at 9 about 3 miles on the Same Road And Encamp'd in an old Field on the Right hand of Said Road, & 20 Miles from Philadelphia.

HEAD QRS Octbr 3rd 1777

Genl Orders

Major Genl for tomorrow..........Green.
Brigadier ....Weeden.
Field Officers, Col. David Hall, Lt. Col. Green, Brigade Major Cox, for Picquett Major Morrill.

The Commander Cheif approves of the Following Sentences of A Genl Court martial whereof Col. James Wood was President.

Nicholas Francis charg'd with Deserting from Col. Hazens Regt & Reinlisting, found guilty & Sentenc'd to Receive 100 Lashes, the above Court is Disolv'd. A Genl Court Martial is

to Sit immedietly at A tent near the Artillery Park, Col. Josia
Parker to Preside; Lewis Fleury is appointed Brigade Major
to Brigadier Count Poleskie of the Light Dragoons, Thomas
Mullen Esqr. is appointed to act as A Brigade Major to Genl
Conway till further orders, they are to be Respected as Such;
the Distribution of tin Cannisters to be made as perticularly
Directed this morning, the Commanding Officers of Regts are
themselves to See that they are put into the hands of proper
men & fill'd with Catridges carefully Stowed in them. The
Engineers are to make Despach in throwing up Works in the
front of the encampment. The Genl has the Satisfaction to
inform the Army that the Continental Frigate the Randolph
fell in with a fleet of 5 of the enemys Ships & took 4 of them,
one mounting 20 Guns, & the others 8 all Richly Laded to the
Southward. At the Northward every thing wears the most
favourable Aspect, every enterprise has been successfull, & in A
Capital Action the left wing only of Genl Gates's army maintain'd its Ground against the main body of the enemy Commanded by Genl Burgoine in person, our troops behaving with
the utmost spirit & bravery during the whole engagement which
lasted from one OClock till dark, in Short every Circumstance
promises Success in that Quarter equal to our most Sanguine
wishes, this Surely must animate every man under the Genls immediate Command; This army the main American Army, will
not suffer itself to be out done by their Nothern Brethern, they
will never Such Disgrace, but with ambition becoming freemen,
contending in A most Rightous Cause rival the Heroic Spirit
which Swell their Bosoms, & which so nobly exerted has pro-
cur'd them Deathless Renown. Covet my Countrymen and
fellow Soldiers Covet a Share of the glory due to Heroick
deeds, let it never be Said in the day of action you turn'd your
backs upon the foe, let the enemy no longer triumph, they brand

you with ignominious epithets, will you patiently enduer that Reproach, will you Suffer the Wounds given your Country to go unrevenged, will you Resign your Parents, Wives, Children, & Friends, to be the wretched Vassals of A proud insulting Foe, & your own necks to the Halter, Genl Howe promised protection to Such as Submitted to his power, & A few Dastard Souls Accepted the Disgracefull boon, but his promises were Deceitfull, the Submitting & Resisting had their property Alike plunder'd & destroy'd, but even these empty promises of Protection have now come to an end, A term of mercy is expired, Genl Howes has within A few days proclaimed all who had not then Submitted to be beyond the reach of it, & left us no Choice but Conquest or Death, nothing then Reamins but nobly to contend for all that is dear to us, every motive that can touch the Humane heart, Call us to the most Vigourous exertions, our dearest Rights, our Dearest friends, our own lives, Honour, Glory, & even Shame urge us to Fight, & my Soldiers when an oppertunity presents itself be firm. behave, & Victory is Yours.

The Cols are to See every Regt Draw up this Afternoon & these orders Distinctly Read to them, Every Officer who Commands Troop or Company in the Several Corps must immedietly make out his muster Rolls to the first of Octbr that the whole army may be muster'd with the greatest expedition, Such Officers as have heretofore neglected A due attention to making Regular Returns, Will be answerable for future Neglects.

Friday 30 Octbr march'd about 7 OClock in the evening down to the Enemys Lines at Germain town being about 13 miles, attacked their Picquett Saturday morning between day & Sun Rise, drove them in uppon which A Genl engagement ensued on our Right Wing, We Caused their Left Wing to

Retreat 3 miles through their own Encampments, but upon their Receiving A Strong Reinforcement & our Amuñition being almost Spent, & not being Supported Sufficiently by the Reserve, were oblig'd to Retreat and Return to our encampment being 13 miles, Sunday 5th Octbr march'd & Cross'd Perkaoming Creek and encamp'd about a mile from Said Creek being in all about 9 miles.

HEAD QRS Skippack Octbr 5th 1777

Genl Orders

> Major Genl for tomorrow........Stephens.
> Brigadier ....Mulenburg.
> Col. Clark, Lt. Col. Conner, Brigade Majr Poors, for
> Picket M Mullen.

The Officers Commanding Regts are to make Returns of the number of Catridges wanting to compleat their men with forty Rounds each, & draw Materials for making them from the park of Artillery to morrow morning, one attentive Officer from each Regt is to Superintended & be present at the making of them & See that they are well made, & the materials not Wasted, the Arms are to be put in good order, Such as are Charged & Cannot be Drawn are to be Discharged at Noon; tomorrow under the Directions of their Officers, each Regt is to Draw 12 Rounds pr man Ready made at the park of artillery besides the Above materials, Small parties of Horse are tomorrow morning to be Sent up the Different Roads above the present encampment of the Army, as far as ten miles in order to Stop all Soldiers & turn them back to the Army, except the two parties under the Command of Craig and Lee.

Returns as Soon as possible to be made of the Killed
Wounded & missing, in the Action of yesterday, and Deliver'd
to the Commander in Chief at 4 OClock to morrow in the
Afternoon, the Brigade Majors will be punctual to this matter,
& where there is no Brigd. Majrs the Brigadiers or Officers
Commanding Brigades are to appoint persons to do their Duty;
One Set of Collums are to Shew the Killed, of the Differrent
Ranks, & Second the wounded, & third the missing.

The Commander in Chief returns his thanks to the Genls
And other Officers and men, concern'd yesterday in the attack
on the Enemys left Wing, for the Spirit and Bravery they
manifested in Driving the enemy from Field to Field, & Although an unfortunate fogg Join'd with the Smoke, prevented
the Differrent Brigades firing & Supporting each other, or Some-
times Distinguishing themselves from the Enemy, & from other
Causes which as yet cannot be accounted for well, they finally
Retreated, they Nevertheless See that the Enemy are not proof
against A Vigorous Attack, & may be put to flight when boldly
push'd this they will Remember & assure themselves that on
the next Occation by A proper exertion of the power which
God has given them, & inspired by the Cause of Freedom in
which we are engaged they will be Victorious.

The Commander in Chief not Seeing the engagement with
the Enemys Right Wing, Desires the Genl Officers who Commanded them to thank those Officers & men, who behav'd with
becoming Bravery, and Such in either wing who behav'd otherwise are to be Reported.   Details for Picquetts as last Settled
they are to parade at 11 OClock in the forenoon, and afterwards at 8 OClock as Usual.

Octbr 6th 1777

Division Orders

With the Highest of gratitude and esteem the General Returns his Cordial thanks to the Officers & Soldiers of his Division who were engag'd against the British troops on the 4th Inst their gallant Beheaviour has endear'd to him every Officer & Soldier who acted A part in that engagement, & has given him the Highest Confidence in them, he Sincerely Laments that the other part of the Army did not Seasonably Advance to Support them which prevented the Victory from being Compleat, & was the means of many A brave mans falling during the Action, rendred it of So much longer Duration, by this Defeat the Genl Congratulates the Officers and Soldiers on the Experience they have gained, that British Troops must give way to the American Valour, & that the Officers & others of the Army must allow, that the Officers & Soldiers of the first Division have a Claim to for the greatest Share of the honour of Demonstrating this to the world.

The Genl Desires that the Greatest attention be paid to the wounded Officers & Soldiers, and that were anything is wanting for the Comfort of either he will exert himself to procure it for them, he Desires the Surjeons to inform him from time to time what necessaries they may Require, that they may be Seasonably provided, Should any of the Officers unfortunately die of their wounds, he desires to have instant notice of it that those Military honours may be paid to them which their bravery Justly merits; The Commanding Officers of Regts are desired to point out Such Officers & non Commissioned Officers, and Soldiers as perticularly Distinguished themselves in the late Action that proper notice may be taken of them, they are also to Report such as behav'd Ill if any Such there were.

A Return of the kill'd wounded & missing of the Delaware Regt in the Action of Germaintown Octbr 4th 1777.

Col.	Capts.	Lts.	Serjts.	R & File	Col.	Capts.	Lts.	Serjts.	R & File	Total	Col.	Capts.	Lts.	Serjts.	R & File	Total
·	·	·	·	3	1	1	3	2	19	26	·	·	·	2	7	9
Killed					Wounded						Missing					

N. B.   Col. Hall Wounded, Capt. Holland do. Since dead,

Lt. McKennan ⎫
Lt. Wilds   ⎬ Wounded
Lt. Purvis   ⎭

HEAD QRS Pertioming Octbr 7th 1777

Genl Orders

Major Genl for tomorrow.........Green
Brigadier ....Smallwood
Field Officers Col. Williams, Lt. Col. Buttler, Major Vaughen.
Brigade Major Platt, Field Officer for Picquett Majr Nicholas.

The State Regt from Virginia is to Supply the place of the 9th Regt in Mulenburg's Brigade; & do Duty there untill further orders, Jno. Fanden of Col. Hartleys found Guilty of the Charge of Desertion and Sentenc'd by death is to be executed tomorrow at 12 OClock The Situation of the Army frequently not admitting of the Regular performance of Divine Service on

Sundays, the Chaplains of the Army are forthwith to meet together & agree on Some Method of performing it at other times, which method they will make known to the Commander in Chief.

Divers Swords and other things have been Stolen from Officers by Some Soldiers; Officers are Requested to take notice of Such things if they See any in the possession of their men & have them taken care of and Advertis'd. The Paymaster Genl is at Genl Conways Qrs at Metivyleers Mils, where he will attend the Buisness of his Department.

Wednesday 8th Octbr Struck tents and march'd on the North Wales Road and encamp'd on a hill in Pownaoming Township Philada County being 8 Miles.

Head Qrs Octbr 8th 1777

Genl Orders

Major Genl for tomorrow.........Sterling

Brigadier ....McDougall

Field Officers Col. Dicky, Lt. Col. Lindsey, Brigade Major Nichols, Field Officer for Picquett Polk.

The Brigade Majors are to morrow to make Returns of the Arms & Accoutriments wanting to their Several Regts of their Brigades in order to have them Compleated without Delay, they are also to make Returns of the number of Tin Cannisters they have in their Brigades.

The Battallion of Militia from Virginia Commanded by Major Pickett is to be attach'd and do Duty with Genl Woodfords Brigade, the mens pouches are to be well greased at least once A Week perticularly that part which covers the Catridges, the better to preserve them from Rain, the Commanding Officers of Corps to attend to this matter, they are also to Select the most Suitable of their men & Set them to making morkesons immedietly for their Corps, the Commissaries are to order the Skins of the Heads & legs of Bullocks to be saved for that use, So far as they will go, the Commissaries are to issue Rawhides for this purpose on orders from Commanders of Corps.

John Findans of Col. Hartleys Regt Sentenc'd to Suffer death for the Crime of Desertion to the Enemy, & was to have been executed this day at 12 OClock, but is to be executed to-morrow at the above mentioned time; A Detachment of 60 men from each Brigade is to parade to See the execution.

Octbr 9th 1777

Division Orders

The Genl Cannot help expressing his Satisfaction on observing the regular & Soldierly desposition in which his division march'd Yesterday, he was pleas'd to hear the Genl Officers mention it Repeatedly in the Course of the day, this must reflect great honour to the Commanding Officers of Corps & Divisions, and upon the Soldiers and as his Division have Distinguished themselves by clear bravery he wishes in Discipline & order to outshine the other Divisions of the Army, everything that may Contribute on his part to bring about the desireable end,

Shall be attended to:— The Genl orders that no Ruff of A Drum or any Compliment or Salute be paid on a march to any Officer whatsoever & that the Compliments of Resting firelocks by the Pickett guard or Sentry from Picquetts be never paid to any Officer, the Sentries are to Stand Shoulder'd when Genl Officers or Field Officers of the Day pass by, & face the way they expect the enemy without turning the head or Looking towards the Visiting Officer, the Guard are to turn out & Stand well Shoulder'd facing toward the enemy the Soldiers not to turn their heads or to take any notice of the Visiting Officer, this to be Observed as A Rule except; when the Grand Rounds visit by night who are to be received as Usual The Division Commissary immedietly to Supply himself with rum & deal one gill Pr day to each man till further orders. Richard Emeroy Esqr. is appointed to act as Brigade Major to Col. Richardson, Col. Commandant till further Orders.

Octbr 9th 1777

Genl Orders

Major Genl for tomorrow.........Stephen.
Brigadier ....Wayne.
Field Officers Col. Swift, Major Mentzies, Brigade
   Major Williams,
Field Officer for Picquett Major Force.

The Genl Court Martial whereof Col. Broadhead is President is to Sit tomorrow at 8 OClock the members to attend precisely at that time, at A horsemans tent by the park of Artillery. By Genl orders of Sepr 13th the destribution of tents was directed 1 Soldiers tent for the Field Officers of Regts 1 Do for every 4 Commissiond 1 Do for 8 non Commissioned officers, 1 Do for 8 Privates.

The Commanding Officers of Regts are instantly to examine into the number of tents, and Cause all above the allowance, to be Collected & given in to the Brigade QRMaster, in the first place to Supply those Corps in their Brigades which are

Short of that Allowance, & the Residue to be Deliver'd to the QRM. Genl to Supply the Militia & Such Corps as are Destitute, the Commander in Chief expects the Genl Officers & those Commanding Brigades will See this order carried in execution Immedietly; Brigadier Genl Nash will be interr'd this forenoon at 10 OClock with military honours, at the place where the Roads forks, where the Troops march'd in yesterday, all Officers whose Circumstances admit of it will attend and pay their last Respects to A Brave man who died in Defence of his Country The execution of John Faindon is to be postponed till tomorrow noon;— The Genl Officers are without Dailey to have the Rolls of Officers Call'd & Such as are absent, and not Sick or wounded or on Command are to be ordred preemtorily to Join their Corps & those that are absent without leave are to be immedietly reported to the Commander in Chief, they are also to Report the number of Blankets, & Shoes, & other Necessaries to Compleat one Suit for each man. True Field Returns are to be made of the Troops under the immediet inspection of the Genl Officers, for this Purpose the Several Corps are to be muster'd & the Rolls Call'd if the weather permits, that the Returns may be made tomorrow at noon, Sign'd by the Major Genls or Officers Commanding Divisions, the Brigadiers or Officers Commanding Brigades are Immedietly to report the number of those Retain'd, missing after the Action of the 4 Inst who have Join'd their Brigades Since the Returns of the Kill'd &c. & those Returns will continue to be made dailey to the Commander in Chief.

If Col. Crawford is in Camp he is desir'd to Call'd at Head Quarters as soon as possible.

Head Qrs Towaininsing Octbr 10th 1777

Genl Orders

> Major Genl for tomorrow..........Sullivan.
> Brigadier ....Scott.
> Field Officers Col. Marshall, Major Hay Brigade Majr
> Cox.
> Field Officer for Picquett Majr Francis Murry.

The Chaplains of the Army are to meet together at the rear of the park of Artillery at 12 OClock to morrow for the purpose mentioned in the order of the 7th inst, the Paymaster Genl will attend the Buisness of his Department at Genl Weedens Qrs in Genl Greens Division at Mr. Tunnells House.

A Court of Inquiry to Consist of 4 members Majr Genl Lord Sterling President to Sit to day at 12 OClock at the Presidents Qrs and examine into the Conduct of Major Genl Sullivan, in the expedition Commanded by him to Staten Island in the month of August last, Major Taylor & others who can give Information of the matter are to attend, but if the Court See Cause to postpone the examination for want of evidence, after Major Taylor has urg'd what he has to Say on that matter they are to do it accordingly;—

Genl MDougal, Genl Knox, Col. Spencer, Col. Clark Members.

The Genl being informed that much provision is wasted, by the Irregular manner in which it is Drawn, & Cook'd does in earnest terms exhort the officers Commanding Corps to look into & prevent Abuse of this kind; and in verry express terms also desires that their men have provisions by them ready on any emergency & moreover that they will be perticulary attentive to the execution of orders both the times & meaning, ardently wishing that the necessaty & Rigid compliance with them may be deeply impressed on the minds of the officers who ought to Consider how impracticable it is to carry many military opperations without it, it is not for every officer to know the principal on which every order is issued, and to Judge how far they may or may not be dispenced with or Suspended, but their duty to carry them into execution with the utmost punctuality & exactness, they are to Consider that military movements are like the working of a Clock, & will go equally Regular & easy if every officer does his duty, but without it, will be as easily disordred, because neglect in any one part (like the Stopping of A Wheel) disorders the whole frame, the Genl expects therefore that every officer will duely Consider the importance of this observation, their own Reputation & the duty they owe their Country; Claims it of them, he earnestly Calls upon them to Act; The Genl Directs that the arms may be put in the best order without loss of time, Amunition Compleat and everything in Readiness against a Sudden Call, if Such Should be made, those wanting arms to be Supplied immedietly be order from the Adjt Genl, an Account is to be Rendred at the foot of the Return how the Difficiencies arrises & promotions in Consequence of the Late Deaths will now take place.

As A reward to the merit of Deserving Officers, the Provision in which they are to be made agreeable to Genl officers of the Regts they belong to; Officers who are under any imputation are to be noted for it, as the Genl is determined to Discriminate, Return the good & bad, this order is Confin'd to Promotion, no new appointments will take place at this time in the weak State of the Regts.

After Orders

Returns are to be brought in to morrow noon of the number of Rounds of Catridges pr man with which each man is furnished in the Different Brigades.

Octbr 11th 1777

Genl Orders

  Major Genl for tomorrow........Green.
  Brigadier ....Mulenburg.

Field officers Col. Chambers, Lt. Col. Nelson, Do for picquett Majr Sommers. The Court of inquiry of which Lord Sterling is President now Sitting at the Presidents Qrs is to inquire into the Charge against Brigadier Genl Wayne, that he had himself notice of the enemies intention to attack the troops under his Command on the night of the 20th Septr & notwithstanding that Intilligence he neglected making disposition till it was too Late either to anoy the enemy or make a Retreat without the utmost Confusion, the president will give notice of the time when the Court can enter on that buisness, when the parties & Evidences are to attend.

A Flag of truce will go to the enemies lines on Monday next at 9 OClock in the morning, all persons who have Letters & other things to Send in must have them in by that time. Twice A Week the Officers of each Company are Carefully to examine the Arms, Amunition & Accoutrements of the men, to See that they are in perfect order, that nothing is wanting in the first inspection, they are to take an exact acctt of every article belonging to each man, if any is missing they are to Report the Same to the Officer Commanding the Regt that the matter may be inquired into if he Judges it proper by A

Regimental Court martial, & the Delinquent punished if Deserving it, & Charg'd with the Articles lost & deducted from his wages.

The Militia from Prince William, Culpepper, Louden, & Bartley in the State of Virginia are to be form'd into a Brigade, and be under the Command of Col. Crawford.

The QRMGenl & Commissary Genl are to appoint persons themselves to do their duty of their Respective Departments, all the Troops last come from Peckskills under the Command of Genls MDougall, Vernon, & Huntington; Malcolms Regt excepted are to be thrown into two Brigades as their Genl Shall think best a Report of which is to be made to the Commander in Cheif for his further orders, Col. Malcolms Regt is to Join Genl Conways Brigade; Twelve Light Horse with an Officer are to mount Guard every day with the Picquett, to be despos'd off at the Differrent Picquetts for the purpose of conveying any intilligence in Such manner as the Majr Genl of the day Shall direct. The Commanding Officers of all those Companies which were Rais'd as A part of the 16 additional Battalions and at differrent times annexed to other Regts to make immediate Returns to the adjutant Genl of their Strength and in what Regt they are now doing duty.—The Commander in Chief has the Pleasure to inform the Army that the Congress have in A Unanimous Resolve express'd their Satisfaction to the officers and Soldiers in the attack on the enemy near Germaintown on the 4th Inst for their brave exertions on that occation; & hopes that the approbation of that Honourable Body will Stimulate them to Still greater Efforts on every future Occation.—Capt. Paul Parker of Col. Hartleys Regt is appointed to do duty of Brigade Major in Genl Waynes Brigade untill further orders, & is to be obey'd & respected as Such;—All guns is absolutely forbid firing without the leave of the Majr Genl of the day, the instant a gun is fired a Serjt and A file of men, Shall be sent to catch the Villain who is thus waisting amunition, & alarming the Camp, all officers are Strictly to See this order put in execution.

HEAD QRS Towarinsing Octbr 12th 1777

Genl Orders

> Majr Genl for tomorrow.........Stephens.
> Brigadier ....Smallwood.

Field Officers Col. Patten, Lt. Col. Mead, Majr Lockart of 3d Carolina Regt is promoted to the Rank of Lt. Col. in the 8th Regt of that State, in the Room of Col. Ingram who has Resigned, Capt. Dixon of N. Carolina Regt is promoted to the Rank of Major in the Room of Majr Lockart.

The Commander in Chief approves of the following Sentences of A Genl Court martial, held the 3rd Inst whereof Col. Josiah Parker was president, Ens. Cannon of the 4th Virginia Regt Charg'd with accusing Ens. Ford with Cowardice also of getting on the morning & behaving in an ungentleman like manner, found guilty of the Charge & Sentenc'd to be discharg'd the Service; Ens. Thomas Shanks of the 10 Pensylva Regt Charg'd with Stealing two pair of Shoes from Lt. Adams, Regimental QRMaster to the Said Regt found guilty of the Charge exhibited against him & Sentenc'd to be discharg'd from the Service.

Major Forrest of Coll. Proctors Regt of Artillery Charg'd with neglect of duty, with Disobedience of Orders to the Prejudice of good order & Millitary Discipline, & with Breaking his arrest found guilty of neglect of Duty & Disobedience of orders but not guilty of Breaking his Arrest it appears by the Evidence, That Major Forrests conduct was highly Reprimandible because of Such nature as tends to Subvert the Foundation of Order in an Army When an Officer is ordre'd to do any thing in A line of his duty, he ought not to Reason on the Propriety of the measure but execute it in the best manner he can remembring that any Implicit Obediance constitutes true Discipline is Essential and Even to the exixtance of an Army it is the ardent wish of the Commander in Chief that the duty of the Camp may be perform'd with the greatest Exactness General and Field Officers of the day to attend the Parade Constantly at Guard mounting and see the Guard on Duty March'd off and every thing carried on with propriety & Conduct.

Thence forward the Guards are To mount at 9 OClock now the Officers have an Oppertunity of Attending to the Descipline of their Men, every day when the weather permitts the Corps are To be turned out and practis'd in the most Essential manner and Exercise particularly in priming, loading, forming, Advancing, retreating, Breaking, Rallying, and no pains are To be spared in Improving the Troops in these Points.

All parties and Witnesses relative to the Charge against General Wayne are To attend the Court of Inquiry at Lord Sterling's Qrs to morrow morning at 9 OClock.

The QrMr Genl is directed to procure paper immediately that the Several Corps may be Furnish'd.

October 13th 1777

Division Orders

The General is extremely sorry to Inform the Officers of his Division that he was yesterday Inform'd in the hearing of the Commander in Chief, That the Officers of the Division were

universilly dissatisfied with being under his Command and had
no Confidence in him as an Officer, and that they had declared
it publickly in many places and at all Oppertunities, This report so to them if False and To him if True, he wishes to
have cleared up, he therefore desires every Commissioned to
give him Candidly Their Sentiments Upon the matter, he
promises them that if any Considerable part of the Officers are
Uneasy under his Command he shall take it kind in them to
let him know it and he will immediately remove that Difficulty
be quitting the Division the Instant he finds them wish For it
but if On the Contrary the report has no foundation or Truth,
he expects and desires them to take the proper Steps to bear the
publick Testimony Against it.

AFTER DIVISION.

October 13th

The Commandants of Brigades are immediately To Order
those men that are in Want of Cathridges Boxes to be Supplied by those men who have Ball Cathridges boxes and Tin
Canisters so that each Soldier may be Supplied with one and
the Other.

Immediate Application is to be made To supply those men
with Arms who are in want no Excuse will be admitted as
plenty of Good Arms are Arived in Camp and are ready to be
deliver'd on an Application.

General Sullivan requires that the Commandants will take
the Size of the bores of their Guns and return a list thereof
Immediatly.

HEAD QUARTERS October 13th 1777

General Orders

Major General For tomorrow Sullivan.

Brigadier Vernan, Field Officer Colonal Broadhead.

Lwt. Colonal Green, for Picket, Major Sterrett.

Brigade Major day.

The sending in Flaggs To the Enemies lines are Defer'd till to morrow at 9 OClock Those Battalions of Militia and Corps that Han't joined the Army sooner than the 3d Instant are To attend to the Orders of that day with regard to makeing Muster-rolls.

AFTER ORDERS.

Athough Orders have been given to Compleat the Army with 40 rounds of Cathridges pr man the General did not intend it shou'd be distributed to the men except so fare as to Fill the Cathridge boxes until further Orders and Tin Canisters all above that number is to be immediatly collected and deposited in a good Covered Waggon of the Brigade or Division no delay of this matter is least the Cathridge be Spoiled and lost.

The Companies raised by Captains shall living Theanly & Calderwood are to join Col. Malcome's Regmt & Compose part of it.

It is with Grief and Amazement that the General Observes by the late returns of Arms and Accoutriments the Continental Troops are not yet Supplied he immediately directs that they may be Supplied with Musketts and if those are any not Sufficiently supplied with Cathridge boxes that the Tin Canisters be taken from them who have Cathridge boxes and distributed to those who are destitute of both.

After this the General positivly orders that the Arms Ammunition and accoutriments be examin'd once a day by an

Officer of each Company that this may be done he expects the Commanding Officers will be particular to the duty here Enjoin'd he also Commands to the Genel Officers as a Matter well worthy of their Care.

Any Soldier after this who shall loose, sell or dispose of their Arms, or accoutriment or Cloathing shall be punish'd in a most Examplary manner without the smallest mittigation.

Colonal Crawford as there are not Spare Cathridges Boxes at this time to supply the Militia it is desired he will use his Utmost Skill and Industry to procure horns and pouches to carry their Ammunition in or To adapt any other method consulting his Officers his Officers find most expedient he is to appoint some person acquainted with the duty of Brigade Major who will be allowed pay during the time he Acts.

As many great and Valuable advantages would result from having the Arms of a Brigade or even a Division of the Same Size the Commander in Chief directs that each Officer Commanding a Brigade would have a return Instantly made to him of the Different Callibres and number of each in his Brigade And that as soon as this is done Major General Sullivan would call in his General Officers commanding Brigades and see if such a Disposition of Arms can be Effected as many happy Consequences would Flow from it.

HEAD QRTS October 14th 1777

General Orders

> Major General For to Morrow........Green.
> Brigadier, Kentington Field Officer, Colonal Evans.

Lieut. Colonal Lynly Brigade Major, Platt the Officer on Guard to make a Report to the Officer of the day who will

report the whole To the Adjutant General Doctor Craig
Director of the Hospital at Reading has sent a list of the
wounded there whose blankets and other necessaries Remain
in Camp the Commanding Officers of Regmts are directed to
make the most diligent Search for all such Necessaries belonging To the wounded in their Respective Regmts, collect them
there togather and Lodge them with all possible Dispatch at
the Quarter Master General's Quarters,   The wounded are
now Suffering for Want of them, and not a moment is to be
lost in relieving those brave men who have Suffered in their
Countries Cause the Brigade Major is To send lists of their
names to the Officers commanding Regmts without Delay.

Hitchcock Esqr. is appointed to do duty as Brigade Major in
the Second Merryland Brigade late Deborres and is to be respected as such John Lawson Esqr. Adjutant to the Prince
William Militia is appointed to do the duty of Brigade Major
of Militia under the Command of Colonal Crawford and to
be respected as Such.

HEAD QUARTER Octr 15th 1777

General Orders

> Majr Genl for tomorrow Stevens.
> Brigadier Wirden, Field Officer Col. Lewis.
> Lieut. Col. Meade, Brigade Major, Parker Officer.
> For Picket Major Richardson.

The General has the expected pleasure of informing the
Army of our Troops under the Command of General Gates
over Genl Burgoin's Army the 7th Instant, The Action began
at 3 OClock in the afternoon between the picket of the Army
which were reinforced on both sides, the Contest was warm &
Continued till evening when our Troops gained the advanced

Lines of the Enemy and encamptd on their Ground all night they Fled and left 330 Tents with Kettles boiling with Corn, 8 Brass Cannon 2 twelve & 6 pounders, upwards of two hundred Dead of their Flying Army Genl Frazier is among their Slain Our Troops took 550 of their non Commissioned Officers and Soldiers Sir Francis Case Clarke A D C to General Burgoine a Qrtt. Genl supposed to be Carlton the Commanding Officers of Artillary of a Forreign Brigade and of the British Granadeers and a number of other Officers of Inferior Rank Two of our Genl Arnold & Lincoln are wounded in the Legs besides our Troops suffered but little they behaved with great bravery and interpidity and have then a Second time triumphed Over Veteran Troops when the last Accompts came away Genl Burgoin's Army was retreating & some perishing the General Congratulates the Troops on this Signal Victory the third Capital advantage under divine Providence we have gain'd in that Quarter and hopes it will prove a powerful Stimulus under his immediate Command at least to Equal their Nothren Brethren in brave and Intrepid Transactions when called thereto the General wishes them to consider that this is the Grand American Army and in Consequence great things are expected of it is the Army of whose superior power some have boasted what Shame then and Dishonour will attend us if wee Suffer ourselves in every instance to be out done, we have Force Sufficient by the Favour of heaven to Crush our Enmies, but nothing is wanting but a Spirited persevering of it To which as before mentioned duly and the love our Country Irrasestably impells us, the Effect of much powerfull Motives no man who posses the Spirit & Soldier can withstand an Oppertunity by those Motives the General assures himself the next Occasion his Troops will be Compleatly Successful.

For honour to the Nothern Army and To Celebrate the Victory thirteen pieces of Canon are to be Discharg'd at the park of Artilary at 5 OClock this afternoon Previous to this the Brigades of Corps are to be Drawn up on their respective Parades the Orders to be Distinctly read by their Officers.

Those men of Colonal Crawford whose pieces cant be Drawn are to be Discharged at 5 OClock this afternoon.

The troops are To march from the right to morrow morning at 10 OClock the Major General of the day will point out the Order of the March.

The brig Adventurers are to be made out of all the Seamen are to be made out of all the Respective Corps of the Army the Brigadier and Officer commanding Brigadiers & Officers commanding Brigades are without delay to make a Strict Enquiry for the Tin Cannisters which have been Delivered them & report those numbers now with them and inform what became of the Rest.

In Consequence of a Representation of the Field Officers of Colonal Stewart's Regmt Captain Patrick Anderson's Company & Liewts Saiobi Militia of that Regmt are thereby Sentenced from their non Attendance and for their unworthy Conduct as Officers their pay is to be Stop'd a Court of Enquiry Consisting of 3 Members one which General Green is to be president To sit at the Presidents Quarters at 3 OClock this afternoon and enquire into the Conduct & Charges against Brigadier Genl Maxwell all Witnesses are to attend at the Same time B: Gen Mulenburgh & Vernon, Colonals Stewart & Richardson are appointed members of this Court.

A General Court Martial of Horse Officers is To Sitt at Col. Moylands Quarters To Morrow morning at 9 OClock for the Tryall of all prisoners of Horse that shall be Brought Before them Col. Moyland President.

15th Octobr 1777

Division Orders

The Court of Enquiry whereof Col. Woodford was President have Determin'd that Thomas Baily a Servant Inlisted in Capt. Pattens Company of the Daleware Regt is the property of Mr. Godden in Maryland, the General Approves of the Determination and Orders that Said Servant be deliver'd to Col. Guest.

The General would be Oblig'd to the Officers Commandants to make Reports of the Vacancies in their Several Regts and what promotion they would wish to take place.

Thursday 16th October Struck tents and marched to the Skippack Road and Encamped on the Same Ground we were at on the 3d Instant being 8 miles and About 20 from Philladelphia in Philladelphia County Wooster Township.

HEAD QUARTERS October 18th 1777

General Orders

Major General for tomorrow Lord Sterling Brigadier Scott.

Field Officers Col. Russell Lieut. Col. Guyney, for picquit

Major Locket B M Emery Detail the Same as Yesterday Saving that Harpein Wain's, Thompsons, Maxwell's, Conway's, and Nashes; Brigades To find Captains in Addition of the Other Detail and the Other Brigades not to find Captains, the Genl has his happiness Compleated relative To the Success of our Nothren Army On the 14th Inst. G: Burgoine and his whole Army Surrendered prisoners of War let every heart brighten themselves and every heart expand with Greatful Joy

To the Supreme Disposer of all Events who has Granted us this Signal Success.

All the Chaplains of the Army to prepare Suited to the Joyful Occasion short discourses To deliver to their Respective Corps and Brigades at 5 OClock this Afternoon immediately after this Thirteen peices of Canon are to be discharg'd at the Artillary Park to be followed by a Fued of Joy with Blank Cathridges or Powder by every Brigade or Corps of the Army, beginning at the Right of the Front line and Running to the left of it and then Instantly beginning at the left of the Second line and running to the Right of it where it will end the Major of the day will Superintend and Regulate the Feu, de, Joy; the Officers Commanding Brigades and Corps are to draw out their men, Excepting those on duty, every day when the weather Permits, to practice the most Necessary Manoevres particularly to Advance in a line, from thence to form Collumns To go through Passes & Oppening Fences, and Reduceing them again To Retire in a Line and Collumn and Form again in a Word Form all Those movements which in Action in a Wooden and Close Country shall make Necessary.

ADVERTISEMENT

A horse Saddle & Bridle came to Genel Knox's quarters; The Owner by applying may have them again.

On Monday 20th October Struck Tents about 4 OClock this morning and marched on the Shippack Road about 5 Miles and within 15 of Philladelphia then halted in an Old Field on the left of said Road then Countermarched to the Wood do.

Then Incampted in Wheppain Township Philadelp: County.

CAMP NEAR SHIPPACK Octr 20th 1777

Proceedings of a Regimental Court Marshall held this day by Order of Colonal David Hall for the Tryal of such persons as Shall be brought before them belonging to said Regmt.

John Larmouth Capt. President

Lwt. Corsse
Ens. Jas. Campbell } members { Lit. Harvey Duff
En: Cal Bennet

Thomas Clark Drummer of Kaptain Kirkwood's Company Confined by Lieut. Brattan for disobedience of Orders.

Prisoner saith he was Sick and went for a Drink of Watter and left his drum with the Rest & went to sleep in the Woods as he thought they would stay all night Lut. Brattan being duely Sworn saith that he did not see the Prisoner after they halted on the Ground they Remain'd on the Court thinks him Guilty of the Charge, & Sentence him to Receive 39 Lashes. Approved by Charles Pope Esqr. Liet. Colonal *D R.*

HEAD QRTS Octr 22 1777

General Orders

Brigadier Smallwood, Field Officers Cols Chambers Lieut. Col. Hashton for Picquet Lieut. Ford, B. M. Peers Such of the Troops as have not drawn Provision for to day and to morrow to do it Immediately and Cook the Whole, and all be Ready to march on the Shortest Notice.

HEAD QUARTERS 22d October 1777

General Orders

Major General for to morrow Sullivan, Brigadier Vernon, Field Officers Col. Prentice Lieut. Col. Willis for Picquet

Lieut. Col. Pope, Brigade Major Olden; many abuses have been made in Impressing horses for the Army, the Commander in Chief possitively orders that no horse henceforth will be Impressed by any member of the Army, without an Order from the Quarter Master Ge. or Some of his Deputies, or Assistants, or Special Order from the Commander in Chief; the Brigade Qr. Mrs are to make Returns tomorrow Afternoon at 5 OClock of all the riding and bad Horses, of their Brigades and their persons and Ranks, in whose Service they are used.

A General Court Martial whereof General Sullivan is President is to Sit tomorrow morning at the Presidents Quarters for the Tryal of Brigadier General Wayne, upon this charge against him (that he had Timely notice of the Enemies Intention to Attack the Troops under his Command on the Night of the 20th September & Notwithstanding that Intelligence neglected making dispositions untill it was too late either to Annoy the Enemy, or make a Retreat without the utmost Danger and Confusion.

Brigadier Genls Mulenburgh, Werden, Conway, Huntington, Colls. Stevens, Denton, Mr. Clahan Stewart, Beadly, Leut. Col. David Deharte Faihlon are appointed Members of this Court.

A Return of the number of Swords is to be made, and wanting in the horse Brigade as Deficiensies may now be Supplied.

Although the Enterprize under Genl Mc Dougal proved fruitless by Reason that the Enemy had abandon'd their Post; Intended to have been attacted yet the Commander in Chief Seems his Thanks due To the Officers and men Detaled for that Service, who two might Succesfully have Crossed and Recrossed the Schuylkill and To Those men under Genl Sulli-

van, & Green, who were designed to facilitate Genl Mc Dougall's Opperation; For the Fortitude and Resolution with
which they went through the night's Marching which was performed in the Expedition.

A Flagg will go into the Enemy to morrow morning at 10
OClock Such persons as have any thing to send to their Friends
are to get them Ready and have them at Head-quarters at that
time.

HEAD QUARTERS Octr 25th 1777

General Orders

> Major General For to morrow, Stevens,
> Brigadier Woodford Field Officers Col. Lawson, Major
> Hail For Picket Major Schull Brigade Major Wil-
> liams.

The Intention of a Certificate upon the pay Abstracts under
the hands of the Brigades was that truth of them shou'd be
made apparent upon Comparisons, the Signing their names is
but an empty Form. The Commander in Chief therefore
Requests that henceforth the Brigadiers or Officers commanding they are Carefully to examine and compare the pay Abstracts with the weekly Returns before they make a Certificate
concerning them. The Commander in Chief Orders that a
Weekly Return be made of each Brigade to morrow morning
at 10 OClock without Fail & and those men Return'd on command & number of each to be pointed out the General will
look to the Brigadiers and Officers commanding Brigades for
the mutual Compliance of this Order.

The Commander in Chief approves of the Sentance of a
General Court Martial held the 14 Inst whereof Col. Broadhead was president Orders them put in execution immediately

Lewt. Nathan Funs chargd with being drunk and uncapable of doeing his duty when the Army engaged the Enemy engaged the Army on the 4th Inst found Guilty and Sentenced to be cashihired, Leut. Joseph Fish of Capt. Lac's Company in Colonal Dukenson's Regmt charged with leaving his Regmt and Platoon which he belong'd to while on the March towards the Enemy on the night of the 3d Inst and also being much disguised in Liquor was acquited of the first charge and found guilty of being in Liquor and Sentenced to be Reprimanded by the Brigadier Genl in prescence of the Officers of the Brigade.

Proceedings of a Regimental court Martial held in camp near Germaintown October 25th 1777 by Order of Col. David Hall.

Captain John Learthmouth President

Lieut: John Wilson ⎱ Members ⎰ Lieut. John Rhodes
Ensign M. Lean ⎰   ⎱ Ensign Hariman

Prisoners Crime

William Dowers of Captain Moors Compy being charg'd with Stealing a five Dollar bill from Serjeant M. Cain pleads not Guilty but says he found a five Dollar bill by the fire.

EVIDENCE—Marmaduke Mc Cain Being duely Sworn deposeth that he was under Guard with the Prisoner, he was Singing and prisoner Sitting Close by him, and asked him to Sing the Song again, after he was Done Singing he mist his pocket Book which had a five dollar Bill in it, and Accus'd the prisoner with Stealing it, but he Denied it, the Prisoner after that Changed a five dollar bill and Said he found it by ye fire.

EVIDENCE—Henry Gardner being duely Sworn Deposeth, that he was On Guard with the prisoner and was ordered up to the Mill and was put on sentry there, the Prisoner Asked him if he would go to the Sutlers, he Said he would, there the Prisoner Changed a 5 Dollar Bill.

EVIDENCE—Jno. Bowden being duely Sworn, Saith that he was prisoner at the time the Prisoner was Search'd, & he had no money about him, & the next day he Chang'd a 5 Doll: bill with the Sutler.—The Court having duely Considre'd the evidence for & Against the Prisoner are of Opinion that he is guilty of the Charge he is accused with, & do Sentence him to Receive 500 Lashes well laid on & pay Serjt M Cain 5 Dollars;

The Above Sentence Approv'd & ordred to be put in execution on Parade Remitting 300 Lashes.

D. HALL
Coll. DR

GENERAL ORDERS HEAD QUARTERS 26th October 1777

Majr Genl for tomorrow Green.
Brigade Maxwell, Field Officers, Col. Brown, Majr Snead.

The Court of inquiry whereof Genl Green was President Relative to the Complaint's against Genl Maxwell

Report their opinion as follows Vizt.

The Court having fully inquired into the complaints exhibited by Lt. Col. Heath against Brigadier Genl Maxwell while Commanding the Light Corps, are Clearly of opinion that they are without foundation Saving that it appears that he once during that time disguis'd with liquor in Such A manner as to disqualify him in Some Measure but not fully from doing his duty & that once or twice besides his Spirits were a little elevated with Spiritous Liquor, the Court Submits to his Excellencys better Judgment whether Genl Maxwell from these instances of deviation ought to be Subjected to A tryal by A Court Martial;—

The Commander in Chief directs that the Genl Court martial of which Genl Sullivan is President; as soon as the tryal before them is finished, proceed to the tryal of Brigadier Genl Maxwell upon the Complaints Refer'd to in the foregoing Report;—

The Commander in Chief approves the following Sentences of A Genl Court Martial of which Col. Broadhead was president held the 17th 18th & 19th Inst and orders that they be put in execution forth with; Lt. Col. Markham of the 8th Virginia Regt Charg'd with having left the Regt in time of Action on the 4th Inst & also on the Retreat ye Same day, & also Charged with delay when ordred to Support the Advanc'd Guard, was by the unanimous opinion of the Court found guilty of the Charges exhibited against him & Sentenc'd to be Cashiered;

Capt. M Cormick of the 13th Virginia Regt charg'd with laying down in time of Action & behaving in A Cowardly & Unofficerlike manner, was Acquited with honour.

Lt. Crane of the 15th Virginia Regt Charged with Disobedience of Orders, also with Breaking his Arrest; Acquitted by the unanimous opinion of the Court Lt. Thos. Moore of Capt. Harrissons Compy in ye 15th Virginia Regt Charg'd with incouraging the men to breed A mutiny & otherwise behaving unbecoming the Character of A Gentleman & Officer, was Acquitted;—

Thos. Roche A Mattross in Capt. Serjeants Compy of Artillery in Col. Cranes Regt Charg'd with Desertion & attempting to escape to the Enemy, the Court are Unanimously of opinion the Prisoner is guilty of the Charges against him & do Unanimously Sentence him to suffer Death.

This Sentence to be put in execution to morrow at 12 OClock near the Artillery Park 60 Men with Officers from each Brigade to attend the Execution.

HEAD QRS Octbr 28th 1777
General Orders

> Majr Genl for tomorrow Stevens.
> Brigadier Wayne, Field Officers Col. Ogdon, Lt. Col. Lytell for Picquett Majr Ross, Brigade Majr Mc Gowen.

The Honble Congress have been pleased to promote Brigadier Genl Robt Howe, & Alxr McDougall to the Rank of Majrs Genls in the Service of the United States;

The Rank of Capts & Sublts In Col. Malcolms Regt are to be established as Settled the 19th Inst by Cols Ogden, & Spencer, & Lt. Col. Brailey. Capt. M Gowen is appointed to do the duty of Brigade Majr in the Brigade late Dehaws & is to be respected as Such.

HEAD QRTRS Octbr 29th 1777
Genl Orders

> Majr Genl for tomorrow Sullivan.
> Brigadier Smallwood, Field Officers Lt. Col. = Majr West for Picquett Majr Smith.

The Seamen mentioned in Genl Mulenburghs, Weedens, Scotts, 2nd Maryland, & MDougalls Brigades are to have three Days provisions Cook'd, & hold themselves ready to march at the Shortest Notice.

HEAD QRTRS Octr 30th 1777

Genl Orders

Majr Genl for tomorrow Green.

Brigadier Huntington, field Officers Lt. Col. Symes, Lt. Col. Green.

For Picquett Majr Haimer: Brigade Majr of ye Day

Detail as Yesterday Save that the Six Brigades that furnish'd Capts then to furnish none, the Brigadiers & Officers Commanding Brigades are without Loss of time to cause the Arms & Accoutrements of their men to be put in the best order & that due care be taken that the Catridges that were damp may be dried & made fit for use. The Seamen in the Six Brigades mentioned in Yesterdays orders are to parade this forenoon at 10 OClock in front of Genl Vernons Brigade with everything Belonging to them & Provisions Ready to march.

The Execution of Thos Roche is Respited till tomorrow; Such Arms as are Loaded & cannot be drawn are to be discharged this Afternoon at 4 OClock under the directions of the Officers no pains to be Spaired to draw all Such as will admit of it.

Divers Horses & Cattle have been brought off by the Detachment commanded by Genl MDougall which lately crossed the Schuylkill, the persons who had or have them in possession are to Report them immedietly to the QRM. Genl Returns of the Sick to go to the Genl Hospital are to be made to morrow morning to the Surjeon Genl at Col. Biddles Qrs. A Sufficient number of Camp kettles are to be Sent with the Sick, those persons whose cases are very bad are to be sent immedietly to the Quaker meetinghouse at the 20 mile Stone on the North Wales Road, where the Surjeon of the hospital will Receive them, the Arms of the Sick to be left with the Regimental QRMasters; who has to deliver them to the Commissary of Military Stores; A few orderly men are to go with the Sick to the Quaker meeting house proportioned to the number of the Sick;

The Commander in Chief approves the following Sentences of A Genl Court Martial held the 13th Inst whereof Col. Broadhead was President, Col. Alexr Martin of the 2nd N. Carolina Regt arrested for Cowardice was acquitted from his Charge, & is therefore discharg'd from his arrest.

Division Orders   Octbr 30th 1777

The Commandants of Brigades to appoint five or more proper Officers to Settle the Rank of Capts & Subalterns in their Respective Brigades, former Rank is to be attended to in Settling. Merit must be Rewarded by Congress or the Commander in Chief, & cannot be Considred as giving preference in Rank by any others, former pretentions are to be considred and extended only in the Corps; Vizt the former Pretentions of Capts among Capts 1st Liets among themselves, so of 2nd Lts & Ensigns, A Report from the Officers appointed to be made as soon as possible that promotions may immedietly take place.

Hall Brigade Orders   Octbr 31st 1777

Col. of the Delaware, Col. Gunby Lt. Col. Ramsey & Adams & Majr Vaughen, are appointed to Settle the Rate of Capts & Subalterns in the Brigade, they are to Sit this morning at 9 OClock at the Presidents Qrtrs & to Report thereon to Genl Sullivan the Committee whereon their buisness will please to have Recourse to the Division orders of Yesterday which they will give due weight to;

Col. Richardson Requires the monthly Returns of the Respective Regts in the Brigade to be made out & delivre'd to him by 12 OClock to day, as he is determin'd to make the Brigade return this evening; the Sick of the Brigades that are to be Sent to the Meeting house Hospital, are to parade this morning at 10 OClock near the Cols Qrtrs in order to Set off.

Octbr 31st 1777

The Brigade will omit Sending the Detachment of 60 men to the parade today.

Timothy Pickring
Adjt Genl

Head Quarters October 31st 1777

Genl Orders

Majr Genl for tomorrow Stevens.

Brigadier Conway, Field Officers, Col. Martin, Majr Bloomsfield Field Officer Picquett Majr Smith, Brigade Major Pearce.

Richd Platt Reynolds Stephens, & M Dougall Esqrs are appointed Aid D. Cs to Majr Genl M Dougall and are to be Respected as Such; The Deputy QRM Genl are to make Returns to the QRM Genls Office of all the Equïpages, Stores, Waggons &c. in their Respective Divisions, these returns are to be made to morrow morning at 9 OClock;

The Commander in Chief approves of the following Sentences of A Genl Court Martial of which Col. Bland was president vizt Col. Moyland Charg'd with disobedience of orders of Genl Poliskey, in A Cowardly & ungenteel like manner, in Strikeing Mr. Ziniskey A Gentleman Officer in the

Polish service when Disarm'd, putting him under Guard & giving initiating language to Genl Polisky, the Court were of opinion that Col. Moyland Was not guilty & therefore Acquit him of the Charge exhibited against him; Col. Moyland is Discharg'd from his Arrest.

Lucas Henly A private in Col. Blands Regt Charg'd with plundering Wm. Lawrence, was found guilty & Sentenc'd to Run the guantlett thr'o A Detachment of 50 men of the Brigade of Horse.

Judah Gridley A Private in Capt. Palmers troop of Col. Feldons Regt Charg'd with extorting money from Jno. Thompson, also refusing to give himself up, attempting to escape from Capt. Richd Francis & attempting to draw his Sword, was found guilty & Sentenc'd to run the guantlett thr'o 100 men of the Brigade of Horse—Some doubts having arisen with Regard to the order of Promotion, the Commander in Chief thinks it again expedient to declare that Promotions Shall be Regimental as high as the Rank of Capts Inclusive, all from that Rank in the line of the State but Subject to Such exceptions as merit or unworthiness Shall Render Just & proper agreeable to the Genl Orders Issued at Middle Brook on this Head.

AFTER ORDERS

A Detachment of 374 men to Parade tomorrow morning at Sunrise on the Grand Parade with Arms & Amunition & one Days Provision Cook'd;—The Details for privates to be the Same as for the daily guards, Hartleys, Humptons, Maxwells, Conways, Huntingdons, & the North Carolina Brigades furnish each A Capt. Sub. Serjt & 2 Corpls Col. Patten Lt. Col. Craig, & Major Morris will take Command of this Party.

Camp October 31st 1777

Proceedings of A Regimental Court Martial of the Delaware Regt held this day by order of Col. David Hall D. R.

Capt. Jno Patten President.

Lt. Corse } Members { Lt. Jos. Wilds
Do Duff   { Ens. Bennett

Serjt M Gennie of Capt. Pattens Compy of Sd Regt being brought Before the Court for fighting & Abusing Serjt Faires (pleads not guilty Serjt Faires of Capt. Moores Compy of Sd Regt being brought before the Court for abusing Serjt M Ginnes (Pleads not guilty).

No Evidence appearing against the above Serjts the Court are of opinion they ought to be acquitted. Cornelius Haigney & Thos M Cann of Capt. Andersons Compy brought before the Court for drunkness & fighting (Cornelius Haigney) pleads guilty) Thos M Cann pleads not guilty & Sayeth the fault was altogether Haigneys, that he also tore his Coat in the Scuffle.

EVIDENCE—David Young of Capt. Andersons Compy being duely Sworn sayeth that Haigney being in Licquor went to M Canns tent, & gave him abusive language telling him he was A mean fellow & tore his Coat, that during the Scuffle M Cann Struck Haigney.

The Court having duely Considred the Crimes & evidences & of opinion that Thos M Cann ought to be acquitted & that C. Haigney is guilty of A breach of the 18th Section of War, and do Sentence him to Receive 39 Lashes on his bare back with the Cat O Nine tails, & to make good the Dammage done to M Cann's Coat, the Court from the good Character of Cor Haigney & being the first Crime that has appeared against him (Recommend him to Mercy) Jas Caton being brought before the Court for going drunk on the parade (Pleads not guilty)

but says he was A little Hearty no Evidence appearing the
Court do Acquit him the Above Sentence Approv'd & C: Haigney's Sentence emitted.

D. HALL

Col. D R

HEAD QRS White Marsh November 2nd 1777

Genl Orders

> Majr Genl for tomorrow Green, Brigadier Ervine.
> Field Officers Col. Broadhead, Lt. Col. Ennis, for Pic-
> quett Lt. Col. Polk Brigade Majr Mullen, Detail the
> Same as yesterday only the North Carolina Brigade
> no men for Picquett.

Each Division to open A Road into the best & nearest Main
Road leading to the Country, by which the Waggons & troops
may move with the greattest ease & dispatch; The Commander
in Chief Relies on the Officers Commanding Divisions to See
this Necessary work Perform'd As soon as possible; the Waggons are to be Drawn up Regularly & in the best order, &
every night the Horses are to be tied to the Waggons, & gear'd
every morning at day break, the Divisions & Brigade QRMasters are to provide Straw for the troops, taking none that is not
thrashed, but the men will Collect leaves they can for that Purpose; The Genl Court Martial whereof Genl Sullivan is
President, to Sit to morrow morning at 9 OClock at the Presidents Qrs for the tryal of Genl Stevens upon the Charge exhibited against him, the delay that may ariss from the appointment of new members & the Impractability of Changing the
Genl Officers without introducing those that have been upon
the Court of Inquiry Relative to the Same Charges, Renders it
Necessary that this tryal Should be Before the Same Court.

November 2nd Sunday Struck tents & Cross'd Whissahicton Creek on Skippack Road, march'd to the left & encamp'd on the brow of an hill on ye North Wales Road White Marsh Township Philada County in all 2 Miles.

Novmbr 3rd 1777

Division Orders

A Court of inquiry to Sit tomorrow morning at 9 OClock to inquire into Some Complaints against major Adams respecting A Waggon and Horses he had in Custody, Belonging to A person in New Jersey, Lt. Col. Pope of the Delaware to Sit as president of this Court, 2 Capts & 2 Subs from each Brigade to compose this Court, the Same Court to enquire into the Conduct of Lt. Jno Moore of Col. Gunbys Regt in the late Battle of Germainton, also of Lt. Skinner of the Same Regt accused of mis conduct in that Action.

The Commandants of the Division are to attend to having A Road opned in the Rear, agreeable to the Orders of yesterday, the Genl being engaged on A Court martial Cannot attend himself to the Buisness, they will please to Consult each other upon the most proper place to make the Road, and have it Compleated as Soon as Possible.

AFTER DIVIS. ORDERS

3d Novmbr 1777

The Officers and men by no means to be absented from Camp, provisions for this day and tomorrow to be Cook'd immedietly & every thing held in Readiness for marching at the Shortest notice, the Officers Commanding Brigades are without loss of time to furnish them Selves with A Guide well acquainted with the Neighbouring Country; Wm Blanch A Private said to belong to Capt. Deans Compy in the 5th M. Regt now Detain'd in Capt Andersons 2nd M Regt is immedietly to Join the 5th M. Regt any Officer who thinks himself agrieved by another, may on application have A Court of inquiry to Determine to what Corps the Soldier Belongs.

HEAD QRS White Marsh Novmbr 3d 1777
General Orders

Majr Genl for tomorrow M Dougall, Brigadier Scott, Field Officers Col. Marshall, Brigade Majr M Gowen, Detail the Same as yesterday, except the two Maryland Brigades, & Wedens, Mulenburghs, Woodfords, & Scotts, furnish Capts, the Post Office is kept at Edward Hopkins near farmers mill by the great Bridge, the post master has paper to Sell for the price it Cost. The Waggoners are to be in the Rear of their Respective Divisions and kept Ready to move as Directed in yesterday Orders, the Q. R. Masters are to Cause necessaries to be made forthwith for the Conveniencies of each Brigade.

The Cols. of each Regt of Horse to make A Return of the Number & condition of their Horses & furniture, & of the Arms & Accoutrements of his men, the Returns to be made by to morrow forenoon without fail.

ADVERTISEMENT

On Saturday was found A Black pocket book with Some money, & A number of Papers dated at Peek's hills, and A Letter directed to Jos. Fatch Col. Chandlers Regt.

3rd Maryland Regt to Send an orderly Scrjt to Head Quarters.

5th Maryland Regt to Send one orderly Serjt to Col. Richardson Qrs.

The Guards to be on the Parade at half after Eight OClock in the Morning.

———————

White Marsh Novmbr 4th 1777

General Orders

> Majr Gel for tomorrow Green, Brigadier Maxwell, Field Officers Col. Swift, Majr Read of Col. Hazens Regt Brigade Majr Hitchpatrick.

Detail the Same as Yesterday; Agreeable to former orders all Reports of the Guards & Scouting are to be made by the Officers Commanding them to the Majr Gel of the Day who is to Report them to the Commander in Cheif; Every Regt is to go on making Catridges every day when the weather will admit of it, the Commissary of Military Stores is to make A Return of the Catridges Return'd to him & by the Regt by which they were made. Lost yesterday afternoon about 2 OClock on the Skippack Road, between the Commissarys Genl & the Mill, A parchment Pocket book Containing about 40 Dollars & Some Papers, any person Leaving it at Genl Sullivans Qrs Shall receive 10 Dollars Reward.

———————

White Marsh Novmbr 5th 1777

General Orders

Majr Genl for tomorrow Sullivan, Brigadier Woodford, Field Officers Col. Hogun, Majr Taylor, Brigade Majr Minnes, Detail the Same as Yesterday; A Genl Court Martial of which Genl Sullivan was President held the 30th Octbr last & the two following days, for the tryal of Brigadier Genl Maxwell on the following Charge Viz. that he was once during the time he Commanded the Light troops disguised in Liquor, in Such A manner as to be Disquallified, in Some measures, but not fully from doing his Duty, & that once or twice Besides, his Spirits were A little elivated with liquor, upon which the Court pronounced Sentence as follows; The Court having Considered the Charge & evidence, are Unanimously of Opinion that Brigadier Genl Maxwell while he Commanded the light Troops was not at any time in any measure unfit from doing his Duty, they do therefore Acquit him of the Charge laid against him; The Paymasters Genls Qrs are at Nathen Clevins, in the Rear of Genl Stevens Division.

5th M. Regt to Send A Captain and one Subaltern to A Court of inquiry to Sit at Col. Popes tent to morrow morning at 9 OClock.

7th M. Regt to Send an Orderly Serjt to Head Quarters.

1st M. Regt to Send one Do to Col. Richardsons.

HEAD QRS White Marsh Novmbr, 6th 1777

Genl Orders

Majr Genl for tomorrow M Dougall, Brigadier Smallwood

Field Officers Col. Gunby, Lt. Col. Brent, Brigade Majr Alder The Independent Compy commanded by Capt. Joshua Williams to be annexed & to do Duty with the 4th Pensylvania Regt till further Orders; all Prisoners not being Continental Soldiers and Suspected persons are to be Carried to the Major Genl of the day to be examin'd and dealt with as he Shall think fit.

The Cols or officers Commanding Regts are to appoint an Officer from each Regt to go with 4 men to Bethlehem to get Such of their Cloathing as is absolutely Necessary and Bring the Same on Waggons, the Waggon Master Genl will make the Necessary provision and Waggons for that end; Any Gentleman of the Army having any effects of the late Majr White A. D. C. to Genl Sullivan are Desired to bring them to Head Qrs to be deliver'd to his Brother.

Brigade Orders   Novmbr 6th 1777

Returns of Cloathing wanted are to be Rendred to morrow morning by the Commandants of the Maryland Continental Regts that A Distribution may be equally made of Such that is now on hand and an application made for the deficiency; for which purpose an Officer will be detached with proper Instructions to the States of Maryland to morrow, and Also like Returns from the Delaware Regt is expected as an Officer will be detatch'd to that State for the Same purpose Col Guest is Required to Detach A Scouting party Consisting of the Same number under Similar Instructions of that Detachmen yesterday.

Detail for Guards 1 Sub 2 Serjts 2 Corpls & 27 Privates.

HEAD QRS White Marsh Novmbr 7th 1777
Genl Orders

     Majr Genl for tomorrow Sullivan, Brigadier Wayn, Field Officers Col. David Hall, Lt. Col. Farmer, Brigade Majr Barker.

Detail the Same as Yesterday, the Independant Compy Commanded by Capt. Weaver is to be Annexed to, and do Duty

with the 10th Pensylvania Regt till further orders, Some Disputes having Arrisen Relative to Certain men enlisted by M
Nelson doing duty in the 7th Pensylvania Regt, A Court of
inquiry is to examine into the Matter & Report their opinions
whether these men Should Remain as they are or be transferred to the 9th Pensylvania Regt for which Regt it is Said
they are Inlisted for; A Field Officer and A Capt. from Maxwells Brigade & one field Officer from Col. Huntingdons Brigade are to Compose this Court which are to Sit to morrow
Morning at 9 OClock at Lt. Col. Brearlys Qrs who is to be
one of the members; It is expected by the Commander in
Chief that all intilligence from the enemies lines which may
Come to the Knowledge of any Officer & bears the mark of
Authority will be immedietly Communicated to him or the
Majr Genl of the Day who will if the Cause Requires it give
immediet information thereof to him.

All Officers Commanding at out posts are to Receive &
detain all pass which are given merely for the purpose of passing them, lest they Should afterwards be put to an improper
use;—Since the Genl left Germaintown in September last, he
has been without his Baggage and on that Acct is unable to
Receive Company in the manner he Could wish, but nevertheless he desires the Genls & Field Officers of the Day and Brigade Majrs to dine with him in future at 3 OClock in the
Afternoon; A Detachment of 370 Men properly Officer'd is
to parade at Sun Rise on the Grand Parade, Detail the Same
as for other Guards, Col. Russell Lt. Col. Mead & Majr Sill
are to Command this Detatchment; A Detatchment of 15
Dragoons under the Command of Capt. Smith to be Composed
according to Instructions he Shall Receive.

HEAD QRS White Marsh Novmbr 8th 1777

Genl Orders

Majr Genl for tomorrow Green, Brigadier Woodford, Field Officers, Col. Davis the Majr of the 10th Pensylvania Regt Brigade Majr of Genl Scotts Brigade Detail the Same as yesterday; the Service requiring that the men be Ready to march on the Shortest notice, the Officers Commanding Brigades & Corps are to be perticularly Carefull to keep their men constantly Supplied with 2 Days Provisions in hand;—To make the more despatch in the Tryal of Officers under Arrest, Brigade Genl Court Martials, are to be held without delay for the tryal of Such Officers under Arrest as Shall apply to Brigadiers or other Officers Commanding Brigades for tryal before their Courts; The Commander in Chief Approves of the Sentence of the Genl Court Martial to Brigadier Genl Maxwell Publish'd in Genl orders of the 4th Inst but through mistake that approbation was not Inserted.

Division Orders   November 8th 1777

The Genl Requests the Commanding Officers of Brigades & Corps, to improve every opportunity of Desciplining & Manauvering their troops two or three hours in the Course of each Day while the Army Lays encamp'd, it will by no means fatague the men, but will tend to give them Confidence in each other, which in time of Action is Essentially necessary, teaching them to move in large bodys will answer the best purpose, moving in lines at open order & forming, Displaying Collumns by their Center are verry Essential;

As soon as the Genl can be Dismiss'd from other duty, he will give every Assistance in his power to promote this desireable End.

Novmbr 8th 1777

Brigade Orders

Col. Hall of the Delaware Regt is appointed President of the Brigade Court Martial ordered yesterday in place of Majr Jos. Vaughen who is Sick, the Same Court is ordred to Sit to morrow morning at 9 OClock, for tryal of Such prisoners as are under Confinement.

HEAD QRS White Marsh Novmbr 9th 1777

General Orders

Majr Genl for tomorrow Sullivan, Brigadier Maxwell; Field Officers Lt. Col. Powell, Majr Hurman; Brigade Majr Day, Detail the Same as Yesterday;—Nicholas Vancourtland Esqr. is appointed A D C. to Majr Genl Sullivan and is to be Respected as Such;

One piece of Cannon at Genl Ervins Brigade is to be discharg'd this evening at 4 OClock it being found impracticable to draw the Charge;—All the empty Waggons or which can be emptied without great inconveniency are to be got Ready in the Several Brigades and to be Assembled this day at Such place and hour as the Forrage master Genl Shall direct to be dispos'd of by him.

The Brigadiers & Officers Commanding Brigades are with as much Despatch as possible to have their Brigades paraded & from their own observation to take an Acct of the Articles of Cloathing indispensably necessary for the men, many of the men mount parade daily who make very unsoldier like appearance, the Adjutants and Brigade Majrs will be Respectively Answerable, that hence forward they Bring no man to the Parade whose appearance is not as decent as his circumstances will permit, having their Beards Shaved, Hair Comb'd, Face

wash'd & Cloath put on in the best manner in their Power;—
Capt. Craig of Col. Moyland's Regt with his party of horse
have taken of Dragoons & 7 Soldiers with their horses, Arms,
& Accoutrements, The Genl desires Capt. Craigs leave &
others who distinguished themselves will accept his Cordial
thanks for the enterprise, Spirit & Bravery they have expati-
ated in harrassing & making Captives of the Enemy; All the
Genl Officers in Camp are to Assemble to morrow at 10
OClock in the forenoon at Genl Greens Qrs to Settle the
Rations, the Genl Officers will attend this in preferrence to
any other Duty and make Report as Soon as they have finished;

A Detatchment of 370 men are to parade precisely at 3
OClock to morrow morning with their Arms & Accoutrements
& 1 Days Provision Cook'd the Brigade Majrs will have their
men turn'd out and See everything in order this afternoon, &
parade them tomorrow morning with the greatest punctuality
the Detail the Same as for other Guards; Col. Spencer Lt.
Col. Starr, & Majr Breuster are to Command this detatchment; 24 Light Dragoons are to parade at the Same time and
place.

———————

Proceedings of A Regimental Court Martial held at Camp
White Marsh Novmbr 9th 1777 by order of Col. David Hall
of the Delaware Regt.

Jno. Larimonth Capt. President.

Lt. Jno. Rhodes, Lt. Jas. Bratten, Lt. Caleb Brown, & Ens.
Horsman members Serjt Dowds, Hugh Coffell & Andrew Pollard Privates of Capt. Kirkwood's Compy, Confin'd by order
of Col. David Hall for burning a tent Serjt Dowds Says he
was Asleep & did not know anything of the tents being burnt;
Hugh Coffell Says he did not know how the tent got afire;

Andrew Pollard Says he did not know how the tent got afire, for he was A Cutting Cabbage at the time. No Evidence Appearing against the Prisoners, the Court are of opinion that they are not guilty of the Crime alledg'd against them, as it appears to have been an Accident.

JNO. LEARMONTH
Capt. President

The Above Sentence approv'd.

D. HALL
Col. D. R

HEAD QRS White Marsh Novmbr 10th 1777

Genl Orders

> Majr Genl for tomorrow Green, Brigadier Smallwood, Field Officers Col. Clark, Majr of Col. Steels Regt Brigade Majr Williams.

Detail the Same as yesterday only Hartleys, Huntingtons, Maxwells, Conways, North Carrolina, & Humptons Brigades furnish Capts Instead of those who furnish'd them yesterday; Col. Stevens is Appointed President of A Court of Inquiry, relative to the Complaint of Jos. Chambers against Lt. Col. Jos. Parker; Lt. Col. Farmer, & 1 Capt. from Genl Wedens Regt & two Capts from Genl Mulenburghs Brigade are appointed members of the Court, which is to Sit at Col. Stevens Qrs to morrow at 10 OClock.

Novmbr 10th 1777

Division Orders

The Court of inquiry whereof Lt. Col. Pope was President to enquire into the conduct of Majr Adams Respecting A

Waggon & Horses taken by him the last Campaign Report their opinions as follows, the Court taken into Consideration Majr Adams Conduct concerning Said Waggon & horses, and from the Several testimonies handed in are unanimously of opinion that he Acted the part of A Gentleman & ought not to bear the least Censure; the Genl cannot help observing that upon perussing the evidence laid before the Court of Inquiry, he not only coincides in opinion with the Court but is fully convinced that few persons in Majr Adam Circumstances that would have taken So much pains to Render Justice to the owner of the Waggon & Horses as he has done.—The Genl has the Satisfaction to Inform his Division that Capt. Pears author of A Letter published in the Virginia Gazette, assuring that this Division first gave way at the Battle of Germaintown, he has wrote another Letter which will be published in the Same paper Contradicting that assertion and rendering them that Justice, which their Bravery will intitle them to, the Resentment Shewn by the Genl Officers of the Army as well as others who were of Different Divisions against the erronious Acct ought to Serve as A Stimulous to excite the Officers & Soldiers on every Similar occation to deserve the good opinion of those Officers who have taken So much pains to do them Justice & Resented A Publication which gave their own Corps A Preference to them & Robbed them of part of the Glory they acquired.

Proceedings of A Regimental Court Martial held by order of Col. Davd Hall of the Delaware Regt Camp White Marsh Novmbr 10th 1777.

Jno. Patten Capt. President

Lt. Wilson, Lt. Wilds, Enss. M Clane, & Hosman Members.

Prisoner Serjt Perry Confin'd by Lt. Duff Charg'd with frequent Drunkeness

Pleads not Guilty

EVIDENCE—Lt. Quenouault being duely Sworn Saith that he Saw the Serjt when the Corporal Confin'd him that he appeared verry much in Liquor, & fell on A tent Just by him, & that he has Seen him in Liquor Several times before; The Court having duely Considred the Evidence are of opinion that he is guilty of a Breach of the 5th A of the 18th Sect of War & do Sentence him to be Reduced to ye Ranks.

Approv'd by COL. D. HALL

D. Regt

HEAD QRS White Marsh Novmbr 11th 1777

Genl Orders

> Parole Hudson.   C. Sign Delaware.   Schuylkill.
> Majr Genl for to morrow Lord Sterling, Brigadier Scott, Field Officers, Col. Beauford, Majr Bryard, Brigade Majr McGowan, the Detail the Same as Yesterday.

The Honourable Continental Congress passed the following Resolves, which has been transmitted hither to be made Publick in the Army; In Congress Novmbr 4th 1777.

Resolv'd that his Excellency Governour Casswell of North Carolina be Requested to errect A monument of the Value of 500 Dollars at the expence of the United States in honour of the Memory of Brigadier Genl Nash, who fell in the Battle of Germaintown of the 4th of Octbr 1777 nobly contending for the Independance of his Country; Resolv'd that the thanks of Congress in their own name & in behalf of the thirteen

United States, be presented to Majr Genl Gates, Commander in Chief to the northern Army & to Majr Genl Francis Lincoln & Arnold, the rest of the Officers & men under his Command, for their brave & Successfull Behaviour in Support of the Independency of their Country, Whereby the Army of the Enemy of 10,000 Men have been totally Defeated, one large Detatchment of it Strongly posted and entrench'd having been Conquer'd at Bennington, another Repuls'd with loss & Disgrace from fort Schuyler & the main Army of 6,000 men after being beat in three Actions, & driven from A Strong post & formidable Intrenchments reduced to the Necessaty of Surrendering themselves upon terms Honourable & Advantageous to these States on the 19th of Octbr last to Majr Genl Gates.

That A Medal be Struck of Gold under the direction of the Board of War in Commemoration of this great event & in the name of these United States presented by the President to Majr Genl Gates.

Resolved that Congress have A high Sence of the merit of Col. Green & the Officers & men under his Command for their late Gallant defence of the fort at Red bank on Delaware River & that An Elligant Sword be provided by the Board of War & presented to Col. Green.

Resolved that Congress have an high Sense of the Merit of Lt. Col. Smith & of the Officers & Men under his Command in their Gallant defence of Fort Mifflin on the River Delaware & that an Elligant Sword be provided by the Board of War, & present to Lt. Col. Smith.

Resolved that the Congress have an high Sense of the merit of Commodore Hazelwood the Commander of the Naval Force in the River Delaware, in the Service of the Commonwealth of Pensylvania, & of the Officers & men under his Command in their late Gallant defence of their Country against the British Fleet, whereby two of their Men of War were Destroyed & four others Compelled to Retire, & that an elligant Sword be provided by the Board of War & presented to Commodore Hazlewood;—A Flag will go to the Enemies lines to morrow morning at 10 OClock.

ADVERTISEMENT

Taken yesterday afternoon from Col. Proctors tent a handSome Silver Mounted Small Sword, with the handle Bound with Gold the Sheath of Parchment, & the Shell verry neatly Chas'd with zays whosoever will bring the same to Lt. Col. North, Shall be handsomely Rewarded at the Park of Artillery.

HEAD QRTRS White March Novembr 12th 1777
General Orders

> Majr Genl for tomorrow Green.
> Brigadier Ewin, Field Officers Lt. Col. Nagle, Majr Stewart Brigade Majr Minnes.

		C	L	S	C	P
Detail for to morrow	1st Maryland Brigade	1	1	2	2	29
	2nd Do. Do.	0	1	2	2	25

The Honble the Continental Congress have been pleased to pass the following Resolves Concerning the opinion of the Court of inquiry mentioned in General orders the 6th Inst Relative to Genl Sullivan, In Congress Octbr 20th 1777 Resolved that the Result of the Court of inquiry into the expedition of Staten Island as Honourable to General Sullivan's Charecter, And highly pleasing to Congress, & that the opinion of the Court be published in Justification of the Charecter of that Injured Officer.

It appears that Some Regiments are destitute of Necessary Cloathing although they have been supplied with their full Suits allowed by Congress this must have arrisen, at least in part from the innatention of the Officers not taking lists of their Mens Necessaries & examining them agreeable to General orders, And Calling delinquents to A Severe Acct for what was missing this under our Circumstances is a Neglect of the worst kind & most fatal tendency & demands a most Speedy & effectual Remedy, and although the articles delivered the men beyond the Stated allowance be Charged to them yet in our Situation this does not lessen the evil Complain'd of; The Commander in Chief therefore most Seriously & positively Requests the Officers Commanding Companies, after taking exact lists of the mens Necessaries to examine them Carefully Once A Week agreeable to Genl orders formerly Issued, & if any Non Commissioned Officer or Soldier Shall Sell or willfully destroy, or Carlessly loose any of the Necessaries, he is to be Severly punished at the direction of A Court martial, this is a matter of So important a nature, that the Commander in Chief expects the Officers will pay the most exact attention to it, & that the Genl Officers & others Commanding Brigades, will see this order Carefully & Regularly Comply'd with, It appears also that many men who go into Hospitals well Cloathed are in A manner almost naked, when they get well & Cannot Return to their Regts till they are new Cloathed, to prevent A continuance of this evil, & that the Guilty may be known & Punished, no man henceforward are to be Sent to the Hospitals with out lists of the Company & Regt they belong to & of every article of their Cloathing, these lists to be Signed by their Captain or those Commanding the Company & Transmitted to the Surjeons of the Hospital to which the Sick are Sent to, and if any men are Sent to the Hospitals without Such lists, the Officers

Sending them Shall be punished for their neglect at the Discretion of A Genl Court Martial, And the Surgeons of the Hospitals are as Soon as Possible to Send A Report of Such Officers to the Adjutant Genl.

That the Arms & Accoutrements of the Sick may not be lost or damaged they are agreeable to Genl orders lately Issued to be delivred to the Regimental QRMasters & by them without delay to the Commissary of Military Stores, & never Carried with the Sick to the Hospitals.

There will be A Discharge of Musquettry this Afternoon at 4 OClock at the burial of an Officer of Genl Maxwells Brigade, the Flag which was to have gone to the Enemy to day, will Set off to morrow morning at 9 OClock from the Qrtrs of the Commissary Genl of Provisions.

November 13th 1777

Brigade Orders

This Instant it is Suggested that many of the men mount Guard daily, make a verry unsoldier like appearance, the adjutants & Brigade Majrs will be respectively answerable hence forward for to bring no men to the Parade, whose appearance is not as decent as his Circumstances will admit, having his beard Shaved, hair Comb'd, face wash'd & his Cloaths put on in the best manner in his power, as this order is extended the Brigade Majors I apprehend is to Caution the Adjutants to bring the details from their Respective Regts in this order, & if not Comply'd with it then becomes the Brigade Majrs duty to Report or put under Arrest the Adjutant in fault, it is therefore Strictly Required to Report Such Adjutant in every instance who do not Comply with this order, in like manner to Report Such Adjutants who furnish their detail for Picquetts without Cartridges Sufficient to mount with these Gentlemen may order their Serjeant Majors to See this duty done, but does not Justify its not being Comply'd with.

The Brigadier is verry Sorry to Observe that there is A General neglect in the Adjutants Department in point of Applying for orders except Col. Richardsons Adjutant who alone Condescends to Apply for them, it is expected this admonition will after the practice; If Cartridges are wanting an order will be given on the Park on Application; The Adjutant General has Complained of the Field Officers appointed from this Brigade for Picquetts not attending, it may not be Improper to Remark that there is not only neglect in them, but perhaps the Adjutants, in Complying or Destributing the orders in their Respective Regiments.

HEAD QRTRS White March Novmbr 14th 1777
General Orders
Major General for tomorrow Green.

Brigadier Maxwell, Field Officer Lt. Col. Barber, For Picquett Majr. Miller, Brigade Major Mullen.—An Officer of the North Carolina Brigade is to be Buried this afternoon at 4 OClock with Military Honours; The Brigadiers & Officers Commanding Brigades, who have not Compleated their Cloathing Returns According to Genl orders of the 9th Inst are to do it without delay, & all the Brigadiers & Officers Commanding Brigades are to meet together to morrow at Genl Hunting's Quarters to Compare the wants of their Brigades & agree on the manner in which the Cloathing Shall be destributed, the wants of Col. Morgans Regt & others not included in the Brigade Returns are to be in like manner Considred, Mr. Rimsier the Deputy Cloathier Genl is to attend the meeting & take

the directions of the board, for the present & further distribution, A Considerable Quantity of Cloathing being on hand
it is the highest importance that this order be executed with
the greatest punctuallity.

The Court of Inquiry held the 11th Inst whereof Col.
Breardly was President relative to the Complaint of Joseph
Chambers late Commissary to Genl Greens Division against
Col. Joseph Parker for ordering A Serjt And file of men to
whip Said Chambers, made the following Report Viz:—

As Col. Parker owns the fact the Court after hearing the
evidence produced by him in his defence are unanimously of
opinion, That however Negligent the Commissary might have
been in the Discharging of the duty of his department, yet
Col. Parker was by no means warrantable to inflict private
punishment upon him, that the punishment was Illegal & his
Conduct highly Reprehensible as being Subversive of Good
order and Discipline.

Such Brigades as Choose to have their flower baked in good
bread may have it done by Sending it with two Bakers from
their Brigades Respectively to Leonard Stone Burners next to
Chewshouse in Germantown where the Baker General will
Superintend the Work.

ADVERTISEMENT

Novmbr 14th 1777

The Riding horse and wearing apparell of Majr White late
Aid-de-Camp to Genl Sullivan will be Sold to morrow at 12
OClock at Genl Sullivans Qrtrs.

Head Qrtrs White March Novmbr 15th 1777

General Orders

Major General for tomorrow Lord Sterling, Brigadier Wayne, Field Officers Lt. Col. Gray Majr Slaughter, Brigade Majr Alder, the detail the Same as Yesterday.—Hence forward & untill further orders the Sick are to be Sent to Buckingham meeting house, with A Suitable number of orderly men to attend them; the troops are to be immediately Supplied with two days provisions exclusive of this day, one of which at least to be Cook'd, no Officer or Soldier is to be absent from Camp but ready for duty at A moments warning; No Scouting party on any pretence whatsoever unless Sent for that purpose is to Seize Horses, Cattle, or other property belonging to the Inhabitants under the plea of taking these things within the enemies lines;—Great & erroneous abuses are Committed and Infringements, therefore A Disobedience of these Orders in either Officers or Soldiers will be punished with the utmost Rigor, Complaint has been made of the Irregularities in point of time with which the Horse mount Guard, the Commander in Chief expects they will parade with more punctuallity for the future, he also desires that the Cols of those Regts which have more horses than men, would immedietly furnish by way of Loan the others that are in want of Horses that men may be mounted & the publick not unnecessarily burthen'd.

After Orders

One Subaltern 1 Serjt 1 Corpl & 17 privates of the 1st Maryland Brigade, are to parade on the Grand parade precisely at 4 OClock this afternoon with their Arms &c to go on detachment for A number of Days, Provision will be Sent after them to morrow.

HEAD QRTRS White March Novr 16th 1777

General Orders

Brigadier Smallwood, Field Officer Col. Fibiger, Majr Skull, Brigade Majr Parker; Detail as Yesterday, A large Quantity of Materials for Cartridges have been Issued & few Cartridges Returned to the Commissary of military Stores; Returns are to be made to morrow afternoon by each Brigade of the number of Cartridges in their possession, the Returns are to Show the number in each Regt how many are in the hands of the Soldiers, & where the residue are Deposited.

Novmbr 16th 1777

Brigade Orders

The Commandants of Regts are Requested to examine the State of and have the arms in their Respective Regts put in the best order, & make Returns of the number of Cartridges on hand, & apply for orders on the Commissary of Millitary Stores to Compleat 40 Rounds, & the Commandants of the Militia in like manner to Compleat to 23 Rounds;

Weekly Returns have not been yet Generally Rendred; the Officers are Required to make out lists of their Companies Clothing & examine once or twice A week into the State of the same to prevent the waste or Sale thereof agreeable to the requisition of A Genl order issued on the 12th Inst; the Capts of Militia Companies are to inspect frequently their mens Cartridge Boxes, to prevent the waste or embezzlement of the amunition, The Col. or Commandants will appoint an Officer from each Regt to attend at the Clothier Genls at 10 OClock in the morning to Receive their proportion of Cloathing which are to be distributed to morrow.

HEAD QRTRS White March Novnbr 17th 1777

General Orders

Major Genl for tomorrow Lord Sterling, Brigadier Scott; Field Officers Col. Summers Majr Lidquish, Brigade Majr from Genl Scotts Brigade, Detail the Same as yesterday 80 men with 1 Capt 4 Subs 8 Serjts & Corporals to parade at 1 OClock this day to Relieve the Residue of the Guard, two Brigades under marching orders not having Sent their Quotas in the morning; Some Officers yet remaining untried & many prisoners in the provost, Brigade Court martials are to be held for trying them without delay.

No pass is to be given to anyone to go into Philadelphia, but by the Majr Genl of the day, who will not grant them without due examination & upon the most Necessary Occations; At the Request of Col. Price A Court of inquiry is to Sit to inquire into his conduct on Sundry occations to morrow forenoon at 10 OClock, at the Tavern next to Col. Biddles Qrtrs, all persons who have any assertions or any Complaints to make against him, or know any thing amiss in his past Conduct are desired to appear & declare the Same before the Said Court; Cols. Hartley, & Humpton & Lt. Col. Craig are appointed members of this Court.

Col. Summers is appointed field Officers of the day for to morrow in the Room of Lt. Col. Pope who is absent.

HEAD QRS White March Novmbr 18th 1777

General Orders

Majr Genl for tomorrow Green, Brigadier from North Carolian Brigade Field Officers Lt. Col. Patten, Majr Vaughen, Brigade Majr Stodert, Detail the Same as Yesterday.

The Goverment of Pensylvania having appointed Commissioners in each County thereof to Collect Blankets & Cloathing for the army; all Officers Sent Round in the State for that purpose are by their Commanding officers to be called in as Soon as possible with what Cloathing they have.

A Detachment equal to the Dailey Guard to parade tomorrow morning at ½ past 3 OClock precisely on the Grand parade, with one days provision Ready Cook'd the Brigade Majrs will have their men drawn out at Retreat beating today, & See that they are properly warn'd for that duty, Col. Joseph Carvel Hall will Command the Detachment, & under him Lt. Col. Burr & Majr Adams. The Remains of the late Capt. Foster of the 15th Virga Regt will be interred this afternoon at 4 OClock with the Honours of War, Richard Clayburn Esqr. is appointed Brigade Majr to Genl Weedens Brigade & is to be obeyed as Such.

HEAD QRS Novmbr 19th 1777

General Orders

Majr Genl for tomorrow Sullivan, Brigadier Woodford, Field Officers Lt. Col. Woolford Majr West, Brigade Majr Williams. The Pensylvania Field Officers are immedietly to bring in their old Commissions & Receive new ones.

The Genl Officers are to assemble to morrow at 10 OClock at Genl Huntingtons Qrs to Settle the Rank of the Field officers of Horse, who are to attend this Board of Genl Officers & exhibit their respective Claims—all the arms unfit for Service deposited in the different Regts & Corps are to be Sent to the Commissary of Military Stores who will have them Repaired.

General Orders

Majr Genl for tomorrow Lord Sterling, Brigadier Maxwell, Field Officers Col. Richardson Major of the 5th North Carolina Regt Brigade Majr M Gowen, Lt. John Marshall is by the Judge Advocate Genl Appointed D. Judge Advocate in the army of the United States And is to be respected as Such, James Munro Esqr. formerly appointed Aid-de-Camp to Lord Sterling, is now appointed A. D. C to his Lordship in the Room of Majr Wilcocks who Resighned the 20th Octbr & is to be Respected as Such; Mr. Wm M Joy is appointed Paymaster to the 9th Virga Regt & is to be Respected as Such. The Clothier Genl has Received about 400 Blankets the Several Brigades are to Send for their Quotas of them. Before the Sick are Removed application is to be made to Doctr Cochran or other Directors to the Hospitals for directions unless the places where they are to be Sent are previously pointed out in Genl orders; no more Sick men to be Sent to Buckingham meeting house to take Care of the Sick; the Serjt & 12 men are to parade at Doctr Cocharn's Qrs at Mr. Wests house precisely at 4 OClock in the afternoon & apply to him for orders; A Genl Court Martial of which Lt. Col. Barber was president held the 15th Inst & proceeded to the tryal of Ens. Clement Wood of the 4th Jersey Regt Charged with absenting himself for upwards of 3 months from the Regt without leave & also of Disobedience of orders, the Court determin'd that Ens. Wood is Guilty of the Charge exhibited against him, that he be dismissed the Service & that he Receive pay no longer than the time he Received orders of Lt. Col. Brearly, which was on the 4th Octbr 1777.

The Commander in Chief approves of the Sentence & orders it to be put in execution immediately; A Genl Court Martial

of which Majr Genl Sullivan was president held the 3rd Inst
& divers other days to the 17th Inst inclusive for the tryal of
Majr Genl Stevens, charged with first Unofficerlike behaviour
on the march from the Clove, Secondly his unofficerlike behaviour in the Action of Brandewine & Germantown, thirdly
Drunkeness, the Court declare their opinion & Sentence as follows; The Court having Considered the Charges against Majr
Genl Stevens are of opinion that he is guilty of unofficerlike
behaviour in the Retreat from Germantown, owing to inattention or want of Judgement & that he has been frequently Intoxicated since in the Service to the prejudice of Good order &
discipline & Contrary to the 9th Article of the 18th Section of
the articles of war, therefore Sentence him to be dismissed from
the Service; they find him not guilty of any other crime he
was Charg'd with, & therefore acquit him as to all others except the two before mentioned, the Commander in Chief approves the Sentence.

HEAD QRS White March Novmbr 21st 1777

General Orders

Major General for tomorrow Sullivan, Brigadier Wayne,
Field Officers Lt. Col. Burr, Majr Adams Brigade Majr
Hitchcock, Detail the Same as Yesterday; Those paymasters of
Regts that have drawn pay for any Officer or Soldier in Col.
Morgan's Rifle Corps are immediately to pay the Sum over to
the Paymaster of that Corps; A Detachment of 80 men with
proper Officers are to parade at 3 OClock this afternoon on the
Grand parade.

Complaints are made that by the Carelissness of the Butchers
the Hydes are greatly Damaged in taking them off, the Issuing
Commissaries are enjoined daily to inspect the Butchers they

imploy & See that they take off the Hydes with proper Care
No more coming out of Philada is to be allow'd to pass the
first Guards without being told that they Cannot Return again,
if upon being inform'd of this, they chuse to come out, they are
to be permitted to pass the Guards into the Country, the Genl
of Horse will give this in Charge to all parties & patroles of
Horse. The Officers of the Day Report that Sentries from the
Picquetts keep fires by them, this dangerous practice is absolutely forbid, And all Officers of Guards are without fail to
Visit all their Sentries between every relief to See that they are
allert & keep no fires, & in cold & bad weather they are to
Relieve the Sentries every hour, they are also to see that the
Sentries are well inform'd of their duty, & to instruct Such as
are deficient.—Advertisement Lost last evening near Col. Biddle's Qrs A pair of Seven barrel Silver mounted Pistols, the
locks on the tops of the Barrells, whoever will bring them to
Genl Waynes or Col. Biddles Qrs Shall Receive 8 Dollars Reward.

Novmbr 21st 1777

Division Orders

  A Court of inquiry to Sit tomorrow morning at 10 OClock
in Such place as the president Shall appoint to enquire into the
Conduct of Lt. John Skinner, of the 7th Maryland Regt at the
battle of Brandewine And also into the behaviour of Lt. Jonathan Morris of the Same Regt in the Action of Germantown
Majr Vaughan of the Delaware Regt President 1 Capt & A
Subaltern as Members. All persons Conscerned will give attendance.

Head Qrs White March Novr 22nd 1777

General Orders

Majr Genl for tomorrow Lord Sterling, Brigadier Smallwood, Field Officers Lt. Col. Ford, Majr Lockart Brigade
Majr Barber; Detail as yesterday. The Genl Court Martial
of the line of which Col. Grayson is president is to Sit to morrow morning at 10 OClock at the house where Genl Huntingtons Qrs for the tryal of all prisoners which Shall be brought
before them, an orderly Serjeant from each Brigade to attend
the Court, Lt. Col. Heath, Lt. Col. Barker, & Majr Taylor
& A Captain from each Continental Brigade to attend the
Court as members all the Genl Officers present in Camp are
desired to meet at Lord Sterling's Qrs to morrow at 10 OClock
in the forenoon to Settle the Rank of the Field Officers of
Horse, who are to attend the board & exhibit their Respective
claims, The Brigades commanded by Genl Patterson, & Leonard are to form A Division, under the Command of Majr Genl
the Baron de Kalb. The Horses taken yesterday by the Scouting party commanded by Col. Bosrit, assisted by A party of
our light Horse, are all to be brought to the QRMGenls
Quarters tomorrow morning at 10 OClock, & Sold at Publick
vendue, the produce of the Sale is immediately to be divided by
the Quarter Master Genl Between the Captors.

After Orders

Lt. Col. Smith will detach from the troops under his Command 1 Capt. 2 Subs & 50 Privates to be Ready to march this
afternoon precisely at 4 OClock with one days provisions
Cook'd, Capt Jarvis will Command the Detachment & apply
immediately to Col. Biddle Forrage Master Genl for A Guide
& further directions; A Subaltern of Horse with 12 Light

Dragoons will parade at Col. Biddle's Qrtrs precisely at 4 OClock tomorrow morning, where orders will be Ready for the Subaltern. _____

Novmbr 22nd 1777

Division Orders

The Division is to be Ready to march in the morning at day light with such provisions as they have on hand, the tents are to be left Standing, no Blankets are to be Carried, as the troops will return again in the evening, as Soon as the Division is form'd they are to march off from their left in Sub divisions on the main Road leading to Germantown.

_____

Head Qrtrs White March Novmbr 23 1777

General Orders

Majr Genl for tomorrow Sullivan, Brigadier Scott, Field Officer Lt. Col. Powell, Lt. Col. Lytell Brigade Major Ridley,—The Court of enquiry held the 18th Inst of which Col. Humpton was President to inquire into the Conduct of Col. Price of the 2nd Maryland Regt Report as follows Viz:

The Court after Considering the evidences against & for him are of opinion that the Reports Circulating to the prejudice of Col. Price are without the least foundation; The Genl Court Martial of the line ordred to Sit today, is to Sit tomorrow morning at 10 OClock, at General Huntington's Quarters. _____

Head Qrtrs Novmbr 24th 1777

General Orders

Majr Genl for tomorrow Lord Sterling, Brigadier, Irvin, Field Officer Col. Price Majr Polk—Brigade Majr Parker.—

Information having been given that divers of the late Sutlers & Some of the Inhabitants have opened tipling houses in & adjacent to the Camp of the Army by which the desighn of banishing Sutlers from the Army is in a Great measure frustrated; The D QR Masters is required forthwith to make deligent inquiry & examination in discovering Such houses & Suppressing them, & assure all Such as have driven Such a pernicious trade that if continued any longer their Liquors Shall be Seized, & they expell'd from the Neighbourhood of the army on pain of the Severest punishment if they Return.—The legislative of New Jersey having made provision for Supplying their troops with Cloaths & Blankets, all officers Sent thither for the purpose of Collecting Cloaths are by their Commanding officer to be immediately recalled.

CAMP WHITE MARSH Novmbr 25th 1777
Regimental Orders

That the muster Rolls for the month of November be immediately made out, and Ready for the Muster Master by the 30th of this Inst. That each Commander of a Company have a roll of the Necessaries each man is at this time possessed of, & what Quality, & that an examination into Such necessaries be made at least once a Week.

HEAD QRTRS White Marsh Novmbr 25th 1777
General Orders

Majr Genl De Kalb, Brigadier Woodford, Field Officers Col. Hanson, Lt. Col. Smith Brigade Majr Stodart.

For the information of the troops lately arrived in Camp, the Genl orders issued Sometime Since is Repeated that Tattoo is not to be beaten in Camp.

White Marsh Novmbr 25th 1777

Brigade Orders

A Brigade Court martial whereof Col. Richardson is President, Consisting of 6 Captains & 6 Subalterns is ordred to Sit this evening at 3 OClock on Lt. Skinner Charg'd with misconduct in the Action of Brandewine, & on Lt. Morris Charg'd with misconduct at the action of Germantown both of the 7th Maryland Regt to morrow at 10 OClock the Said Court is Required to proceed to the Tryal of all prisoners belonging to this Brigade now under Confinement. Col. Gunby 2 Capts 2 Subs are to compose a Court of inquiry, to inquire into the Conduct of Lt. Hilmot of the 3d Maryland Regt Charg'd by Capt. Maxwell of the 2nd Jersey Regt with having possession of A parcell of Sd Maxwells Baggage which never has been rendred or Accounted for to him, this Court is to Sit at 3 OClock.

HEAD QRS White Marsh Novmbr 26th 1777

General Orders

Majr Genl for tomorrow Sullivan, Brigadier Maxwell, Field Officer Lt. Malcom, Noah Cato Majr Brigade Majr Paterson;—If any Gentleman of the Army can give information to the General of Shoes, Stockings, or leather breeches in Quantities he will be exceedingly oblidg'd to them, & will likewise be oblidg'd to any Gentleman officer for recommending proper persons to be employed in Collecting those Articles.

General Smallwood & the Colonells of the Maryland Regts are to meet to morrow morning at 9 OClock at Genl Smallwoods Qrs to state as far as they can the Rank of the other Officers in those Regts & the dates which their Commissions ought to bear, where there are Compositions for Rank among the Cols they are to Settle their Claims; The money for the payment of the Army for Septr is expected every moment, the Regimental Paymasters are immediately to make out their abstracts for Octbr & deliver them to the Paymaster Genl for examination; As an alteration in the payment of Rations is now under Consideration of Congress it is Recommended to the Commanding Officers of Regts not to add their Ration Accts to their Pay rolls untill the determination is known it will be signified in Genl orders. The Paymaster Genl has complain'd of the Slovenly careless manner in which Some Captains make out their Pay Rolls; Regimental Paymasters are not to Receive any but Such as is made out fair & agreeable to a Coppy sometime Since given by the Paymaster Genl, which the Regimental Paymasters are to furnish Such Captains; which have not already Received the Same; No Regimental Paymaster is to leave the Service without first applying to the Commander in Chief, or any new paymaster appointed without his approbation.

Camp at White Marsh Novmbr 27th 1777

Proceedings of A Regimental Court Martial held this day by order of Col. David Hall for Such Prisoners as may be brought before them.

Cord Hazzard Capt. President

Lt. Quenouault }
Lt. Duff   }

{ Lt. Bratten
{ Lt. Jos Wilds

Prisoners Crime—Wm Howell of Capt. Hazards Compy Confin'd by order of Majr Vaughen for abusing Serjt Thompson, Pleads Guilty but says he was headdy, & was Rather rash in contradicting Serjt Thompson; Evidence—Serjt Thompson being duely Sworn deposeth that the prisoner yesterday evening

on Parade was told by him to incline to the left & Join his
Compy he told him he would not, upon which the Serjt Shov'd
him in his place, the Prisoner then called him a Chuckleheaded
Son of a bitch, the Court after Considering the nature of the
offence And evidence, are of opinion that the Prisoner is Guilty
of a Breach of the 15th Artcle of the 18th Section of the Articles of War & do Sentince him to Receive 20 Lashes for abusing the Serjt & 10 for being disguised in Liquor.   John Blake
& Thos Giles Confin'd by Lt. Rhodes Blake for giving Giles
his Shirt & Giles for Selling it; Both pleads guilty but Blake
Sais it was A Shirt he brought from home with him & that he
had three more; the Court are of opinion they are Guilty of A
breach of the 3d Article of the 12th Sect. of the Articles of
War & do Sentence Blake to Receive 39 Lashes & Thos Giles
30 on the bare back.

The above Sentence approv'd omitting 24 of Blakes & 18 of
Giles.
                                          D. HALL
                                            Col. D R

HEAD QRS Novmbr 27th 1777

General Orders

Majr Genl for to morrow Lord Sterling, Brigadier Patterson, Field Officers Col. Bailey Lt. Col. Cobb Brigade majr
Williams, A Detachment of 300 men to parade to morrow
morning on the Grand Parade precisely at half past 3 OClock
Col. Hall, Lt. Col. Craig, & Majr Taylor are appointed field
officers for the Detachment.   A Detachment of 100 men to be
under the Command of Capt. M Lane are to Parade to morrow morning at Sun Rise on the Grand Parade with one or
two days provisions & Boxes full of Amunition they will be
absent from Camp one week near the Enemies lines.

WHITE MARSH Novmbr 28th 1777

Brigade Orders

The Commandants of Regular & Militia Regts are requested to Render Returns immediately of Such Arms & Accoutrements as are wanting that they may be Supplied to morrow morning. The Brigadier is sorry to find the Arms in Such bad order.

Novmbr 28th 1777

Division Orders

The Commanding Officers of Corps is to See that their mens arms are in proper order that they be furnished with Cartridges Sufficient to fill their Boxes, & that each Regt have in reserve A Sufficient number of Cartridges to compleat them to 40 Rounds, Ready to be delivered at a moments Warning, the Reserve Cartridges not to be deliv'd out without Special orders, unless the approach of the Enemy is announced by three pieces of Cannon from the Artillery Park, the Soldiers are to have one days provision Cook'd by them from day to Day; the Officers to be perticularly attentive to these orders, & see that they are carried into execution. No Officer or Soldier to be out of Camp upon any pretence whatsoever.

HEAD QRS White Marsh Novmbr 28th 1777

General Orders

Majr Genl for tomorrow De Kalb, Brigadier Learned, Field Officers Col. Gunby, & Majr Hogg Brigade Majr M Cleave. A Genl Court Martial held the 24th Inst of which Col. Grayson was President, Major Ross Charged with leaving his arms in the field in the Action of the 4th Octbr near Germantown was tried & Acquitted with the highest honour; the Commander in Cheif approves the Courts Judgment, & orders Majr Ross releas'd from his Arrest.

HEAD QRS White Marsh Novmbr 29th 1777

General Orders

Majr Genl for tomorrow Sullivan, Brigadier Wayne; Field Officers Col. Marshall Lt. Col. Caryle Brigade Majr M Clinton—The Commanding Officers are to See that their mens Arms are put in the best order possible, & the loaded Arms Such as Cannot be drawn to be Discharged the first fair day at 11 OClock in the fore noon, & them that can be drawn to be drawn immediately, to prevent the want of lead the men of each Regt or Brigade are to Discharge their pieces into A bank of dirt from whence the lead may be taken again, A Court on inquiry is to Sit tomorrow morning at 9 OClock at Col. Gists Qrtrs to inquire into the conduct of Capt. Edward Scull of the 4th Pensulvania Regt.

In ordering the Paymaster of that Regt. to pay Capt. Wicks a Sum of money for A purpose Suggested to be Unwarrantable, Col. Gist President of this Court, Lt. Col. Barber & Majr Ross members; Col. Spencer is appointed President & Majr Byard & A Capt of Col. Lees Regt members of A Court of inquiry into the Conduct of Lt. Reynolds of Col. Malcolms Regt for Abusing Danl Whesserly Esqr. & other persons on the 2nd Augst last as exhibited in their Deposition.

HEAD QRS White Marsh Novmbr 30th 1777

General Orders

Majr Genl for to morrow Green, Brigadier Smallwood, Field Officers Col. Coatland & Majr Smith of 5th Maryd

Regt Brigade Majr of Learnerds Brigade, Detail the Same as yesterday, On the 25th Novembr the Honourable the Continental Congress passed the following Resolution, Resolved that Genl Washington be directed to publish in Genl orders that Congress will Speedily take into Consideration the merits of Such Officers as have distinguished them Selves by their intrepidity & attention to the Health & discipline of their men, & adopt Such Regulations as Shall tend to introduce order & good Discipline into the army & to Render the Situation of the Officers & Soldiers with Respect to their Cloathing & other Necessaries more eligible then it has hitherto been; Forasmuch as it is the indispensible duty of all men to adore the Superintending Providence of Almighty God; to acknowledge with Gratitude their obligations to him for benefits Received & to implore Such further blessings as they Stand in need of, And it having pleased him in his Abundant Mercies; Not only to Continue to us the innumerable bounties of his Common Providence, but also to Smile upon us in the prosecution of Just and present War, for the Defence of our infallable Rights, & Liberties, Its therefore Recommended by Congress that Thursday the 18th day of December next be Set apart for Solemn thanksgiving & praise; that at one time & with on one Voice the Good People may express their Gratefull feelings of their hearts & Consecrate themselves to the Service of their Divine Benefactor, & that together with their Sincere Acknowledgements & offerings they may Join their penitent Confession of their lives, & Supplications for Such further Blessings as they Stand in need of; The Chaplains will take proper notice of this recommendation that the day of Thanksgiving may be duely observed in the Army Agreeable to the Intention of Congress; The Regimental Paymasters are to Call upon the Paymaster

Genl & Receive the pay for the month of September, those who have delivered in their abstracts for the month of October, may Receive for that month also.

CAMP WHITE MARSH Novr 30th 1777

Proceedings of A Regimental Court Martial of the Del. Regt Commanded by Col. David Hall & by his order.

Capt. John President.

Lt. Rhodes }   { Lt. Brown
Ens. Berry }   { Ens. Campbell.

The Court having met according to order proceeded to Buisness, When Martenius Sipple of Capt. Mores Compy was brought before them Charged with abusing Serjt Johnston when he ordered him on duty; prisoner pleads Guilty; And says it was A private of the Same Compy which he was abusing & not him, EVIDENCE—Serjt Johnston being duely Sworn deposeth that in the morning as usual he went to turn out the men for Picquett of Capt. Moores Compy at which time the prisoner was Sitting at A fire at his tent doore, he asked the prisoner why he did not repair to the parade, and if he did not hear the Serjt Majr calling for the Picquett, that the Prisoner made no answer to this, that he called him again & Asked him why he did not come along to which he Replied as the Serjt pass'd him, Go along you yellow Son of A Bitch; The Court asked the deponent if he firmly believed that the prisoner intended the Abuse for him; Answr—He is not Certain, but understood it so at that time EVIDENCE—Benjamin Modey Private of Capt. Moores Compy being duely Sworn Deposeth that he heard the Prisoner & Wm Ploughman of Sd Compy disputing & that the prisoner repeated the words, Yellow Son of A Bitch but does not know whether he intended it for the

Serjt or Plowman; The Court having duely Considred the Crime & evidence & are of opinion that the abuse was meant for Ploughman & not for Serjt Johnston, & are farther of opinion that he is Guilty of A Breach of the 1st Article of ye 7th Sect. of War, & do Sentence him Agreeable to Sd Article to ask pardon of the party offended in presence of his Commanding Officer. Cornelius M Glaughlen of Capt. Learmonth's Compy brought before the Court, Charged with Neglect of duty & drunkeness; Pleads not Guilty, but says he was A little Groggy but not so as to Render him unfit for duty; EVIDENCE—Capt. Hugh Kirkpatrick waggon Master being duely Sworn Deposeth that he ordered the Prisoner to go for his Waggon which was at the Wheel-Wrights to be mended, but found him So drunk that he was uncapable of doing it; Ques.—Did he Refuse to obey your orders, Answr—No but I Judged it would be unsafe to Send him in the Situation he appeared to be in, & farther Says he had no further Complaint against him Since he has been under his Care but that of Drunkencss.

The Court having duely Considered the Crime & Evidence are of opinion he is Guilty of A Breach of the 5th Article of the 17th Section of War, & do Sentence him to Receive 39 Lashes on his bare back well laid on the Court from the Age of the Prisoner & at the Request of the Waggon Master Recommend him to mercy—

JNO. PATTEN
President

The within Sentence's approved & Cornelius M Laughlen being Recommended to mercy by the members of the Court is pardoned.

DAVID HALL
Col. Delaware Regt

Decembr 1st. The Court met according to Adjournment & Reasumed the tryal of Wm. Peat when Ens. Hosman took the place of Ens. Berry, as member of Said Court;— The Prisoner being brought before the Court pleads not Guilty; Capt. James Moore being duely Sworn Deposeth that after the Prisoner Returned from the Fort he applied to the Paymaster for A months pay but was Refused in Consequence of Capt. Moores requesting him not to let him have it, that the prisoner then Came to this Deponent & asked him in A Verry abrupt manner if he did not intend to let him have any more money, upon which he told him to Remember the Contract he had made with his mistress (To Wit) that half his pay was to be Stop'd for her use, & that he had Received his whole pay in the Deponents absence for which Reason he Stopp'd his pay at present, that the prisoner in an angry manner that if that was the Case he would Stay no longer in the Company, but would go into the Artillery upon which the Deponent having A Stick in his hand Said that if he did not go about his buisness he would beat him, & that if he wanted to go into the artillery he would See to the placing him there (but in a tone that the prisoner could not understand for his assent) that Some time after the prisoner again mentioned his desire to the Deponent of going into the Artillery upon which he told the prisoner that he must be Sensible he had used him Verry ill, upon which the prisoner told him he had not before Rightly understood how much of his pay was to be Stopp'd that the Deponent then told him, that if he went to the artillery he would Receive no more of his pay than if he Staid, that it would be Still in his hands & that he would Retain one half for the use of his Mistress, & farther told him to be content & let him hear no more of it, upon which the prisoner went away contented as this Deponent thought, that in a Day or two after this Deponent was informed, that the Prisoner had taken all his Cloaths & gone to the Artillery, upon which he Sent for him & put him under Guard; EVIDENCE—David Miller Drummer being duely Sworn Deposeth that the Prisoner came into his tent & took up his Kanpsack with his Cloaths & Said he would not Stay any longer in the Company, that he had not been used well, & would go into the Artillery upon which he went off.—EVIDENCE—Serjt Pharis being duely Sworn, Deposeth that Ens. Berry Sent Serjt Johnston to look for the Prisoner & the Deponent went with him, that they found the prisoner with the Train Standing at A fire, that they ordered him back to his Regiment, that the Prisoner Refused & began to abuse the Serjt upon which the Deponent Struck the prisoner with A Switch he had in his hand, that the prisoner then made an attempt to Seize a pole at which time the Serjts laid hold on him & brought him off;— The Court having duely Considred the Crimes & Evidences are of opinion that the Prisoner is Guilty of A breach of the 2nd Article of the 6th Section & 5th Article of the 18th Section of War & do Sentence him to Receive 100 Lashes on his bare back with the Cat of Nine Tails well laid on.

JOHN PATTEN

D. Regt Presdt

The Above Sentence is approved & ordered to be put into execution at Retreat Beating.

JOS. VAUGHAN

Majr D. Regt

HEAD QRS White March Decmbr 1st 1777

General Orders

Majr Genl for tomorrow Lord Sterling, Brigadier Ervine, Field Officers Col. Wilson & Lt. Col. Stodard; Brigade Majr

M Gowen, Detail as yesterday   Mr. Robt Duncan is appointed Paymaster to the 4th North Carolina Regt & is to be Respected as Such; A Genl Court Martial is to Sit to morrow morning at the Tavern next to Col. Biddles Quarters for the tryal of all Such Prisoners as Shall be brought before them; Col. Ogden is appointed President, Lt. Col. Syms, Majr Wallace, & Majr North 1 Capt from the 1st & 2nd Pennsylvas Maxwells, Conways, Woodfords, Scotts, Poors, Pattersons & Learnerds Brigades, are to be members of this Court; the Officers are to make out their Muster Rolls to the first of December immediately, the term of time for which they are Inlisted in every muster Roll, the Non effective are not to be inserted A Second time Officers must pay A Strict attention to the orders, which have been Issued respecting this part of their Duty.

HEAD QRS White March 2nd Decmbr 1777

General Orders

Majr Genl for to morrow De Kalb, Brigadier Mulenburgh, Field Officers Col. Bradford Majr Thomas; Detail as yesterday: Returns are to be made out early tomorrow morning of all Officers & men in the Several Brigades & Corps who have not had the Small Pox; Every Col. or Officers Commanding Regts or Corps to make out A Return to the Paymaster Genl of every Paymaster that has belonged or done duty as Such in Regiments, or Corps, the place of their abode & ye time when they left the Service.

Advertisement A young likely Bay mare, Some Cloaths & linnen the effects of the late Lt. Col. Smith will be Sold to morrow morning at 10 OClock, in front of Genl Scotts Brigade;—After Orders Decmbr 2nd 1777   When the alarum is given by firing three guns, the whole Baggage & provisions of the Army, tents included to be put in Waggons, & immediately march the following Roads Viz. The right Wing of both lines, by the North Wales Road & the Road by Edgers mill & proceed to the 24 mile Stone on those Roads, unless further orders are Received; The left Wing by the two Roads leading from the left of the army into the old York Road, at 13 & 15 mile Stones untill further orders;—Whether the alarum is given or not, the whole Army is to be under Arms at daylight, when the lines will be properly formed by their Respective Majr Genls.

————————————

Friday December 5th Struck tents about 4 OClock this morning & Sent the Baggage away March'd about 8 OClock in the evening about one mile to our left & took Ground to our allarum post at the foot of a hill opposite a paper mill & lay under arms this night, Monday evening the 8th the Enemy retreated into Philadelphia, Thursday 11th December, at 4 OClock this morning Struck tents & March'd to Matsons Ford on Schuylkill & there cross'd the Bridge being 8 miles Recross'd it again & in the evening march'd about 4 miles & incamp'd on a hill opposite to the Swedes ford in all 12 miles, Friday 12th March'd about sun set cross'd the Bridge at Matsons ford & encamp'd on a Hill near the Gulph mill in Chester County being 6 miles.

————————————

HEAD QRTR's Gulph Mill December 13th 1777

General Orders

Maj'r Genl for tomorrow Green, Field Officer Col. Fibeger Majr Miller Brigade Majr MClare, The Officers without delay are to examine the Arms & Accoutriments of their men & see that they are put in good order, Provisions are to be drawn & Cook'd for tomorrow & next day, a Gill of Whiskey is to be issued immediately to each Officer Soldier & Waggoner, the weather being likely to be fair the tents are not to be pitch'd, but the axes that are in the Waggons to be Sent for without delay that the men may make fires and keep them selves Comfortable for the ensuing night— The Army is to march precisely at 4 OClock to morrow morning, an Officer from each Regt is to be sent forth with to the encampment on the other side Schuylkill to Search that & the Houses for all Straglers & bring them into their Corps, all the Waggons not yet over are to be sent for & got over as soon as possible.

Mr. Archibald Read is appointed Pay Master to the 8th Pennsylvania Regt & is to be respected as such.

DIVISION ORDERS

The Officers who go from the Division to the old encampment on the other side Schuylkill are to examine all houses for Sick, & impress Waggons to Convey them to Reading Sending a Carefull Officer with them.

HEAD QRTRS Gulph Mill Decr 14th 1777

General Orders

Majr Genl for to morrow Lord Sterling, Brigadier Woodford, Field Officers Col. Biglow Brigade Majr McClintic, Col. Steward is appointed Field Officer of this day in the room of Col. Fibiger absent: Details for guard the same as yesterday, only Genl Weedens, Learneds, Nernons and Scotts Brigade, Give Capts in room of those who furnished them yesterday, the Guards parade at 3 OClock Delawares to furnish

1 L, 2 S, 2 C, 24 P for Guard, the Regts of Horse are to draw Provisions from any issuing Commissary laying most Convenient to them upon proper return thereof, Such Baggage as is not absolutely Necessary for the troops, and all Commissaries & other Stores to remain on this side the Gulph.

HEAD QRTRS Gulph Decembr 15th 1777
General Orders

Majr Genl for to morrow Marquis La Fait, Brigadier Maxwell, Field Officer Col. Swift Lt. Col. Wozinbuk Brigade Majr from Larnerds Brigade: Detail of Guards to morrow morning at 9 OClock, the same as this day, only the 1st & 2nd Maryland Brigades 2d Pennsylva & Maxwills furnishes Capts instead of those Brigades which gave them to day, A field Officer of each Brigade to Inspect immedietly all the men of this Brigade now with the Baggage, & take from thence every man who is fit to duty in the lines; Majr Snead is until further orders to take Charge of the men left for the Baggage Guard, & report any left Contrary to orders.

HEAD QRTRS Gulph Decembr 16th 1777
General Orders

Majr Genl for to morrow DeKalb, Brigadier Nernom, Field Officers Col. Brook Majr Gitmore Brigade Majr McGowen: In an order the supplies of Clothing Imported by the Honble the Congress, they have earnestly recommended to the several States to exert their utmost indeavours to procure all kind of Cloathing for the Comfortable Subsistance of the Officers & Soldiers of their respective Battalions, & to appoint one or more persons to dispose of Such Articles to Officers &

Soldiers at Such reasonable prices as Shall be best by the Clothier Genl or his Deputy & be in just proportion to the Wages of the Officers & Soldiers, Charging the Supplies of the Costs to the United States Congress have also resolved that all Cloathing hereafter to be Supplied to the Officers & Soldiers of the Contenental Army out of the Publick Stores of the United States, Beyond the Bounties already granted shall be charged at the like prices, the supplies to be refunded by the United States. The tents to be Carried to the Encampment of the troops & pitched immediately.

HEAD QRTRS Gulph Decembr 17th 1777

General Orders

Majr Genl for tomorrow Sullivan, Brigadier Huntington, Field Officers Col. Chambers Col. Carleton, Brigadier Majr Day. The Commander in Chief with the highest Satisfaction expresses his thanks to the Officers & Soldiers for the Fortitude & patience which they stand the fatigue of the Campaign, although in some instances we have unfortunately failed, yet upon the whole Heaven has Smiled upon our Arms & Crown'd them with Signal Success, & we may upon the best ground conclude that by a Spirited Continuance of the means Necessary for our Defence, we shall finally gain the end of the Warfare Independent Liberty & peace, these are blessings worth Contending for at every Hazard, but we Hazard nothing to power of America alone, duely exerted would have nothing to fear from the force of Great Brittan, yet we Stand not alone on our own Ground, France yields us every aid we ask & there reasons to believe the period is not verry far distant when she will take A more Active part by declaring War against the British Crown, every motive therefore immediately obliges may command us to affirm a manly perseverence in our opposition to our Cruel oppressors to slight difficulties indure hardships & contemn every danger. The Genl ardently wishes it was in his power to conduct the troops into the best Winter Quarters but Where are they to be found Should we retire into the Interior parts of the States we Should find them Crowded with Virtious Citizens who Sacrifised their all left Philada & fled there for protection to their Distress humanity forbids us not to add; this is not all, we Should have vast extent of fertile Country to be Spoiled & ravaged by the Enemy, from which they would draw large supplies, & where many of our friends would be exposed to all the miseries of insulting & wanton depredations, a train of evils might be enumerated but these will Suffice, the Consideration will make it, indispensably necessary for the Army to take Such position as will enable most effectually to prevent distress & to give the most extensive security, & an inposition we must make our Selves the Best Shelter in our power with Activity & diligence huts may be errected that may be warm & dry. In these the troops will be Compleat & more Secure against Surprise then if in Divided States and at hand to protect the Country these Cogent Reasons has determined the General to take post in the neighborhood of this Camp, & influenced by them he persuades himself, that the Officers, & Soldiers with one heart & with one mind will resolve to remount every difficulty with a fortitude & patience becoming their profession, & the Sacred cause in which they are engaged he himself will pertake of the hardships & likewise of every inconveniency. To morrow being the day set apart by the Honble Congress to publick Thanksgiving & praise, duty calls us devoutly to express our gratefull acknowledgments to God for the manifold Blessings he has granted us, the Genl directs that the Army remain in its present Qrtrs that the Chaplains preform Divine Service & earnestly excites all Officers & Soldiers, whose absence is not indispensably necessary, to attend with reverence the Solemnity of the Day.

HEAD QRTRS Gulph Decr 18th 1777.

General Orders

Majr Genl for to morrow Green, Brigadier Smallwood, Field Officers Lt. Col. Carson Lt. Col. Sproat Brigade Majr Hitchcock.   Persons having passes from Majr Jno. Clark are to pass all Guards the Commander in Chief approves the following Sentences of A Genl Court Martial held the 22nd Octbr last, where of Majr North was President Viz.   Adjutant Walston of the 1st Pennsilva. Brigade charg'd with making a false return & Signing it, & with ungentelman like behavour, Disobedience of orders, & leaving his Arrest; by the Unanimous opinion of the Court was found guilty of making a False return, contrary to the first Article of the 5th Section of War & Sentenc'd to be Cashier'd, Jos. Cann Qr Mastr of ye 1st Pennsylva. Regt charg'd with disobedience of orders, & neglect of duty, & fraudulent Conduct was acquitted of the Charge of Fradulent Conduct, but found guilty of Disobedienc of orders & Neglect of Duty, & Sentenc'd to be discharged the Service—The Majr Genls & Officers Commanding Divisions are to appoint an Field Officer in & for each of their respective Brigades, to Superintend the Business of Hutting agreeable to the Directions they shall Receive, and in addition to these Command'g Officers of Regts is to appoint an officer of each Regt which Officer is to take his orders from the Field Officer of the Brigade he belongs to, who is to mark out the respective Spots, that every Hutt for Officers & Soldiers is to be plac'd,

as that uniform may be observ'd; an exact return of all Tools
in the hands of every Regt is to be made immediately to the
Qr.M. Genl who with the Adjt Genl is to see that they are
to gether with those in Store duty Justly allow'd to Regimental
Officers of the Work, Who are to keep an exact account of the
mens names into whose hands they are Plac'd that they may
be accountable for them, Superintendents and overseers will be
exempted from all other duties & will moreover be allow'd for
their trouble, the Col. or Commandts of Regts with their Capts
are immediately to Cause their men to be divided into Squads
of 12 men, & see that each Squad has their proportions of tools,
& set about A hut for themselves, & as encouragment to industry & art the Genl promises to Reward the party in each Regt
which furnishes their hutt in the Quickest & most workman
like with 12 Dollars, and there is Reason to believe that boards
for Covering may be found Scarse & difficult to be had, he
Offers 100 Dollars to either Officer or Soldier who in the
opinion of three Gentlemen he shall appoint, as Judges, shall
Substitute Covering that may be Cheaper & Quicker made &
will in every respect answer the end; Plan for the Construc-
tion of Hutts dimensions 14 by 16 Foot Sides Ends & Roof
made of Logs, the Roof made light with Split Slabs, the Sides
made tight with Clay; the fire places made of wood & Secured
with Clay in the Inside 18 Inches thick, this fire place to be
in the rear of the hutt, the door to be in the end next the Sreet
—the door to be made of oak Split Slabs unless boards Can be
procured, Side Walls 6½ feet high, the Officers Hutts to form
a line in rear of the Whole; One hut to be allow'd each Genl
Officer, one to the Staff of each Division, one to the Staff of
each Brigade one to the Field of each Regt one to the Staff of
each Regt, one for the Commsn'd Officers of two Companies,
& one to every 12 men non Commiss'd Officers & Soldiers.

Saturday 20th Decmbr. This morning at 4 OClock our Division march'd under the Command of Brigadier Genl Smallwood to Dilworth town in Chester County being 25 Miles.

Dilworth Town Decr 20th 1777

Division Orders

The Commissaries to furnish one days provisions to the Division immediately, & to provide another days for tomorrow at Such place & time as will be pointed out to them in the morning, they will also provide Liquor for the troops, the alarm post to be in line of the Camp fires, the troops to march at 4 OClock precisely, 5th Maryland Regt. Such as are in uniform to Compose the advance Guard, follow'd by the Artillery & the Main body, the rear Guard to be taken from 4th May. Regt & D. R 50 men from each Regt 1 Capt. 2 Subs. Serjts & Corpls.

Monday 21st. March'd this morning to Wilmington Delaware State and there took up our Quarters (I hope for this Winter) being 12 miles.

WILMINGTON Delaware State Decmbr 21st 1777. Division Orders by Genl Smallwood.

The Commissaries to Supply the troops with one days provision immdeiately, & one Gill of rum pr man, & provide Whiskey to serve one Gill pr man tomorrow morning and one days provision only, & to provide Stores of every kind Necessary in their department without delay to support the troops in the most Comfortable manner, the forrage masters Likewise to provide Forrage for the present, & endeavour by every means in his power to lay in the Supplies Necessary, the Regimental Qr Masters are immdeiately to procure all the Pick Axes, Spades & Shovels in the town for fatigue duty; Picquett 2 C, 4 L, 8 S, 8 C, 100 P with Intrenching tools to parade at the Bridge properly Officer'd for fatigue duty, the Officers will prevent their men from Injuring or disturbing the Inhabitants Regimental Qr Masters to provide wood for the Barracks, A Field Officer from each Regt to report Such Houses as are proper for Barracks by 5 OClock.

Two Field Officers for Picquett to attend at 4 OClock.

Marches made by the Delaware Regt. this Campaign From May 17th to Decembr. 21st, being the time we Came into Winter Quarters	Through what States	Number of Miles
1777		
May		
17th & 18th. From Philadelphia to Trenton	Jersey	30
19th. From Trenton to Princetown	....	12
June		
13th. From Princetown to Rockey hill	....	4
From Rockey hill to Corryells Ferry on the Delaware River	....	24
From Corryells ferry to Flemington	....	18
From Flemington to Sowerlands Mountain.	....	10
From Sowerland Mountain to Rocky Hill..	....	8
From Rocky hill to Brunswick	....	12
From Brunswick to Sampton	....	6
From Sampton to Lincoln Hill ...	....	3
From Lincoln hill to Morristown..	....	18
From Morristown to Pumpton	....	12
From Pumpton to Ramapaugh Clove	New York	14
July		
14th & 15th. From Ramapaugh Clove to New Windsor North River	....	30
From New Windsor to New borough, Higher up the river and opposite Fish kill landing	....	3
16th. From New Borough Cross'd the North River being two miles to Fish Kills Landing, then march'd to Fish kill Town which is 5 Miles from the Landing	....	7

Note: The leftmost margin of the table carries the vertical note "Dont know the Exact dates of these Marches" spanning the June entries, and the vertical note "Commanded by General Sullivan" spanning the Rocky hill to Brunswick through Pumpton to Ramapaugh Clove entries.

		Through what States	Number of Miles
July			
21st.	From Fishkill to Peekskill		18
22d.	From Peekskill on the North Castle Road		5
23d.	From thence to Cortlands Mannor..		4
26.	From Cortlands Manor to Kings Ferry		14
27.	From Cross'd the North River to Haverstraw ferry & March'd one mile		2
28.	From thence to Cackyatt		9
29.	From thence to Perramus	Jersey	13
30.	From thence down the Psaic River 3 Miles below Acquackanack Bridge		20
31.	From thence to Springfield		13
Augst.			
1st.	From thence to Quible Town		15
2nd.	From thence to Bond Brook		8
3.	From Bond Brook to Vealtown		15
4.	From Veal town to Hannover		10
21st.	From Hannover to Elizabeth town Point...		22
22.	From Elizabethtown point Cross'd the Rarington River on to Staten Island....... Recrossed the River & came to Spanktown.		30
23.	From Spank town to Springfield		12
24.	From Springfield to Spicatua		14
25.	From Spicatua Brunswick		5
26.	From Brunswick to Princetown		15
28.	From Princetown to Trenton		12
29.	From Trenton Cross'd the river Delaware to Bristol	Pennsulv.	10
			477

(marginal notes: Commanded by Brigadier General De Jbore Genl Sullivan being Sick; Commanded by General Sullivan)

	Through what States	Number of Miles
Brought over		477
1777		
Augst.		
30th. From Bristol to Philadelphia	Pennsulv.	20
31st. From Philada Cross'd Schuylkill	....	2
Septr.		
1st. From Schuylkill to Chester	....	15
2nd. From Chester to Wilmington	Del. State	13
9th. From thence to Chadds Ford	....	10
11. From Do to Chester	Pennsl.	15
12. From Do to Schuylkill	....	12
13. From Do to Germantown	....	8
14. From Do to the Sign of the Buck on ye Lan-chester Road	....	11
15. From Do On the Same Road.....Do.....	....	14
16. From Do to Yellow Springs	....	11
17. From Do About 3 Miles beyond French Creek Bridge	....	9
18. From thence to Reading Furnace	....	12
19. From Do to Richardson's ford	....	29
21. From Do to the banks of the Schuylkill.....	....	2
22. From Do to Faulkners Swamp	....	15
26. From Do to Parkaoming Creek	....	7
29. From Do to the Skippack Road	....	5
Octbr.		
2nd. From Do 3 miles lower down S'd Road.....	....	3
3. From Do to Germantown	....	13
4. From Do Back to our last encampment.....	....	13
5. From Do Parkaoming Creek	....	9
16. From Do to the Skippack where we was en-camp'd 3 days	....	8

		Through what States	Number of Miles
Octbr.			
20.	From Do on Said Road within 15 Miles of Philada	....	5
Novr.			
2nd.	From Do to White Marsh	....	2
Decr.			
11.	From Do to Mattsons ford then to Swedes ford	....	13
12.	From Do Cross'd Schuylkill to the Gulph Mill	....	6
20.	From Do to Dilworths town	....	25
21.	From Do to Wilmington to Winter Quarters Under the Command of Brigadr Genl Smallwood	....	12
	Total....	....	796

The Scouts & Marches made at Different times to the Enemies lines & Returning again are not included; this is only the different places we have Encamp'd in.

By ROBT KIRKWOOD
Capt D. R